FUTURAMA™
ADVENTURES
Perennial
Currents
An Imprint of HarperCollinsPublishers
P9-BHW-354

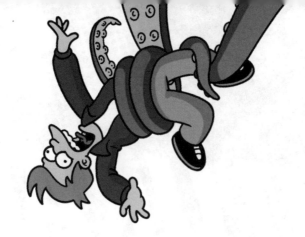

FUTURAMA ADVENTURES

FIRST EDITION

ISBN 978-0-06-073909-6

07 08 QWM 10 9 8 7 6 5 4 3 2

Publisher: MATT GROENING
Creative Director: BILL MORRISON
Managing Editor: TERRY DELEGEANE
Director of Operations: ROBERT ZAUGH
Special Projects Art Director: SERBAN CRISTESCU
Art Director: NATHAN KANE
Production Manager: CHRISTOPHER UNGAR
Administration: SHERRI SMITH
HarperCollins Editors: SUSAN WEINBERG, KATE TRAVERS
Legal Guardian: SUSAN A. GRODE

Trade Paperback Concepts & Design: SERBAN CRISTESCU

Contributing Artists:
KAREN BATES, TIM BAVINGTON, SERBAN CRISTESCU, JOHN DELANEY, MARK ERVIN,
CHIA-HSIEN JASON HO, NATHAN KANE, TOM KING, JAMES LLOYD, RICK REESE, MIKE ROTE,
STEVE STEERE JR., DAVE STEWART, BILL MORRISON, SCOTT MORSE, CARLOS MOTA,
PHYLLIS NOVIN, CHRIS UNGAR, ART VILLANUEVA

Contributing Writers:
BILL MORRISON, ERIC ROGERS, MILI SMYTHE

PRINTED IN CANADA

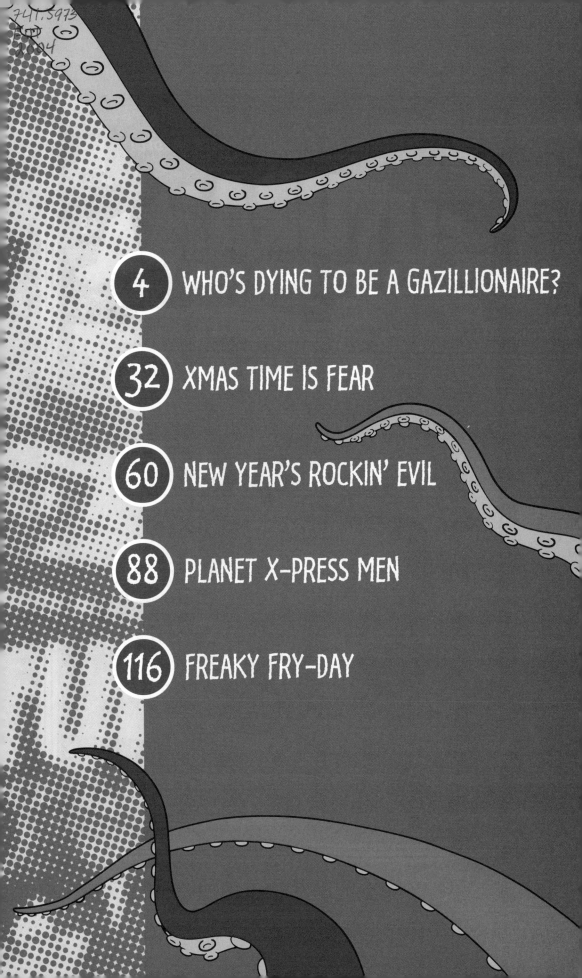

BONGO COMICS GROUP
PRESENTED IN 2-D! NO GLASSES NEEDED!
(UNLESS YOU NEED GLASSES)
APPROVED BY THE COMICS CODE AUTHORITY
US $2.50
CAN $3.50
MARS 4.50
FUTURAMA COMICS
#5
WHAT IS WRONG WITH THIS PICTURE? MORBO DEMANDS AN ANSWER!
MORBO SEES ONLY ONE THING WRONG! THE EARTHLINGS ARE NOT UNDER THE MALEVOLENT TYRANNY OF MORBO'S SUPERIOR RACE! OH, AND ALSO, AMY ONLY DRINKS DIET SLURM.
MATT GROENING
©2001 BONGO ENTERTAINMENT, INC. FUTURAMA ©&TM TWENTIETH CENTURY FOX FILM CORPORATION. ALL RIGHTS RESERVED.

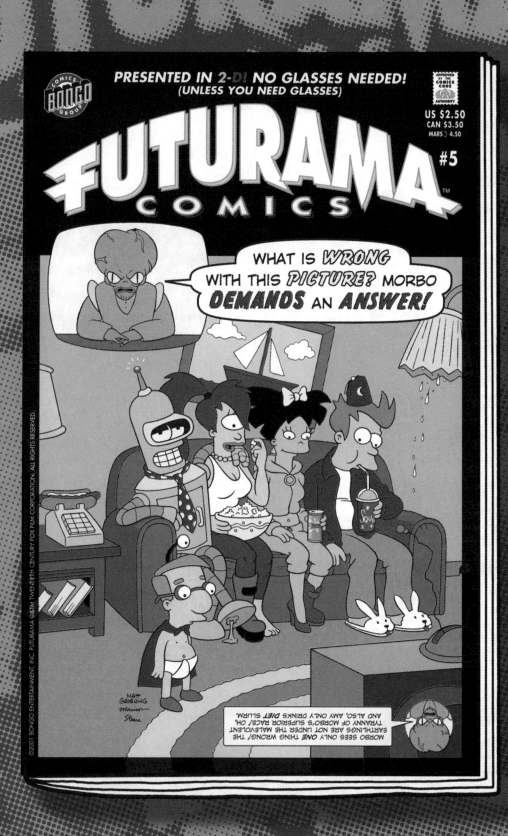

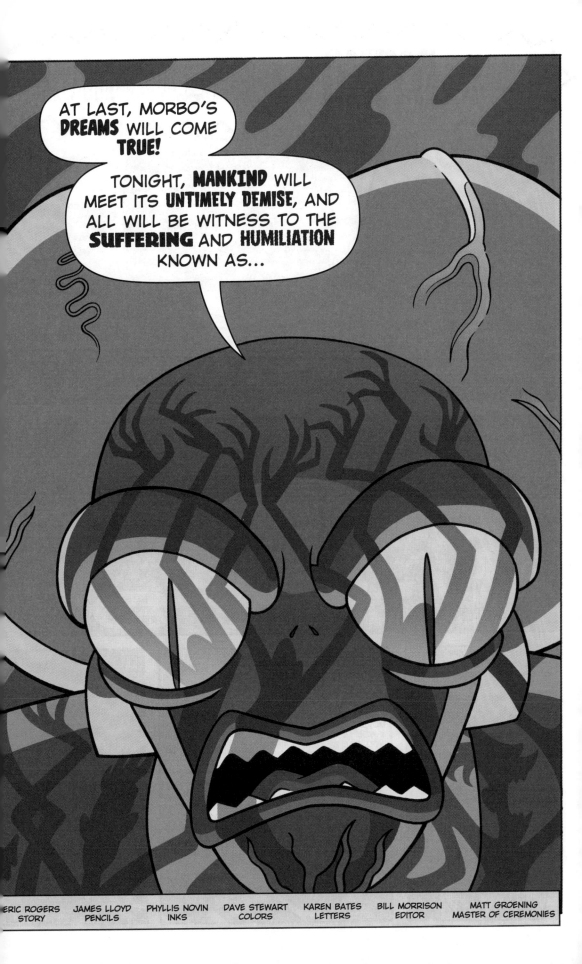

ERIC ROGERS
STORY

JAMES LLOYD
PENCILS

PHYLLIS NOVIN
INKS

DAVE STEWART
COLORS

KAREN BATES
LETTERS

BILL MORRISON
EDITOR

MATT GROENING
MASTER OF CEREMONIES

..."WHO'S DYING TO BE A GAZILLIONAIRE?"

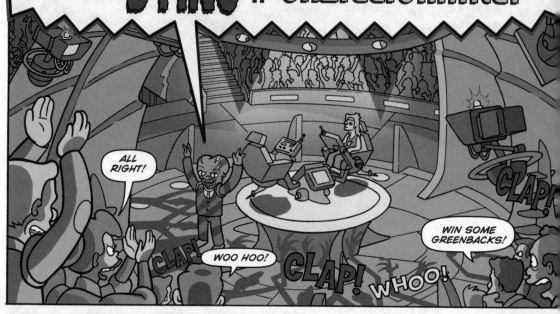

ALL RIGHT!

WOO HOO!

CLAP!

CLAP!

CLAP!

WHOO!

WIN SOME GREENBACKS!

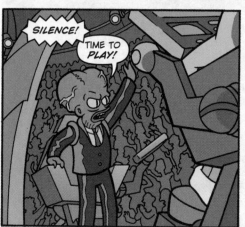

SILENCE!

TIME TO PLAY!

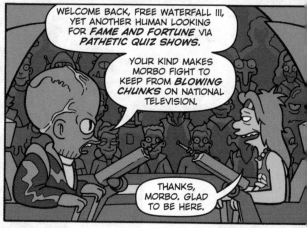

WELCOME BACK, FREE WATERFALL III, YET ANOTHER HUMAN LOOKING FOR *FAME AND FORTUNE* VIA *PATHETIC QUIZ SHOWS*.

YOUR KIND MAKES MORBO FIGHT TO KEEP FROM *BLOWING CHUNKS* ON NATIONAL TELEVISION.

THANKS, MORBO. GLAD TO BE HERE.

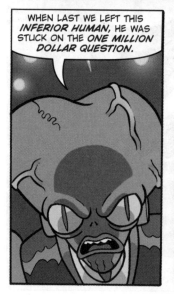

WHEN LAST WE LEFT THIS *INFERIOR HUMAN*, HE WAS STUCK ON THE *ONE MILLION DOLLAR QUESTION*.

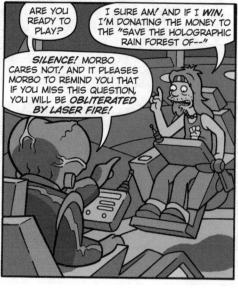

ARE YOU READY TO PLAY?

I SURE AM! AND IF I *WIN*, I'M DONATING THE MONEY TO THE "SAVE THE HOLOGRAPHIC RAIN FOREST OF--"

SILENCE! MORBO CARES NOT! AND IT PLEASES MORBO TO REMIND YOU THAT IF YOU MISS THIS QUESTION, YOU WILL BE *OBLITERATED BY LASER FIRE!*

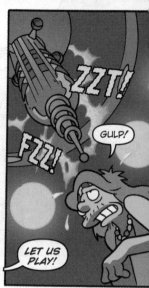

ZZT!

FZZ!

GULP!

LET US PLAY!

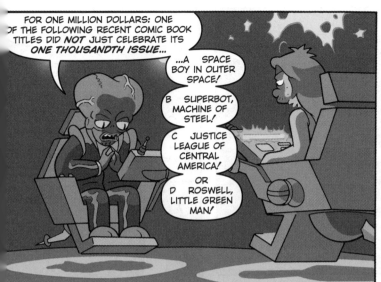

FOR ONE MILLION DOLLARS: ONE OF THE FOLLOWING RECENT COMIC BOOK TITLES DID *NOT* JUST CELEBRATE ITS *ONE THOUSANDTH ISSUE*...

...A SPACE BOY IN OUTER SPACE!

B SUPERBOT, MACHINE OF STEEL!

C JUSTICE LEAGUE OF CENTRAL AMERICA!

OR

D ROSWELL, LITTLE GREEN MAN!

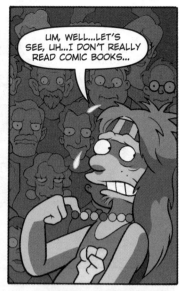

UM, WELL...LET'S SEE, UH...I DON'T REALLY READ COMIC BOOKS...

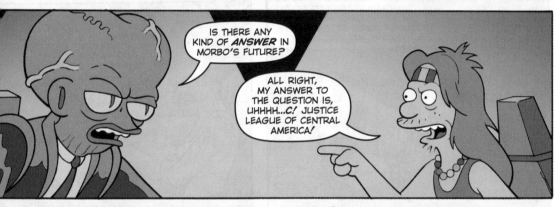

IS THERE ANY KIND OF *ANSWER* IN MORBO'S FUTURE?

ALL RIGHT, MY ANSWER TO THE QUESTION IS, UHHHH...*C!* JUSTICE LEAGUE OF CENTRAL AMERICA!

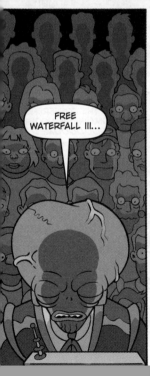

FREE WATERFALL III...

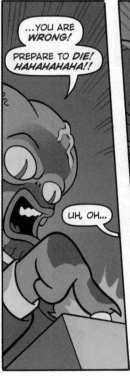

...YOU ARE *WRONG!*

PREPARE TO *DIE!* HAHAHAHAHA!!

UH, OH...

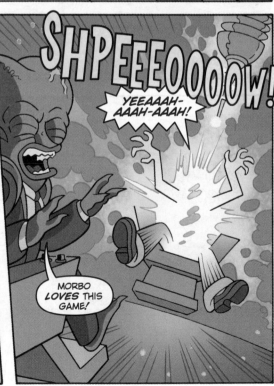

SHPEEEOOOOW!

YEEAAAH-AAAH-AAAH!

MORBO *LOVES* THIS GAME!

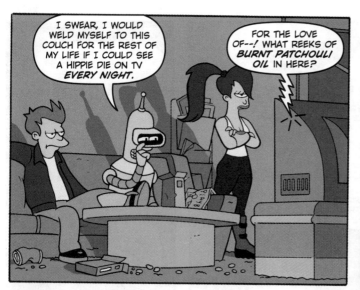

I SWEAR, I WOULD WELD MYSELF TO THIS COUCH FOR THE REST OF MY LIFE IF I COULD SEE A HIPPIE DIE ON TV *EVERY NIGHT.*

FOR THE LOVE OF--! WHAT REEKS OF *BURNT PATCHOULI OIL* IN HERE?

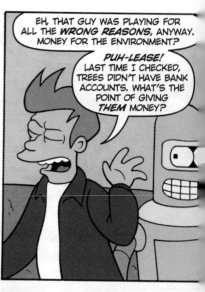

EH, THAT GUY WAS PLAYING FOR ALL THE *WRONG REASONS,* ANYWAY. MONEY FOR THE ENVIRONMENT?

PUH-LEASE! LAST TIME I CHECKED, TREES DIDN'T HAVE BANK ACCOUNTS. WHAT'S THE POINT OF GIVING *THEM* MONEY?

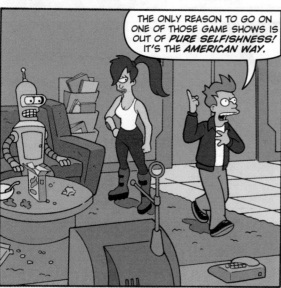

THE ONLY REASON TO GO ON ONE OF THOSE GAME SHOWS IS OUT OF *PURE SELFISHNESS!* IT'S THE *AMERICAN WAY.*

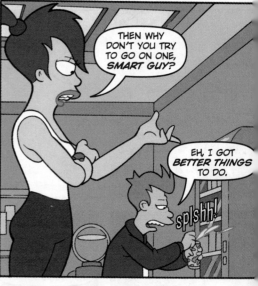

THEN WHY DON'T YOU TRY TO GO ON ONE, *SMART GUY?*

EH, I GOT *BETTER THINGS* TO DO.

splshh!

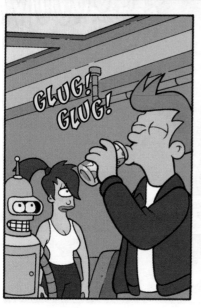

GLUG! GLUG!

BRAAAP!

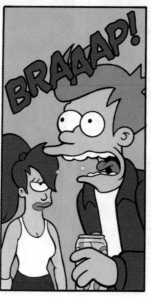

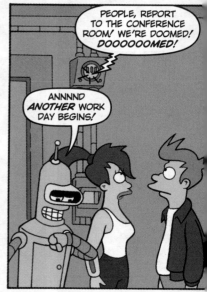

PEOPLE, REPORT TO THE CONFERENCE ROOM! WE'RE DOOMED! *DOOOOOOMED!*

ANNNND *ANOTHER* WORK DAY BEGINS!

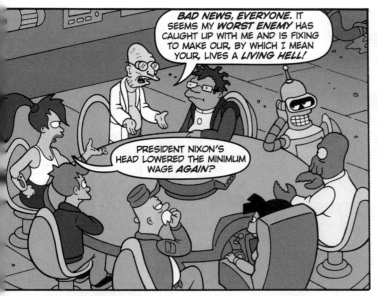

BAD NEWS, EVERYONE. IT SEEMS MY *WORST ENEMY* HAS CAUGHT UP WITH ME AND IS FIXING TO MAKE OUR, BY WHICH I MEAN YOUR, LIVES A *LIVING HELL!*

PRESIDENT NIXON'S HEAD LOWERED THE MINIMUM WAGE *AGAIN?*

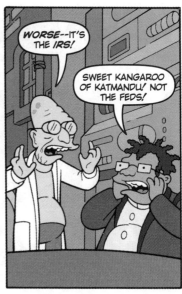

WORSE--IT'S THE *IRS!*

SWEET KANGAROO OF KATMANDU! NOT THE FEDS!

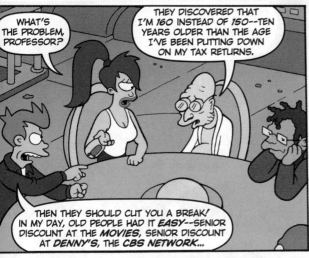

WHAT'S THE PROBLEM, PROFESSOR?

THEY DISCOVERED THAT I'M *160* INSTEAD OF *150*--TEN YEARS OLDER THAN THE AGE I'VE BEEN PUTTING DOWN ON MY TAX RETURNS.

THEN THEY SHOULD CUT YOU A BREAK! IN MY DAY, OLD PEOPLE HAD IT *EASY*--SENIOR DISCOUNT AT THE *MOVIES*, SENIOR DISCOUNT AT *DENNY'S*, THE *CBS NETWORK*...

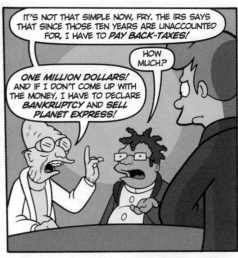

IT'S NOT THAT SIMPLE NOW, FRY. THE IRS SAYS THAT SINCE THOSE TEN YEARS ARE UNACCOUNTED FOR, I HAVE TO *PAY BACK-TAXES!*

HOW MUCH?

ONE MILLION DOLLARS! AND IF I DON'T COME UP WITH THE MONEY, I HAVE TO DECLARE *BANKRUPTCY* AND SELL PLANET EXPRESS!

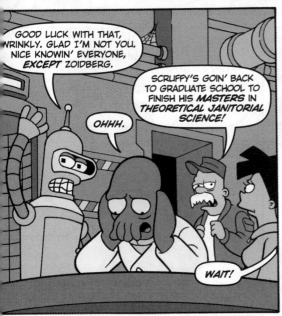

GOOD LUCK WITH THAT, WRINKLY. GLAD I'M NOT YOU. NICE KNOWIN' EVERYONE, *EXCEPT* ZOIDBERG.

SCRUFFY'S GOIN' BACK TO GRADUATE SCHOOL TO FINISH HIS *MASTERS* IN *THEORETICAL JANITORIAL SCIENCE!*

OHHH.

WAIT!

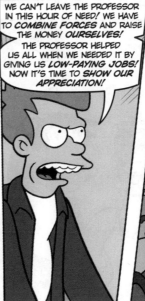

WE CAN'T LEAVE THE PROFESSOR IN THIS HOUR OF NEED! WE HAVE TO *COMBINE FORCES* AND RAISE THE MONEY *OURSELVES!*

THE PROFESSOR HELPED US ALL WHEN WE NEEDED IT BY GIVING US *LOW-PAYING JOBS!* NOW IT'S TIME TO *SHOW OUR APPRECIATION!*

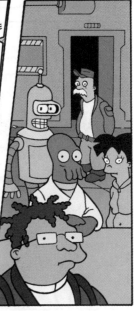

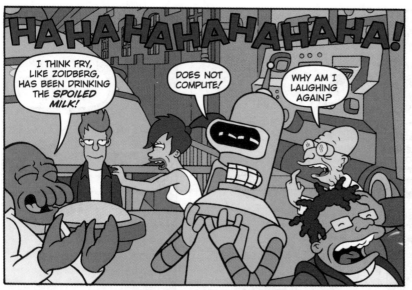

HAHAHAHAHAHAHAHA!

I THINK FRY, LIKE ZOIDBERG, HAS BEEN DRINKING THE *SPOILED MILK!*

DOES NOT COMPUTE!

WHY AM I LAUGHING AGAIN?

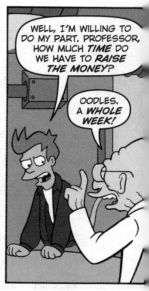

WELL, I'M WILLING TO DO MY PART. PROFESSOR, HOW MUCH *TIME* DO WE HAVE TO *RAISE THE MONEY?*

OODLES. A *WHOLE WEEK!*

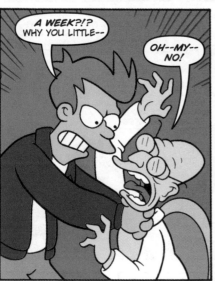

A *WEEK?!?* WHY YOU LITTLE--

OH--MY-- NO!

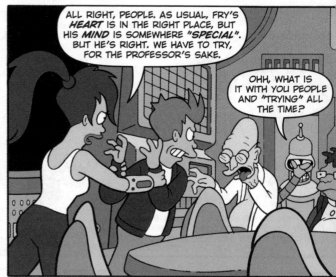

ALL RIGHT, PEOPLE. AS USUAL, FRY'S *HEART* IS IN THE RIGHT PLACE, BUT HIS *MIND* IS SOMEWHERE *"SPECIAL"*. BUT HE'S RIGHT. WE HAVE TO TRY, FOR THE PROFESSOR'S SAKE.

OHH, WHAT IS IT WITH YOU PEOPLE AND *"TRYING"* ALL THE TIME?

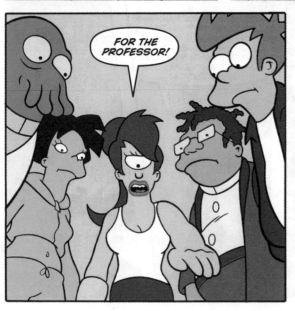

FOR THE PROFESSOR!

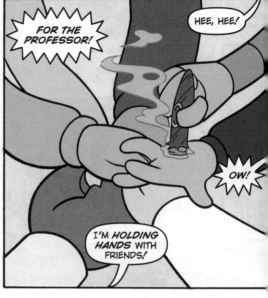

FOR THE PROFESSOR!

HEE, HEE!

OW!

I'M *HOLDING HANDS* WITH FRIENDS!

LANET EXPRESS HOVER CAR WASH!
ASH AND WAX ANY VEHICLE FOR ONLY 10$
BENDER'S TASTY YUMMIES AND YUMMY TASTIES
♪There ain't no tellin' who you might meet...
oo-ooo!♪ ♪You might not ever get rich! ♪ Let me tell you it's better than diggin' a ditch!♪
a movie star or maybe even an...Indian chief! ♪ Workin' at the car wash, workin' at the car wash, yeah...♪
♪C'mon and sing it with me!♪ ♪Car wash! Sing it♪ ...
♪♪ Workin' at the car wash!♪ Singin' it with feelin' now!♪ ♪Car wash yeah!♪

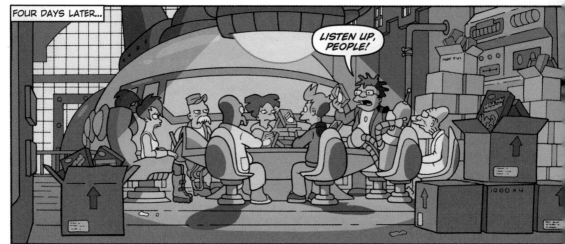

FOUR DAYS LATER...

LISTEN UP, PEOPLE!

DESPITE THE *GANGBUSTER SALES* OF THE *"WILD GIRLS OF THE WORKPLACE"* VIDEO, *AMY'S BIKINI HOVER-CARWASH*, AND, AGAIN, *AMY'S FRENCH-KISSING LESSONS,*

WE'RE STILL *SHORT* OF PAYING THE PROFESSOR'S DEBT BY *993,422.*

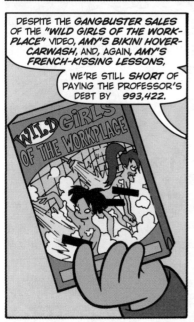

WHEW! I WAS AFRAID THAT TAKING MY 5,000 CUT OF THE *VIDEO SALES* WAS GOING TO MAKE A DIFFERENCE*!*

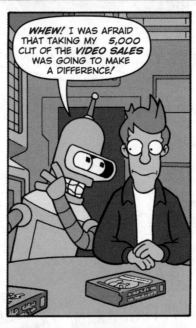

OH, LET'S FACE IT. PLANET EXPRESS IS *DONE FOR,* AND YOU'RE ALL GOING TO BE OUT ON YOUR HEINIES*!*

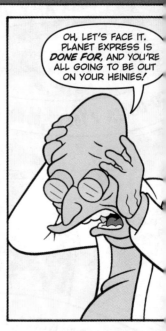

SO ALL THAT FRENCH-KISSING WAS FOR *NOTHING?!*

NOT *ALL.* SCRUFFY CAN TIE A *KNOT* IN A CHERRY STEM WITH HIS TONGUE NOW.

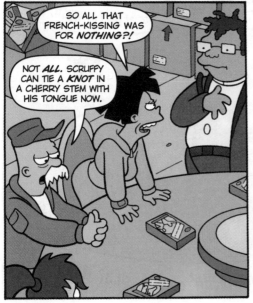

WELL, THERE'S NOT MUCH LEFT TO DO NOW BUT WALLOW IN *MISERY* AND BLAME OUR INACTIVITY ON *SEVERE DEPRESSION* AND A *LOSS OF HOPE.*

LIKE *ANY OTHER* WORK DAY.

CAN DO!

HMMM...

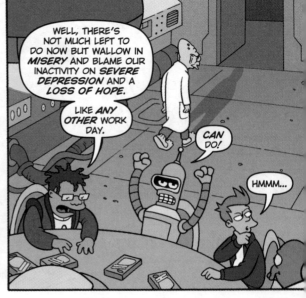

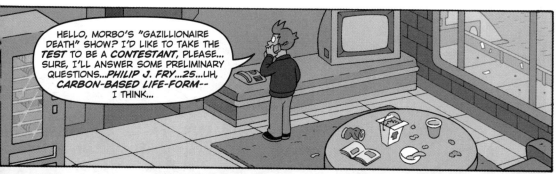

HELLO, MORBO'S "GAZILLIONAIRE DEATH" SHOW? I'D LIKE TO TAKE THE *TEST* TO BE A *CONTESTANT*, PLEASE... SURE, I'LL ANSWER SOME PRELIMINARY QUESTIONS...*PHILIP J. FRY...25...*UH, *CARBON-BASED LIFE-FORM--* I THINK...

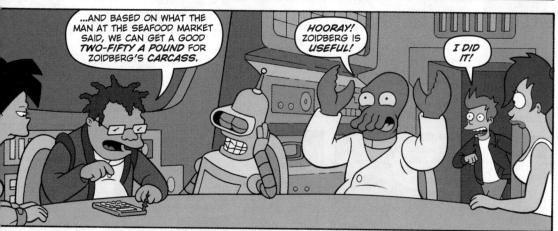

...AND BASED ON WHAT THE MAN AT THE SEAFOOD MARKET SAID, WE CAN GET A GOOD *TWO-FIFTY A POUND* FOR ZOIDBERG'S *CARCASS*.

HOORAY! ZOIDBERG IS *USEFUL!*

I DID IT!

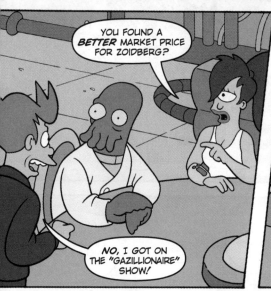

YOU FOUND A *BETTER* MARKET PRICE FOR ZOIDBERG?

NO, I GOT ON THE "GAZILLIONAIRE" SHOW!

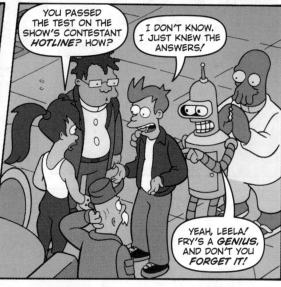

YOU PASSED THE TEST ON THE SHOW'S CONTESTANT *HOTLINE?* HOW?

I DON'T KNOW. I JUST KNEW THE ANSWERS!

YEAH, LEELA! FRY'S A *GENIUS,* AND DON'T YOU *FORGET IT!*

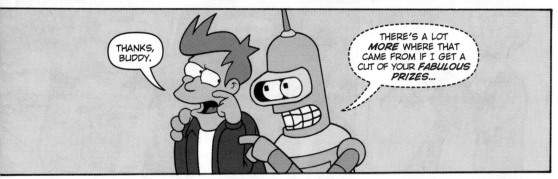

THANKS, BUDDY.

THERE'S A LOT *MORE* WHERE THAT CAME FROM IF I GET A CUT OF YOUR *FABULOUS PRIZES*...

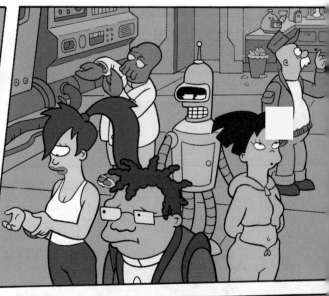

FRY, YOU CAN'T GO ON THAT SHOW! IF YOU LOSE, *YOU'LL DIE!*

I'M NOT GONNA LOSE. LOSING'S FOR *LOSERS!* DO I LOOK LIKE A *LOSER?*

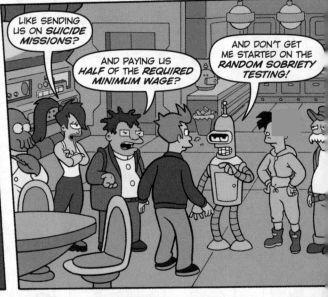

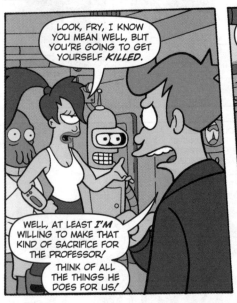

LOOK, FRY, I KNOW YOU MEAN WELL, BUT YOU'RE GOING TO GET YOURSELF *KILLED.*

WELL, AT LEAST *I'M* WILLING TO MAKE THAT KIND OF SACRIFICE FOR THE PROFESSOR! THINK OF ALL THE THINGS HE DOES FOR US!

LIKE SENDING US ON *SUICIDE MISSIONS?*

AND PAYING US *HALF* OF THE *REQUIRED MINIMUM WAGE?*

AND DON'T GET ME STARTED ON THE *RANDOM SOBRIETY TESTING!*

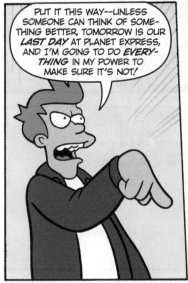

PUT IT THIS WAY--UNLESS SOMEONE CAN THINK OF SOMETHING BETTER, TOMORROW IS OUR *LAST DAY* AT PLANET EXPRESS, AND I'M GOING TO DO *EVERYTHING* IN MY POWER TO MAKE SURE IT'S NOT!

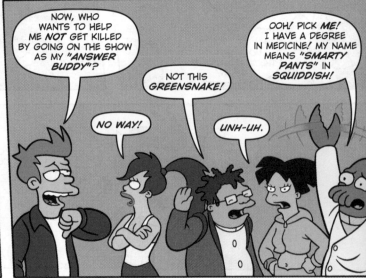

NOW, WHO WANTS TO HELP ME *NOT* GET KILLED BY GOING ON THE SHOW AS MY *"ANSWER BUDDY"?*

OOH! PICK *ME!* I HAVE A DEGREE IN MEDICINE! MY NAME MEANS *"SMARTY PANTS"* IN *SQUIDDISH!*

NOT THIS GREENSNAKE!

NO WAY!

UNH-UH.

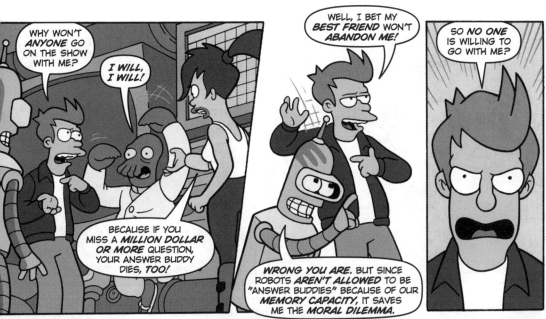

WHY WON'T *ANYONE* GO ON THE SHOW WITH ME?

I WILL, I WILL!

BECAUSE IF YOU MISS A *MILLION DOLLAR OR MORE* QUESTION, YOUR ANSWER BUDDY DIES, *TOO!*

WELL, I BET MY *BEST FRIEND* WON'T *ABANDON ME!*

WRONG YOU ARE. BUT SINCE ROBOTS *AREN'T ALLOWED* TO BE "ANSWER BUDDIES" BECAUSE OF OUR *MEMORY CAPACITY*, IT SAVES ME THE *MORAL DILEMMA.*

SO *NO ONE* IS WILLING TO GO WITH ME?

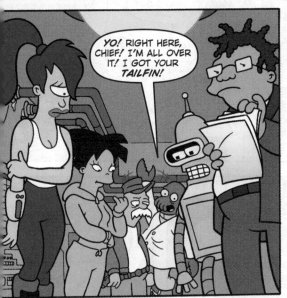

YO! RIGHT HERE, CHIEF! I'M ALL OVER IT! I GOT YOUR *TAILFIN!*

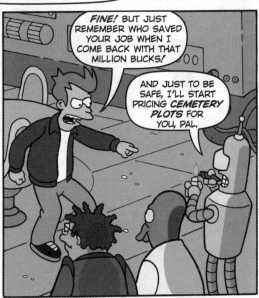

FINE! BUT JUST REMEMBER WHO SAVED YOUR JOB WHEN I COME BACK WITH THAT MILLION BUCKS!

AND JUST TO BE SAFE, I'LL START PRICING *CEMETERY PLOTS* FOR YOU, PAL.

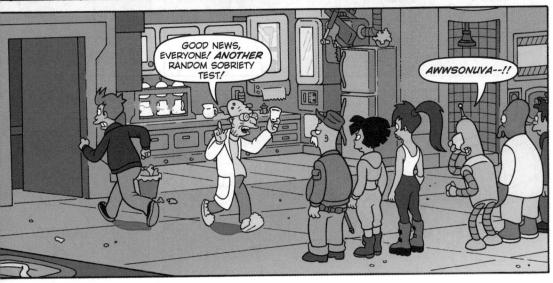

GOOD NEWS, EVERYONE! *ANOTHER* RANDOM SOBRIETY TEST!

AWWSONUVA--!!

THAT AFTERNOON...

WE HAVE TO DO SOMETHING TO *STOP* THIS...

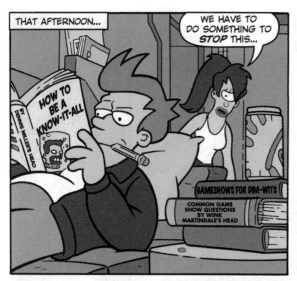

HOW TO BE A KNOW-IT-ALL

BY DENNIS MILLER'S HEAD

GAMESHOWS FOR DIM-WITS

COMMON GAME SHOW QUESTIONS BY WINK MARTINDALE'S HEAD

FRY'S GOING TO GET HIMSELF *KILLED* ON THAT GAME SHOW! IT'S A *SUICIDE MISSION!*

JUST LIKE *EVERY OTHER DAY* OF HIS LIFE.

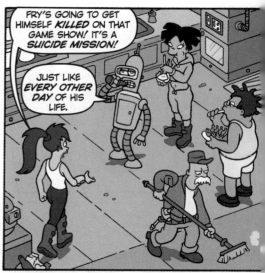

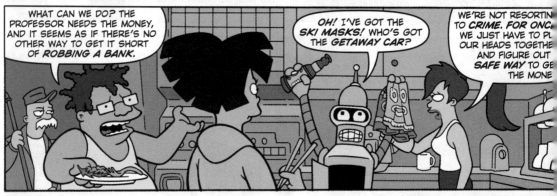

WHAT CAN WE DO? THE PROFESSOR NEEDS THE MONEY, AND IT SEEMS AS IF THERE'S NO OTHER WAY TO GET IT SHORT OF *ROBBING A BANK.*

OH! I'VE GOT THE *SKI MASKS!* WHO'S GOT THE *GETAWAY CAR?*

WE'RE NOT RESORTIN TO *CRIME. FOR ONC* WE JUST HAVE TO P OUR HEADS TOGETHE AND FIGURE OUT *SAFE WAY* TO GE THE MONE

I DON'T KNOW *WHO* THE PROFESSOR KNOWS THAT HAS THAT KIND OF JACK!

WHO COULD POSSIBLY HAVE THAT MUCH?

NO ONE COMES TO MIND!

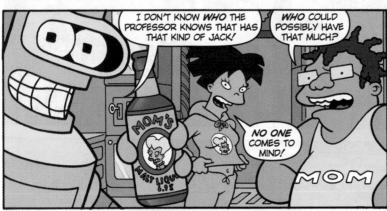

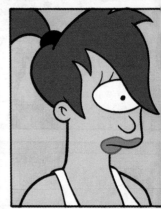

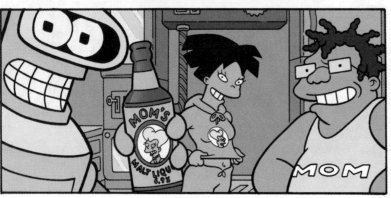

SCRUFFY KNOWS SOMEONE...

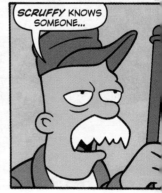

16

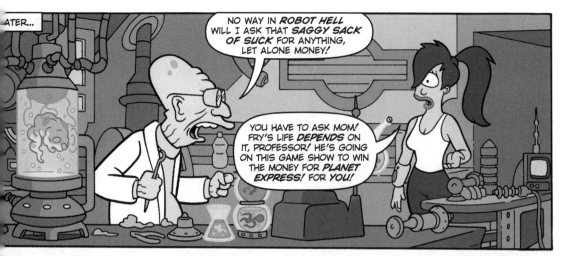

ATER...

NO WAY IN *ROBOT HELL* WILL I ASK THAT *SAGGY SACK OF SUCK* FOR ANYTHING, LET ALONE MONEY!

YOU HAVE TO ASK MOM! FRY'S LIFE *DEPENDS* ON IT, PROFESSOR! HE'S GOING ON THIS GAME SHOW TO WIN THE MONEY FOR *PLANET EXPRESS!* FOR *YOU!*

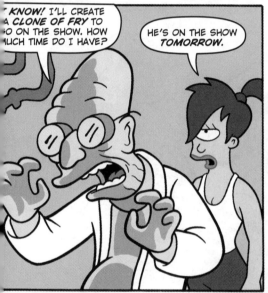

KNOW! I'LL CREATE A *CLONE OF FRY* TO GO ON THE SHOW. HOW MUCH TIME DO I HAVE?

HE'S ON THE SHOW *TOMORROW.*

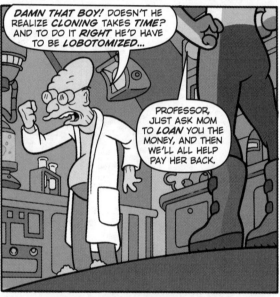

DAMN THAT BOY! DOESN'T HE REALIZE *CLONING* TAKES *TIME?* AND TO DO IT *RIGHT* HE'D HAVE TO BE *LOBOTOMIZED...*

PROFESSOR, JUST ASK MOM TO *LOAN* YOU THE MONEY, AND THEN WE'LL ALL HELP PAY HER BACK.

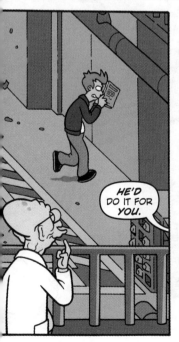

HE'D DO IT FOR *YOU.*

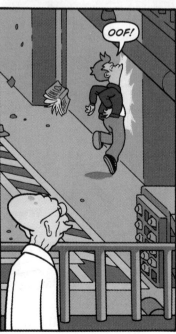

OOF!

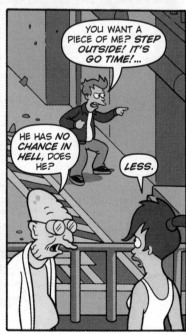

YOU WANT A PIECE OF ME? *STEP OUTSIDE! IT'S GO TIME!...*

HE HAS *NO CHANCE IN HELL,* DOES HE?

LESS.

YOU WANT HOW MUCH MONEY?!?
BWAHAHAHA!!!...
WHO WANTS TO BE...
CONQUERED AND ANNIHILATED,
TUESDAYS AT 9 PM
THE EARTH BROADCAS

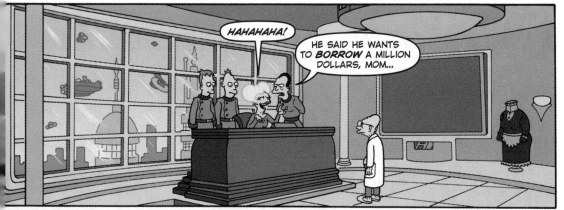

HAHAHAHA!

HE SAID HE WANTS TO *BORROW* A MILLION DOLLARS, MOM...

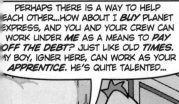

QUIET, YOU CRUD-EATING *CRETINS!*

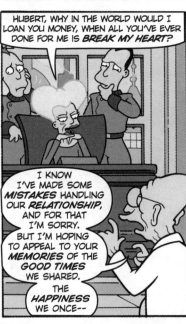

HUBERT, WHY IN THE WORLD WOULD I LOAN YOU MONEY, WHEN ALL YOU'VE EVER DONE FOR ME IS *BREAK MY HEART?*

I KNOW I'VE MADE SOME *MISTAKES* HANDLING OUR *RELATIONSHIP*, AND FOR THAT I'M SORRY. BUT I'M HOPING TO APPEAL TO YOUR *MEMORIES* OF THE *GOOD TIMES* WE SHARED. THE *HAPPINESS* WE ONCE--

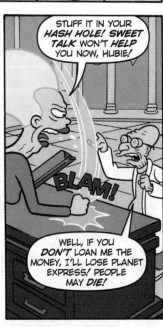

STUFF IT IN YOUR *HASH HOLE! SWEET TALK* WON'T *HELP* YOU NOW, HUBIE!

BLAM!

WELL, IF YOU *DON'T* LOAN ME THE MONEY, I'LL LOSE PLANET EXPRESS! PEOPLE MAY *DIE!*

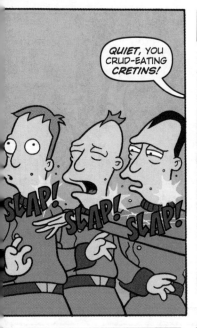

PERHAPS THERE IS A WAY TO HELP EACH OTHER...HOW ABOUT I *BUY* PLANET EXPRESS, AND YOU AND YOUR CREW CAN WORK UNDER *ME* AS A MEANS TO *PAY OFF THE DEBT?* JUST LIKE OLD *TIMES*. MY BOY, IGNER HERE, CAN WORK AS YOUR *APPRENTICE*. HE'S QUITE TALENTED...

I INVENTED A *POOPY*.

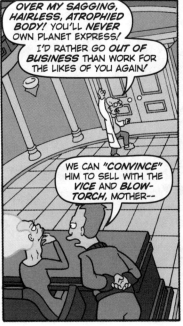

OVER MY SAGGING, HAIRLESS, ATROPHIED *BODY!* YOU'LL *NEVER* OWN PLANET EXPRESS! I'D RATHER GO *OUT OF BUSINESS* THAN WORK FOR THE LIKES OF YOU AGAIN!

WE CAN *"CONVINCE"* HIM TO SELL WITH THE *VICE* AND *BLOW-TORCH*, MOTHER--

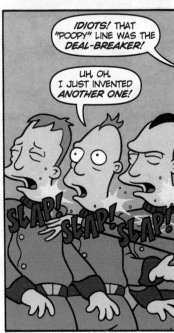

IDIOTS! THAT *"POOPY"* LINE WAS THE *DEAL-BREAKER!*

UH, OH. I JUST INVENTED *ANOTHER ONE!*

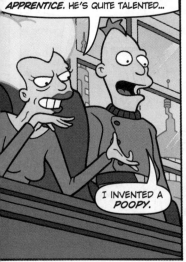

19

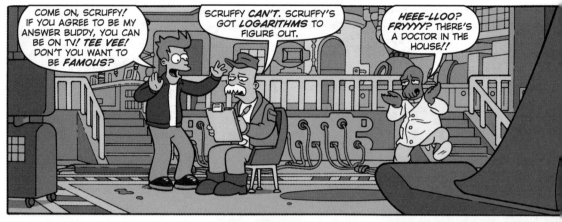

COME ON, SCRUFFY! IF YOU AGREE TO BE MY ANSWER BUDDY, YOU CAN BE ON TV! *TEE VEE!* DON'T YOU WANT TO BE *FAMOUS?*

SCRUFFY *CAN'T.* SCRUFFY'S GOT *LOGARITHMS* TO FIGURE OUT.

HEEE-LLOO? FRYYYY? THERE'S A DOCTOR IN THE HOUSE!!

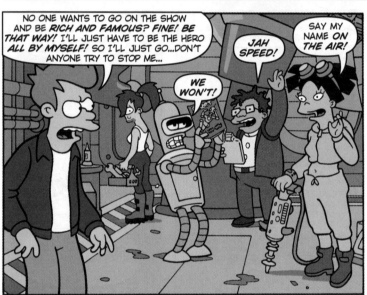

NO ONE WANTS TO GO ON THE SHOW AND BE *RICH AND FAMOUS? FINE!* BE *THAT WAY!* I'LL JUST HAVE TO BE THE HERO *ALL BY MYSELF!* SO I'LL JUST GO...DON'T ANYONE TRY TO STOP ME...

JAH SPEED!

SAY MY NAME *ON THE AIR!*

WE WON'T!

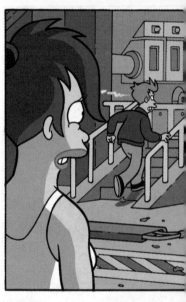

LATER...

WHO'S DYING TO BE A GAZILLIONAIRE? TAPING TODAY!

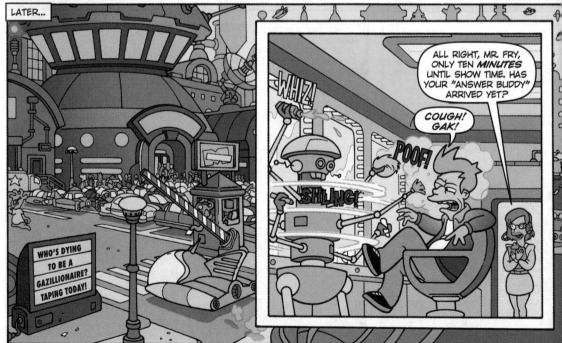

ALL RIGHT, MR. FRY, ONLY TEN *MINUTES* UNTIL SHOW TIME. HAS YOUR "ANSWER BUDDY" ARRIVED YET?

WHIZ!

POOF!

SHLING!

COUGH! GAK!

20

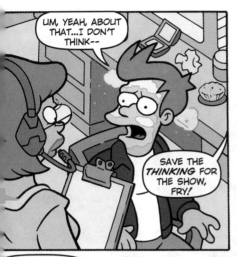

UM, YEAH, ABOUT THAT...I DON'T THINK--

SAVE THE *THINKING* FOR THE SHOW, FRY!

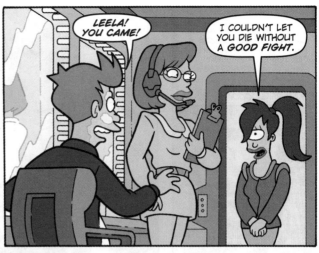

LEELA! YOU CAME!

I COULDN'T LET YOU DIE WITHOUT A *GOOD FIGHT*.

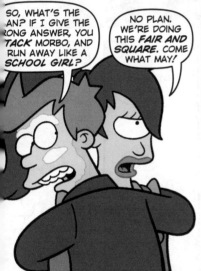

SO, WHAT'S THE [PL]AN? IF I GIVE THE [W]RONG ANSWER, YOU [AT]TACK MORBO, AND [I] RUN AWAY LIKE A *SCHOOL GIRL?*

NO PLAN. WE'RE DOING THIS *FAIR AND SQUARE.* COME WHAT MAY!

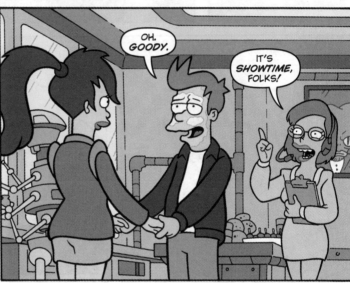

OH. GOODY.

IT'S *SHOWTIME,* FOLKS!

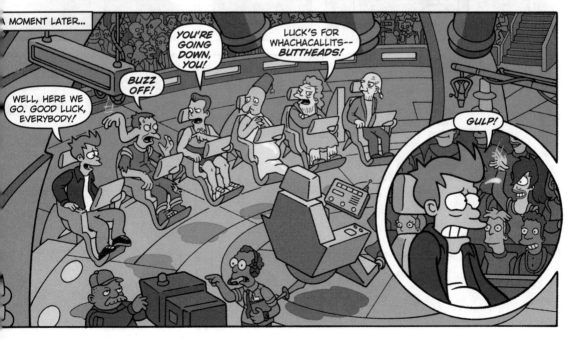

A MOMENT LATER...

YOU'RE GOING DOWN, YOU!

LUCK'S FOR WHACHACALLITS-- *BUTTHEADS!*

BUZZ OFF!

WELL, HERE WE GO. GOOD LUCK, EVERYBODY!

GULP!

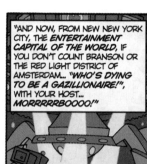

"AND NOW, FROM NEW NEW YORK CITY, THE *ENTERTAINMENT CAPITAL OF THE WORLD*, IF YOU DON'T COUNT BRANSON OR THE RED LIGHT DISTRICT OF AMSTERDAM... *"WHO'S DYING TO BE A GAZILLIONAIRE!"*, WITH YOUR HOST... *MORRRRRBOOOO!"*

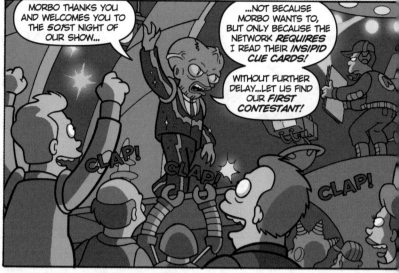

MORBO THANKS YOU AND WELCOMES YOU TO THE *501ST* NIGHT OF OUR SHOW...

...NOT BECAUSE MORBO WANTS TO, BUT ONLY BECAUSE THE NETWORK *REQUIRES* I READ THEIR *INSIPID* CUE CARDS!

WITHOUT FURTHER DELAY...LET US FIND OUR *FIRST* CONTESTANT!

CLAP! CLAP! CLAP!

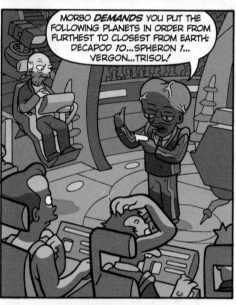

MORBO *DEMANDS* YOU PUT THE FOLLOWING PLANETS IN ORDER FROM FURTHEST TO CLOSEST FROM EARTH: DECAPOD 10...SPHERON 1... VERGON...TRISOL!

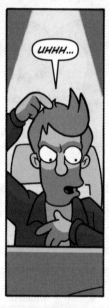

UHHH...

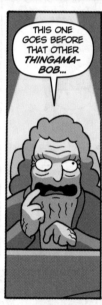

THIS ONE GOES BEFORE THAT OTHER *THINGAMA-BOB...*

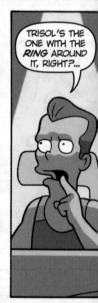

TRISOL'S THE ONE WITH THE *RING* AROUND IT, RIGHT?...

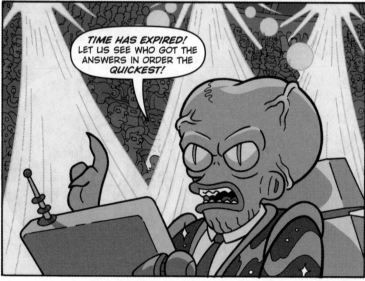

TIME HAS EXPIRED! LET US SEE WHO GOT THE ANSWERS IN ORDER THE *QUICKEST!*

OGDEN WERNSTROM	8.36
HATTIE MCDOOGAL	10.66
GORGAX OF TRISOL	6.03
PHILIP J. FRY	6.89
RANDY MUNCHNIK	12.30
RAOUL INGLIS	7.54

AND OUR FIRST CONTESTANT IS...*PHILIP J. FRY FROM NEW NEW YORK!* MORBO ORDERS YOU JOIN HIM AT THE PODIUM!

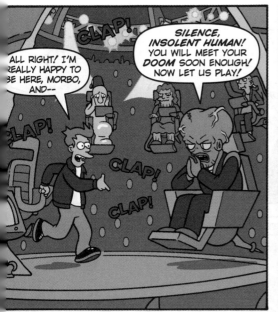

CLAP! CLAP! CLAP! CLAP!

ALL RIGHT! I'M REALLY HAPPY TO BE HERE, MORBO, AND--

SILENCE, INSOLENT HUMAN! YOU WILL MEET YOUR *DOOM* SOON ENOUGH! NOW LET US PLAY!

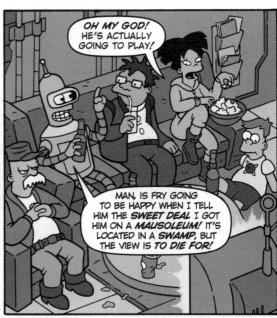

OH MY GOD! HE'S ACTUALLY GOING TO PLAY!

MAN, IS FRY GOING TO BE HAPPY WHEN I TELL HIM THE *SWEET DEAL* I GOT HIM ON A *MAUSOLEUM!* IT'S LOCATED IN A *SWAMP,* BUT THE VIEW IS *TO DIE FOR!*

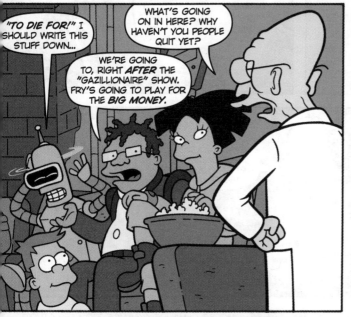

"*TO DIE FOR!*" I SHOULD WRITE THIS STUFF DOWN...

WHAT'S GOING ON IN HERE? WHY HAVEN'T YOU PEOPLE QUIT YET?

WE'RE GOING TO, RIGHT *AFTER* THE "GAZILLIONAIRE" SHOW. FRY'S GOING TO PLAY FOR THE *BIG MONEY.*

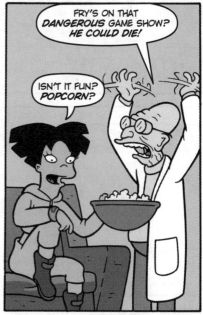

FRY'S ON THAT *DANGEROUS* GAME SHOW? *HE COULD DIE!*

ISN'T IT FUN? *POPCORN?*

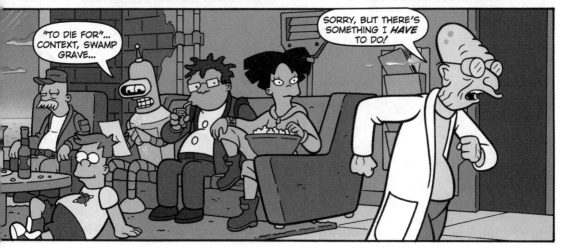

"*TO DIE FOR*"... CONTEXT, SWAMP GRAVE...

SORRY, BUT THERE'S SOMETHING I *HAVE* TO DO!

23

MEANWHILE...

FOR FIVE HUNDRED DOLLARS, WHICH OF THE FOLLOWING ATHLETES DID *NOT* MURDER HIS EX-WIFE?

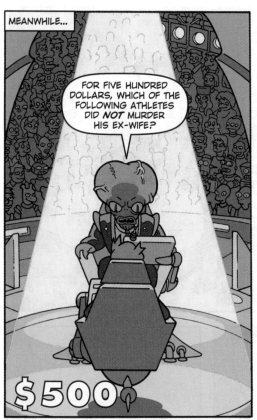

$500

A MOMENT LATER...

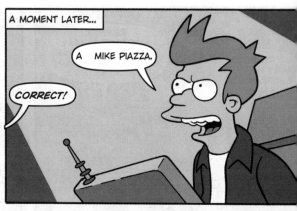

A   MIKE PIAZZA.

CORRECT!

A LITTLE AFTER THAT...

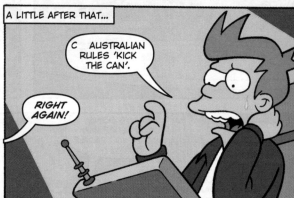

C   AUSTRALIAN RULES 'KICK THE CAN'.

RIGHT AGAIN!

GETTING EVER CLOSER TO THE MILLION...

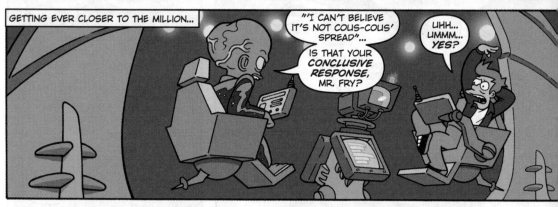

"'I CAN'T BELIEVE IT'S NOT COUS-COUS' SPREAD"...

IS THAT YOUR *CONCLUSIVE RESPONSE*, MR. FRY?

UHH... UMMM... *YES?*

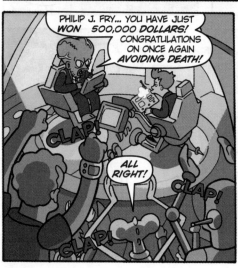

PHILIP J. FRY... YOU HAVE JUST *WON* 500,000 *DOLLARS!* CONGRATULATIONS ON ONCE AGAIN *AVOIDING DEATH!*

CLAP!

ALL RIGHT!

CLAP!

CLAP!

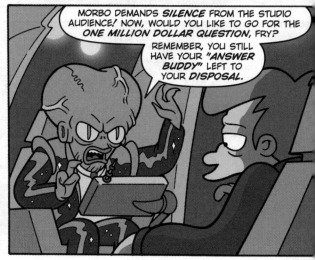

MORBO DEMANDS *SILENCE* FROM THE STUDIO AUDIENCE! NOW, WOULD YOU LIKE TO GO FOR THE *ONE MILLION DOLLAR QUESTION*, FRY?

REMEMBER, YOU STILL HAVE YOUR *"ANSWER BUDDY"* LEFT TO YOUR *DISPOSAL.*

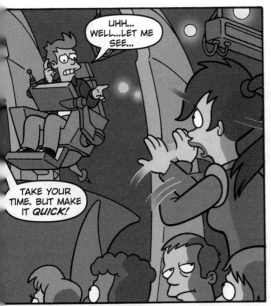

UHH... WELL...LET ME SEE...

TAKE YOUR TIME, BUT MAKE IT *QUICK!*

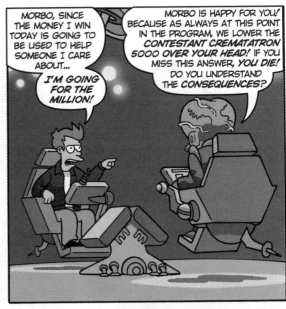

MORBO, SINCE THE MONEY I WIN TODAY IS GOING TO BE USED TO HELP SOMEONE I CARE ABOUT...

I'M GOING FOR THE MILLION!

MORBO IS HAPPY FOR YOU! BECAUSE AS ALWAYS AT THIS POINT IN THE PROGRAM, WE LOWER THE *CONTESTANT CREMATATRON 5000 OVER YOUR HEAD!* IF YOU MISS THIS ANSWER, *YOU DIE!* DO YOU UNDERSTAND THE *CONSEQUENCES?*

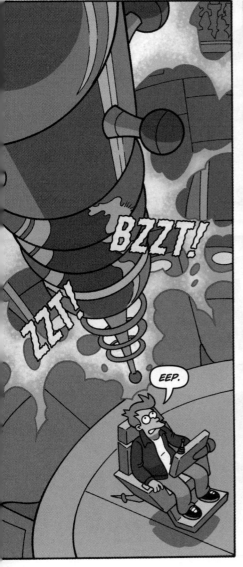

BZZT!

ZZT!

EEP.

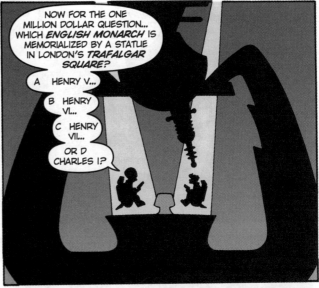

NOW FOR THE ONE MILLION DOLLAR QUESTION... WHICH *ENGLISH MONARCH* IS MEMORIALIZED BY A STATUE IN LONDON'S *TRAFALGAR SQUARE?*

A   HENRY V...

B   HENRY VI...

C   HENRY VII...

OR D   CHARLES I?

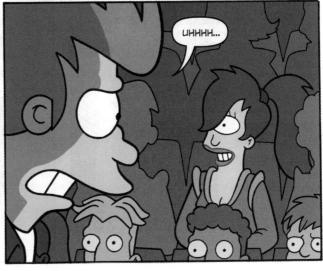

UHHHH...

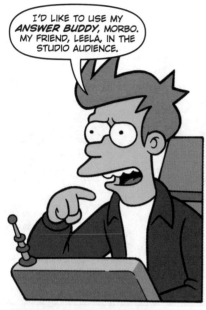

I'D LIKE TO USE MY **ANSWER BUDDY**, MORBO. MY FRIEND, LEELA, IN THE STUDIO AUDIENCE.

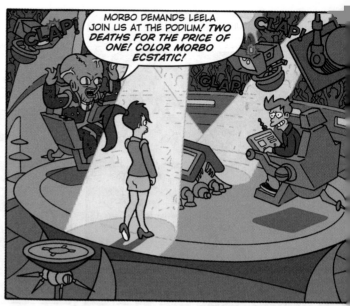

MORBO DEMANDS LEELA JOIN US AT THE PODIUM! **TWO DEATHS FOR THE PRICE OF ONE! COLOR MORBO ECSTATIC!**

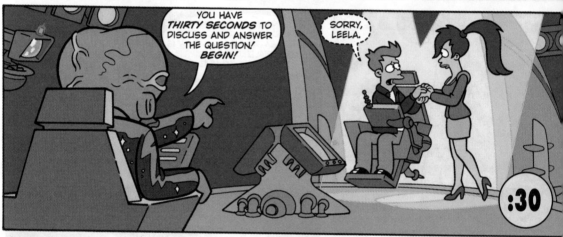

YOU HAVE **THIRTY SECONDS** TO DISCUSS AND ANSWER THE QUESTION! **BEGIN!**

SORRY, LEELA.

:30

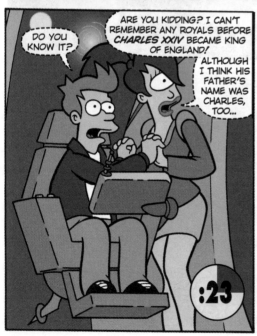

DO YOU KNOW IT?

ARE YOU KIDDING? I CAN'T REMEMBER ANY ROYALS BEFORE **CHARLES XXIV** BECAME KING OF ENGLAND! ALTHOUGH I THINK HIS FATHER'S NAME WAS CHARLES, TOO...

:23

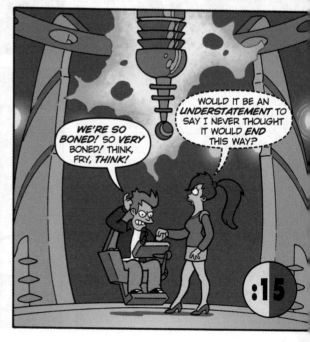

WE'RE SO BONED! SO VERY BONED! THINK, FRY, **THINK!**

WOULD IT BE AN **UNDERSTATEMENT** TO SAY I NEVER THOUGHT IT WOULD **END** THIS WAY?

:15

...AMONG *OTHER THINGS*, IT SAYS HERE CHARLES I WAS THE FIRST ENGLISH KING TO BE *BEHEADED* WHILE ON THE THRONE, WHICH IS WHY THAT STATUE OF HIM ON HIS HORSE SITS IN *TRAFALGAR SQUARE* TO THIS DAY.

WAIT A SECOND...

:9

HISTORY'S *BAD GIRLS* OF BUCKINGHAM PALACE

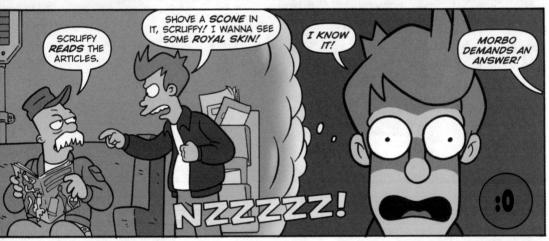

SCRUFFY *READS* THE ARTICLES.

SHOVE A *SCONE* IN IT, SCRUFFY! I WANNA SEE SOME *ROYAL SKIN!*

I *KNOW* IT!

MORBO DEMANDS AN ANSWER!

NZZZZZ!

:0

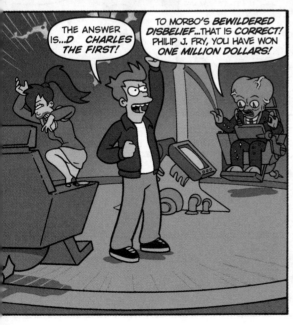

THE ANSWER IS...*D CHARLES THE FIRST!*

TO MORBO'S *BEWILDERED DISBELIEF*...THAT IS *CORRECT!* PHILIP J. FRY, YOU HAVE WON *ONE MILLION DOLLARS!*

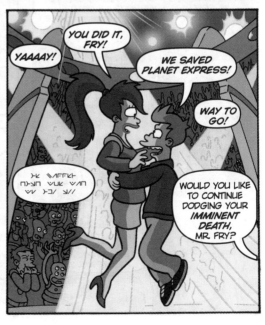

YOU DID IT, FRY!

YAAAAY!

WE SAVED PLANET EXPRESS!

WAY TO GO!

WOULD YOU LIKE TO CONTINUE DODGING YOUR *IMMINENT DEATH*, MR. FRY?

27

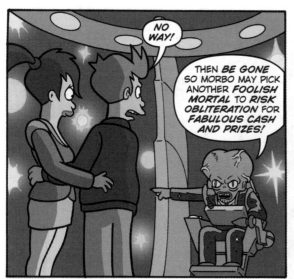

NO WAY!

THEN *BE GONE* SO MORBO MAY PICK ANOTHER *FOOLISH MORTAL* TO *RISK OBLITERATION* FOR *FABULOUS CASH AND PRIZES!*

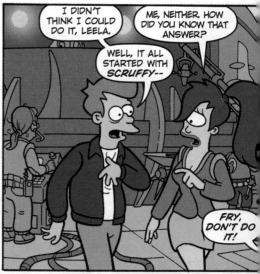

I DIDN'T THINK I COULD DO IT, LEELA.

ME, NEITHER. HOW DID YOU KNOW THAT ANSWER?

WELL, IT ALL STARTED WITH *SCRUFFY--*

FRY, *DON'T DO IT!*

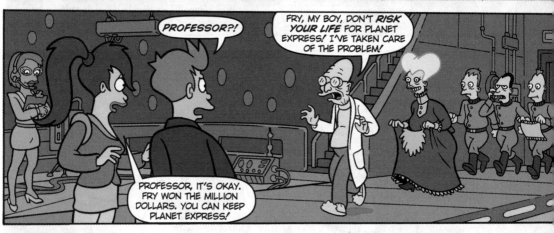

PROFESSOR?!

FRY, MY BOY, DON'T *RISK YOUR LIFE* FOR PLANET EXPRESS! I'VE TAKEN CARE OF THE PROBLEM!

PROFESSOR, IT'S OKAY. FRY WON THE MILLION DOLLARS. YOU CAN KEEP PLANET EXPRESS!

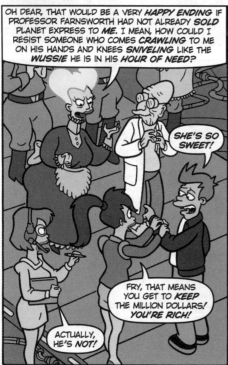

OH DEAR, THAT WOULD BE A VERY *HAPPY ENDING* IF PROFESSOR FARNSWORTH HAD NOT ALREADY *SOLD* PLANET EXPRESS TO *ME.* I MEAN, HOW COULD I RESIST SOMEONE WHO COMES *CRAWLING* TO ME ON HIS HANDS AND KNEES *SNIVELING* LIKE THE *WUSSIE* HE IS IN HIS *HOUR OF NEED?*

SHE'S SO *SWEET!*

FRY, THAT MEANS YOU GET TO *KEEP* THE MILLION DOLLARS! *YOU'RE RICH!*

ACTUALLY, HE'S *NOT!*

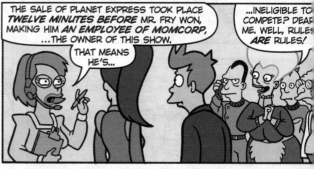

THE SALE OF PLANET EXPRESS TOOK PLACE *TWELVE MINUTES BEFORE* MR. FRY WON, MAKING HIM *AN EMPLOYEE OF MOMCORP,* ...THE OWNER OF THIS SHOW.

THAT MEANS HE'S...

...INELIGIBLE TO COMPETE? DEAR ME. WELL, RULES *ARE* RULES!

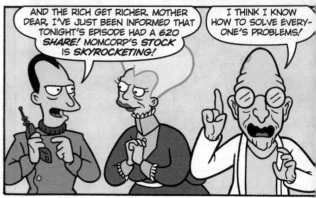

AND THE RICH GET RICHER. MOTHER DEAR, I'VE JUST BEEN INFORMED THAT TONIGHT'S EPISODE HAD A *620 SHARE!* MOMCORP'S *STOCK* IS *SKYROCKETING!*

I THINK I KNOW HOW TO SOLVE EVERY-ONE'S PROBLEMS!

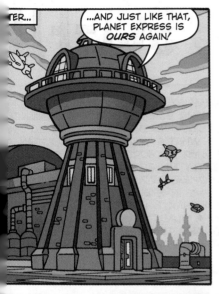

TER...

...AND JUST LIKE THAT, PLANET EXPRESS IS **OURS** AGAIN!

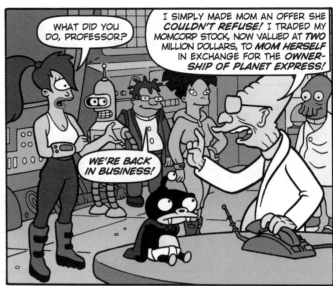

WHAT DID YOU DO, PROFESSOR?

I SIMPLY MADE MOM AN OFFER SHE **COULDN'T REFUSE!** I TRADED MY MOMCORP STOCK, NOW VALUED AT **TWO** MILLION DOLLARS, TO **MOM HERSELF** IN EXCHANGE FOR THE **OWNER-SHIP OF PLANET EXPRESS!**

WE'RE BACK IN BUSINESS!

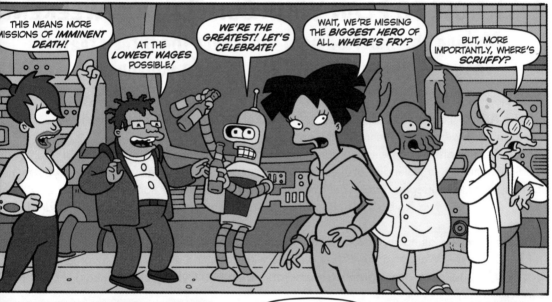

THIS MEANS MORE MISSIONS OF **IMMINENT DEATH!**

AT THE **LOWEST WAGES** POSSIBLE!

WE'RE THE **GREATEST!** LET'S CELEBRATE!

WAIT, WE'RE MISSING THE **BIGGEST HERO** OF ALL. **WHERE'S FRY?**

BUT, MORE IMPORTANTLY, WHERE'S **SCRUFFY?**

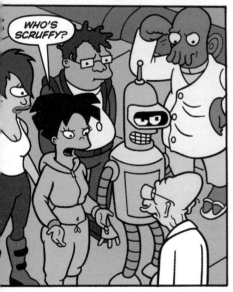

WHO'S **SCRUFFY?**

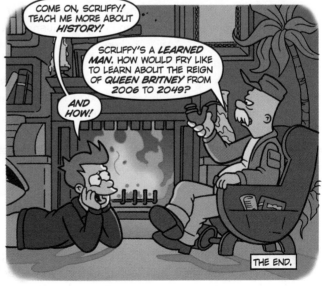

COME ON, SCRUFFY! TEACH ME MORE ABOUT **HISTORY!**

SCRUFFY'S A **LEARNED MAN.** HOW WOULD FRY LIKE TO LEARN ABOUT THE REIGN OF **QUEEN BRITNEY** FROM 2006 TO 2049?

AND HOW!

THE END.

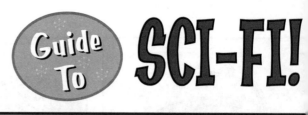

GUBERT'S Guide To SCI-FI!

"GREETINGS, MY SCI-FI LOVING BRETHREN! WELCOME TO THE FIRST EDITION MY GUIDE ON HOW TO MAKE THE MOST OF YOUR SCIENCE FICTION EXPERIENCE YOUR DAILY LIVES. USING MY EXTENSIVE GENIUS AND BURNING DESIRE TO KN ALL, I HAVE COMPILED THIS SYLLABUS OF WHAT'S WHAT IN SCI-FI TODAY A BEYOND. I ASSURE YOU, THERE IS NO HIGHER AUTHORITY ON THE SUBJECT SCIENCE FICTION THAN I, AS I WAS RECENTLY NAMED 'MR. SCI-FI GOD' BY WEBSITE '*CUBERTFARNSWORTHFUTUREOVERLORD.COM*', A HOMELESS M WHO I GAVE A DOLLAR TO, AND WENDELL, MY INVISIBLE FRIEND, ALTHOUGH PROFESSOR PERSISTS ON CALLING HIM 'IMAGINARY'. PFFT! BIG WORDS COMI FROM SOMEONE WHO CAN'T EVEN TELL ME WHY A 'BLACK HOLE' IS BLACK! ANYWAY HOPE YOU FIND MY GUIDE INFORMATIVE AND ENTERTAINING. AND TO THOSE OF YOU WHO DON YOU'RE PROBABLY THE TYPE WHO PREFERS PICARD TO KIRK! AND WE ALL KNOW WHAT KIND LOSER THAT IS!"

PT. 1: HOW TO PLAN YOUR CONVENTION WEEKEND
Making the most of your time over the three greatest days of your life (until next year's convention).

FRIDAY

1. **4:32 A.M.** – Parental unit drops you off in front of the convention. Make way towards the ga of heaven, or if we must be technical, the entrance.

2. **10 A.M.** – Register upon entering convention center. Receive complimentary bag of free goodi including nametag, a calendar of the events, a bumper sticker for some TV show you've nev watched, a button for some book you'll never read, a keychain for some videogame they'll ne actually make, and two 'CyberBucks' good for two dollars off any purchase of two hundred doll or more.

3. **10:50 A.M.** – Call home, check in with parental unit.

4. **11 – 2 P.M.** – Wander around. Get pictures with costumed villains from favorite TV show. B trade novels, posters, and autographed memorabilia. Spend 'CyberBucks' immediately. Eat in fo court. Go to ATM.

5. **2 – 4 P.M.** – Attend screening of latest stupid sci-fi film involving an asteroid headed towar Earth, a time machine, and/or kung-fu fight sequences. Unless it's animated. Animation blows!

6. **4 – 6 P.M.** – Q and A with makers of stupid film. Ask about the sequel, which you don't want see but would like to post information about on your website before anyone else does.

7. **6 – 7:45 P.M.** – Go to hotel, check in. Talk shop with fellow attendees by the ice machine. (online, post info about sequel. Get dressed for opening night party.

8. **7:45 P.M.** – Call home, check in with parental unit.

9. **8 – 11 P.M.** – Attend party. Rub elbows with elite of sci-fi television, film, and books. Pass out d to shortness of breath while trying to talk to fave starlet from fave TV show.
Blame blackout on 'one too many Shirley Temples'.

SATURDAY

1. **9 – 9:45 A.M.** – Have breakfast.

2. **9:45 A.M.** – Call home, check in with parental unit.

3. **10 – 2 P.M.** – Attend autograph signings. Get autographs from fave film director, comic book artist, syndicated series villain, sidekick robot, mad scientist, and various oth 'artists' who seem to have nothing better to do with their time. Not like you at all.

CUBERT? I DON'T KNOW ANY CUBERT! STOP CALLING ME!

2 – 3:45 P.M. – Eat in food court. Go to ATM. Withdraw last dollar.

3:45 P.M. – Call home, check in with parental unit. Beg for money.

4 – 6 P.M. – More autograph signings. Pick on ~~by~~ walking around convention in alien bad guy ~~co~~stume from latest Star Trek TV show. Flee for ~~life~~ as it turns out the guy is the real alien bad guy ~~wh~~o's there looking for foolish humans to enslave.

6 – 8 P.M. – Make it back to hotel. Trade autographs ~~wi~~th fellow attendees by the ice machine. Get dressed for ~~"H~~ump Day" party. (People always giggle when I ~~me~~ntion this part – I don't understand why!)

8 – 8:22 P.M. – Attend party. Start fight with lame ~~ac~~tor who took place of your fave alien sidekick on ~~lo~~ve TV show. Get thrown out. Go back to hotel.

~~SU~~NDAY

9 A.M. – 9:12 A.M. – Wander beautiful town in ~~w~~hich convention is set. See sights. Get bored. Walk ~~ba~~ck to convention.

9:55 A.M. – Call home, check in with parental unit.

3. **10 A.M. – 2 P.M.** – Wander convention buying wares sold at half-price from over-stocked vendors.

4. **2 P.M. – 4 P.M.** – Eat at food court. Spend last dollar on side of cheese for nachos (this is all you can afford).

5. **4 P.M. – 6 P.M.** – Sell back wares to vendors packing up for half of the half price you originally paid. Eat at food court.

6. **6 P.M. – 8 P.M.** – Back to hotel. Put on costume for Closing Night Gala and Costume Contest.

7. **8 P.M. – ???** – Attend gala and roam freely although your picture is given to all security to keep ~~y~~ou out. Register for costume contest. Lose to a robot ~~dr~~essed as HAL from 2001: A Space Odyssey. ~~(P~~fft! Like that's original!) Par-tay. Win dance contest, beating a robot whose patented move is 'The ~~Ro~~bot'. See fave starlet again, stalk her back to her hotel. Encounter her bodyguards. Black out.

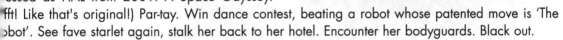

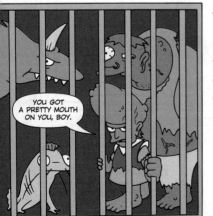

MONDAY

1. **9 A.M.** – Awaken in jail (pray they put you in the 'all-human' holding cell!) Use one phone call to call home, beg for parental unit to get you out. Post bail after parental unit arrives. Get out of town at warp speed. Say goodbye to another year. Mail in registration for next year's convention as soon as you get home.

Look for the next installment...

PT. 2: The Guide to the Sci-Female!

PRINTED IN MINT CONDITION!
COMICS BONGO GROUP
APPROVED BY THE COMICS CODE AUTHORITY
US $2.50
CAN $3.50
#6
FUTURAMA
COMICS
MATT GROENING
J.Ho

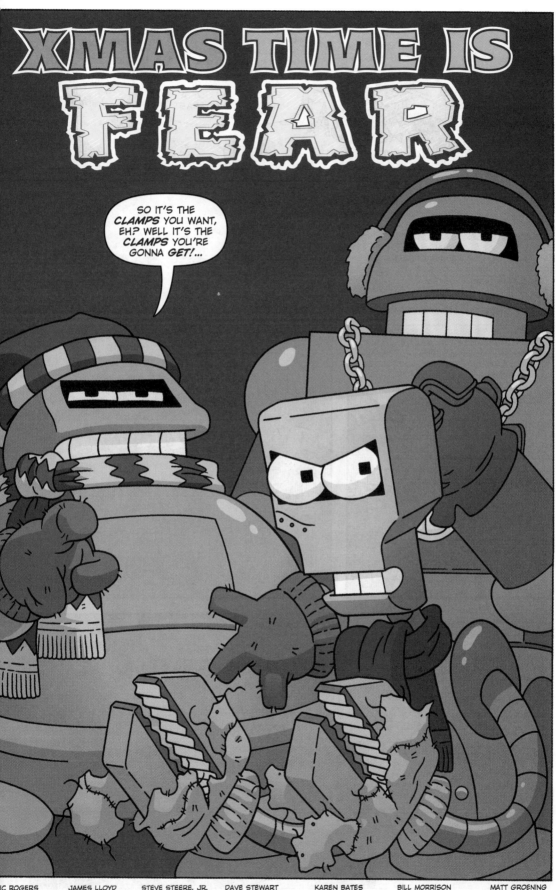

XMAS TIME IS FEAR

SO IT'S THE *CLAMPS* YOU WANT, EH? WELL IT'S THE *CLAMPS* YOU'RE GONNA *GET!*...

ERIC ROGERS
WRITER

JAMES LLOYD
PENCILS

STEVE STEERE, JR.
INKS

DAVE STEWART
COLORS

KAREN BATES
LETTERS

BILL MORRISON
EDITOR

MATT GROENING
NAUGHTY BUT NICE

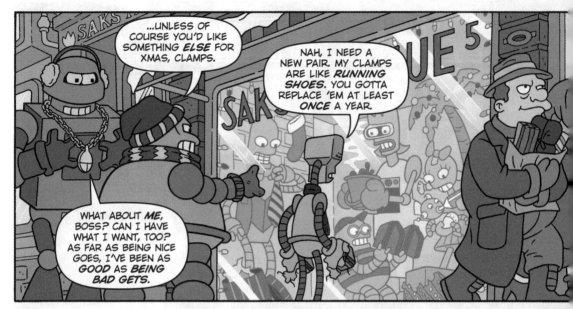

...UNLESS OF COURSE YOU'D LIKE SOMETHING *ELSE* FOR XMAS, CLAMPS.

NAH, I NEED A NEW PAIR. MY CLAMPS ARE LIKE *RUNNING SHOES.* YOU GOTTA REPLACE 'EM AT LEAST *ONCE* A YEAR.

WHAT ABOUT *ME,* BOSS? CAN I HAVE WHAT I WANT, TOO? AS FAR AS BEING NICE GOES, I'VE BEEN AS *GOOD* AS *BEING BAD GETS.*

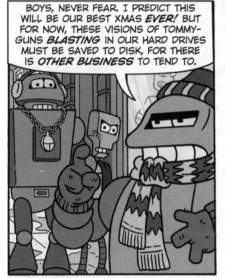

BOYS, NEVER FEAR. I PREDICT THIS WILL BE OUR BEST XMAS *EVER!* BUT FOR NOW, THESE VISIONS OF TOMMY-GUNS *BLASTING* IN OUR HARD DRIVES MUST BE SAVED TO DISK, FOR THERE IS *OTHER BUSINESS* TO TEND TO.

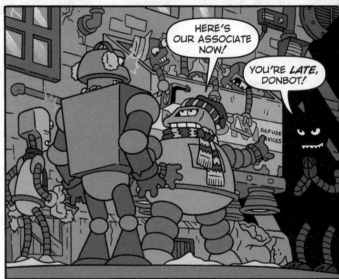

HERE'S OUR ASSOCIATE NOW!

YOU'RE *LATE,* DONBOT!

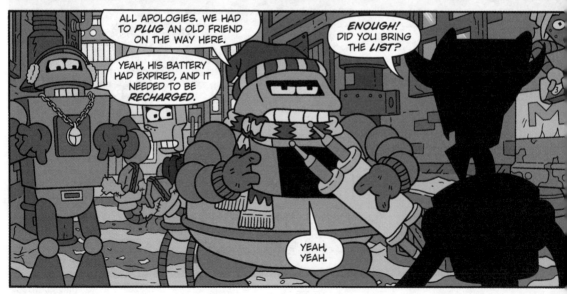

ALL APOLOGIES. WE HAD TO *PLUG* AN OLD FRIEND ON THE WAY HERE.

YEAH, HIS BATTERY HAD EXPIRED, AND IT NEEDED TO BE *RECHARGED.*

ENOUGH! DID YOU BRING THE *LIST?*

YEAH, YEAH.

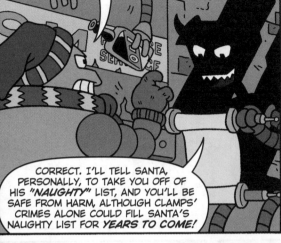

SO LET ME GET THIS STRAIGHT. WE GET *IMMUNITY* FROM THE *ROBOT SANTA CLAUS* JUDGING US NAUGHTY AND TRYING TO MURDERIZE US ON XMAS EVE. IN EXCHANGE, WE GIVE YOU THE NAMES AND MARKERS OF ALL ROBOTS WHO *OWE* US MONEY, RIGHT?

CORRECT. I'LL TELL SANTA, PERSONALLY, TO TAKE YOU OFF OF HIS *"NAUGHTY"* LIST, AND YOU'LL BE SAFE FROM HARM, ALTHOUGH CLAMPS' CRIMES ALONE COULD FILL SANTA'S NAUGHTY LIST FOR *YEARS TO COME!*

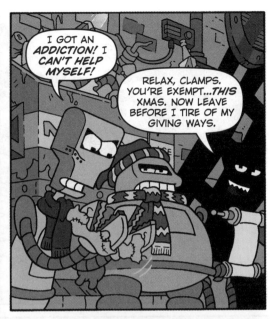

I GOT AN *ADDICTION!* I *CAN'T HELP MYSELF!*

RELAX, CLAMPS. YOU'RE EXEMPT...*THIS* XMAS. NOW LEAVE BEFORE I TIRE OF MY GIVING WAYS.

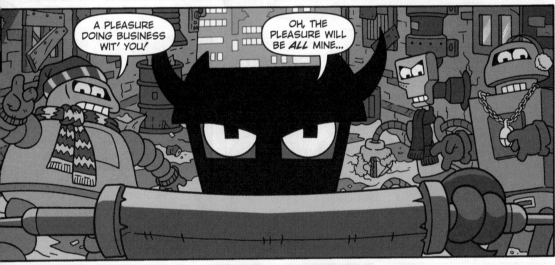

A PLEASURE DOING BUSINESS WIT' YOU!

OH, THE PLEASURE WILL BE *ALL* MINE...

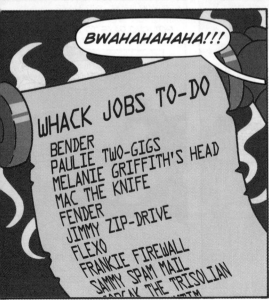

BWAHAHAHAHA!!!

WHACK JOBS TO-DO

BENDER
PAULIE TWO-GIGS
MELANIE GRIFFITH'S HEAD
MAC THE KNIFE
FENDER
JIMMY ZIP-DRIVE
FLEXO
FRANKIE FIREWALL
SAMMY SPAM MAIL
~~~~ THE TRISOLIAN

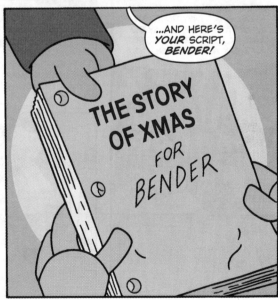

...AND HERE'S *YOUR* SCRIPT, BENDER!

THE STORY OF XMAS FOR BENDER

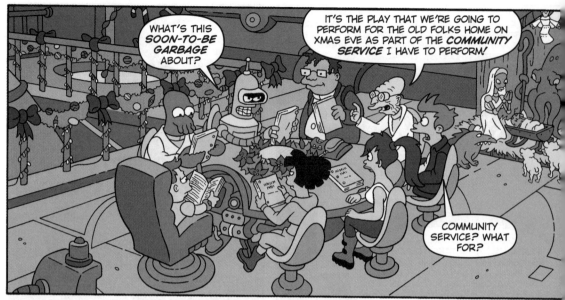

WHAT'S THIS *SOON-TO-BE GARBAGE* ABOUT?

IT'S THE PLAY THAT WE'RE GOING TO PERFORM FOR THE OLD FOLKS HOME ON XMAS EVE AS PART OF THE *COMMUNITY SERVICE* I HAVE TO PERFORM!

COMMUNITY SERVICE? WHAT FOR?

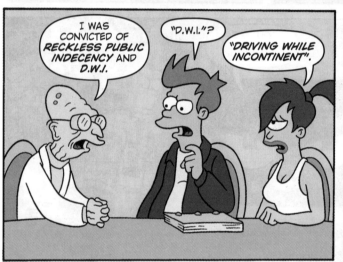

I WAS CONVICTED OF *RECKLESS PUBLIC INDECENCY* AND *D.W.I.*

"D.W.I."?

"DRIVING WHILE INCONTINENT".

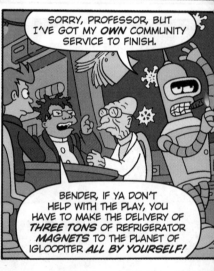

SORRY, PROFESSOR, BUT I'VE GOT MY *OWN* COMMUNITY SERVICE TO FINISH.

BENDER, IF YA DON'T HELP WITH THE PLAY, YOU HAVE TO MAKE THE DELIVERY OF *THREE TONS* OF REFRIGERATOR *MAGNETS* TO THE PLANET OF IGLOOPITER *ALL BY YOURSELF!*

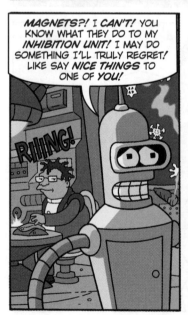

MAGNETS?! I *CAN'T!* YOU KNOW WHAT THEY DO TO MY *INHIBITION UNIT!* I MAY DO SOMETHING I'LL TRULY REGRET! LIKE SAY *NICE THINGS* TO ONE OF *YOU!*

RIIING!

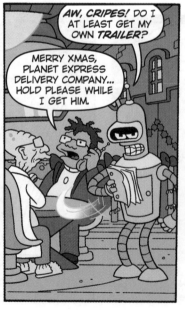

AW, CRIPES! DO I AT LEAST GET MY OWN *TRAILER?*

MERRY XMAS, PLANET EXPRESS DELIVERY COMPANY... HOLD PLEASE WHILE I GET HIM.

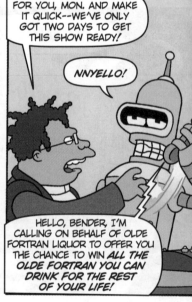

FOR YOU, MON, AND MAKE IT QUICK--WE'VE ONLY GOT TWO DAYS TO GET THIS SHOW READY!

NNYELLO!

HELLO, BENDER, I'M CALLING ON BEHALF OF OLDE FORTRAN LIQUOR TO OFFER YOU THE CHANCE TO WIN *ALL THE OLDE FORTRAN YOU CAN DRINK FOR THE REST OF YOUR LIFE!*

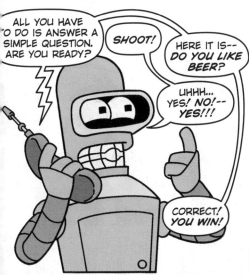

ALL YOU HAVE TO DO IS ANSWER A SIMPLE QUESTION. ARE YOU READY?

SHOOT!

HERE IT IS-- *DO YOU LIKE BEER?*

UHHH... YES! NO!-- YES!!!

CORRECT! YOU WIN!

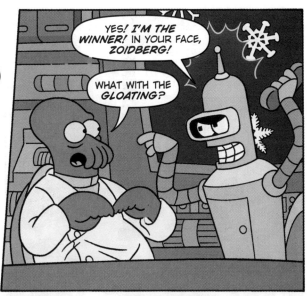

YES! *I'M THE WINNER!* IN YOUR FACE, ZOIDBERG!

WHAT WITH THE *GLOATING?*

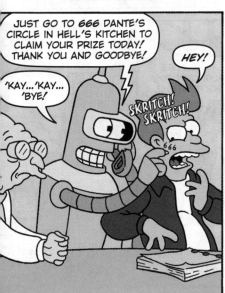

JUST GO TO *666* DANTE'S CIRCLE IN HELL'S KITCHEN TO CLAIM YOUR PRIZE TODAY! THANK YOU AND GOODBYE!

HEY!

'KAY...'KAY... 'BYE!

SKRITCH! SKRITCH!

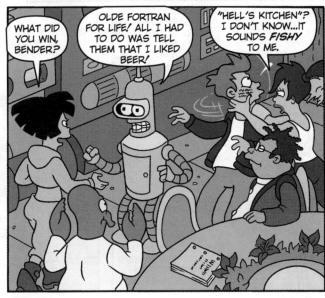

WHAT DID YOU WIN, BENDER?

OLDE FORTRAN FOR LIFE! ALL I HAD TO DO WAS TELL THEM THAT I LIKED BEER!

"HELL'S KITCHEN"? I DON'T KNOW...IT SOUNDS *FISHY* TO ME.

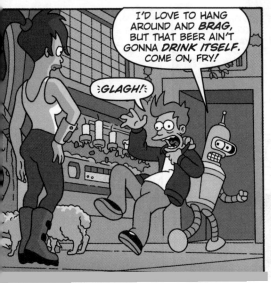

I'D LOVE TO HANG AROUND AND *BRAG*, BUT THAT BEER AIN'T GONNA *DRINK ITSELF.* COME ON, FRY!

GLAGH!

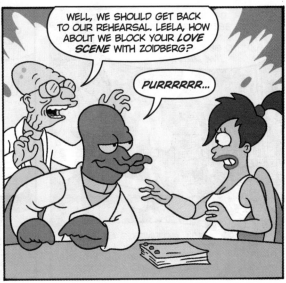

WELL, WE SHOULD GET BACK TO OUR REHEARSAL. LEELA, HOW ABOUT WE BLOCK YOUR *LOVE SCENE* WITH ZOIDBERG?

PURRRRRR...

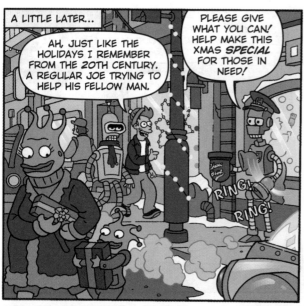

A LITTLE LATER...

AH, JUST LIKE THE HOLIDAYS I REMEMBER FROM THE 20TH CENTURY. A REGULAR JOE TRYING TO HELP HIS FELLOW MAN.

PLEASE GIVE WHAT YOU CAN! HELP MAKE THIS XMAS SPECIAL FOR THOSE IN NEED!

RING!

RING!

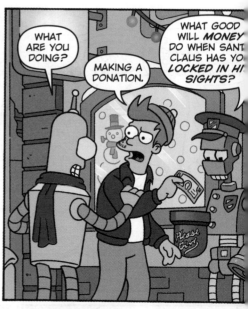

WHAT ARE YOU DOING?

MAKING A DONATION.

WHAT GOOD WILL MONEY DO WHEN SANT CLAUS HAS YO LOCKED IN HI SIGHTS?

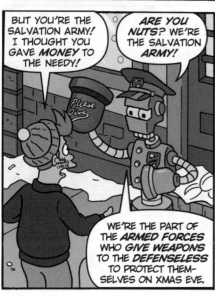

BUT YOU'RE THE SALVATION ARMY! I THOUGHT YOU GAVE MONEY TO THE NEEDY!

ARE YOU NUTS? WE'RE THE SALVATION ARMY!

WE'RE THE PART OF THE ARMED FORCES WHO GIVE WEAPONS TO THE DEFENSELESS TO PROTECT THEM-SELVES ON XMAS EVE.

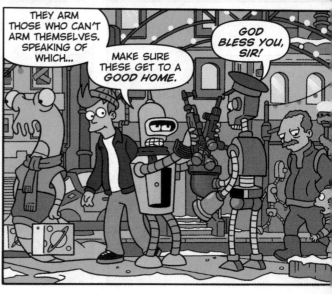

THEY ARM THOSE WHO CAN'T ARM THEMSELVES. SPEAKING OF WHICH...

MAKE SURE THESE GET TO A GOOD HOME.

GOD BLESS YOU, SIR!

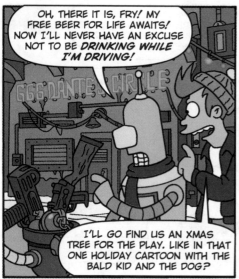

OH, THERE IT IS, FRY! MY FREE BEER FOR LIFE AWAITS! NOW I'LL NEVER HAVE AN EXCUSE NOT TO BE DRINKING WHILE I'M DRIVING!

I'LL GO FIND US AN XMAS TREE FOR THE PLAY. LIKE IN THAT ONE HOLIDAY CARTOON WITH THE BALD KID AND THE DOG?

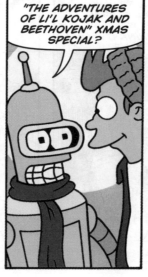

"THE ADVENTURES OF LI'L KOJAK AND BEETHOVEN" XMAS SPECIAL?

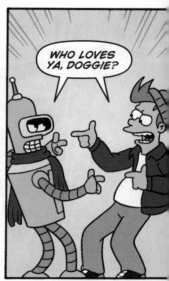

WHO LOVES YA, DOGGIE?

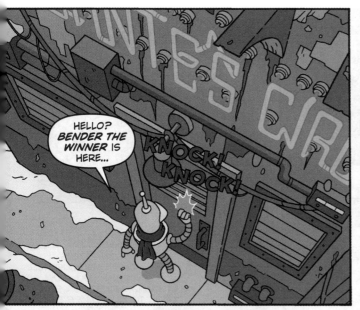

HELLO? BENDER THE WINNER IS HERE...

KNOCK! KNOCK!

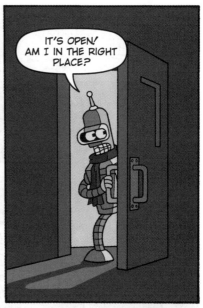

IT'S OPEN! AM I IN THE RIGHT PLACE?

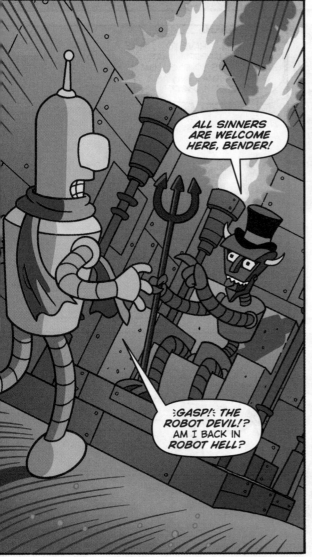

ALL SINNERS ARE WELCOME HERE, BENDER!

:GASP!: THE ROBOT DEVIL!? AM I BACK IN ROBOT HELL?

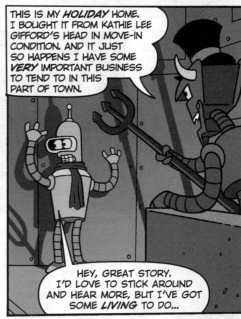

THIS IS MY *HOLIDAY* HOME. I BOUGHT IT FROM KATHIE LEE GIFFORD'S HEAD IN MOVE-IN CONDITION. AND IT JUST SO HAPPENS I HAVE SOME *VERY* IMPORTANT BUSINESS TO TEND TO IN THIS PART OF TOWN.

HEY, GREAT STORY. I'D LOVE TO STICK AROUND AND HEAR MORE, BUT I'VE GOT SOME *LIVING* TO DO...

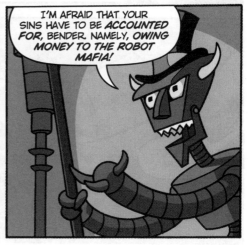

I'M AFRAID THAT YOUR SINS HAVE TO BE *ACCOUNTED FOR*, BENDER. NAMELY, *OWING MONEY TO THE ROBOT MAFIA!*

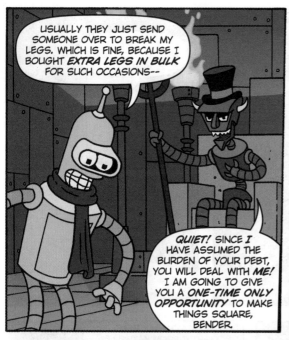

USUALLY THEY JUST SEND SOMEONE OVER TO BREAK MY LEGS. WHICH IS FINE, BECAUSE I BOUGHT *EXTRA LEGS IN BULK* FOR SUCH OCCASIONS--

QUIET! SINCE *I* HAVE ASSUMED THE BURDEN OF YOUR DEBT, YOU WILL DEAL WITH *ME!* I AM GOING TO GIVE YOU A *ONE-TIME ONLY OPPORTUNITY* TO MAKE THINGS SQUARE, BENDER.

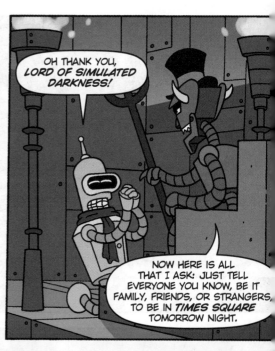

OH THANK YOU, *LORD OF SIMULATED DARKNESS!*

NOW HERE IS ALL THAT I ASK: JUST TELL EVERYONE YOU KNOW, BE IT FAMILY, FRIENDS, OR STRANGERS, TO BE IN *TIMES SQUARE* TOMORROW NIGHT.

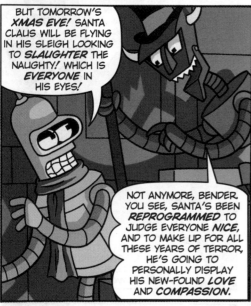

BUT TOMORROW'S *XMAS EVE!* SANTA CLAUS WILL BE FLYING IN HIS SLEIGH LOOKING TO *SLAUGHTER* THE NAUGHTY! WHICH IS *EVERYONE* IN HIS EYES!

NOT ANYMORE, BENDER. YOU SEE, SANTA'S BEEN *REPROGRAMMED* TO JUDGE EVERYONE *NICE*, AND TO MAKE UP FOR ALL THESE YEARS OF TERROR, HE'S GOING TO PERSONALLY DISPLAY HIS NEW-FOUND *LOVE* AND *COMPASSION.*

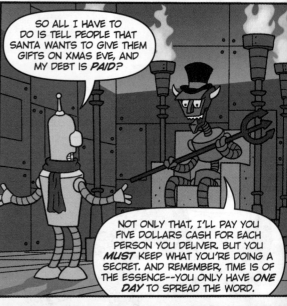

SO ALL I HAVE TO DO IS TELL PEOPLE THAT SANTA WANTS TO GIVE THEM GIFTS ON XMAS EVE, AND MY DEBT IS *PAID?*

NOT ONLY THAT, I'LL PAY YOU FIVE DOLLARS CASH FOR EACH PERSON YOU DELIVER. BUT YOU *MUST* KEEP WHAT YOU'RE DOING A SECRET. AND REMEMBER, TIME IS OF THE ESSENCE--YOU ONLY HAVE *ONE DAY* TO SPREAD THE WORD.

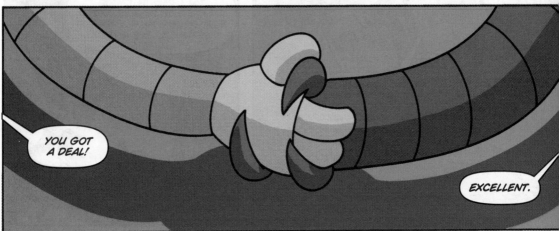

YOU GOT A DEAL!

EXCELLENT.

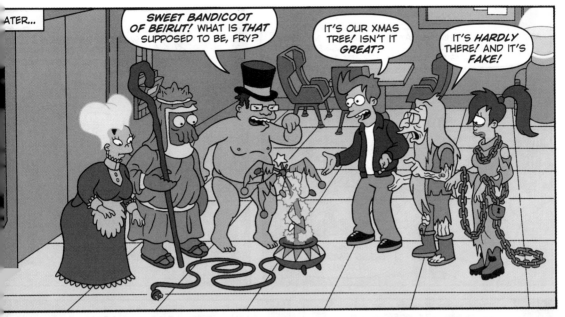

...ATER...

SWEET BANDICOOT OF BEIRUT! WHAT IS **THAT** SUPPOSED TO BE, FRY?

IT'S OUR XMAS TREE! ISN'T IT **GREAT?**

IT'S **HARDLY** THERE! AND IT'S **FAKE!**

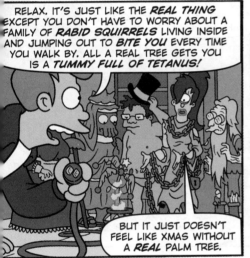

RELAX. IT'S JUST LIKE THE **REAL THING** EXCEPT YOU DON'T HAVE TO WORRY ABOUT A FAMILY OF **RABID SQUIRRELS** LIVING INSIDE AND JUMPING OUT TO **BITE YOU** EVERY TIME YOU WALK BY. ALL A REAL TREE GETS YOU IS A **TUMMY FULL OF TETANUS!**

BUT IT JUST DOESN'T FEEL LIKE XMAS WITHOUT A **REAL** PALM TREE.

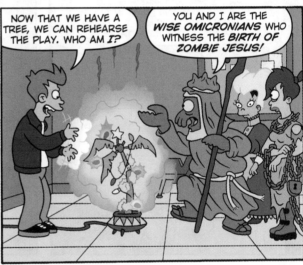

NOW THAT WE HAVE A TREE, WE CAN REHEARSE THE PLAY. WHO AM **I?**

YOU AND I ARE THE **WISE OMICRONIANS** WHO WITNESS THE **BIRTH OF ZOMBIE JESUS!**

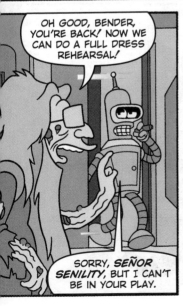

OH GOOD, BENDER, YOU'RE BACK! NOW WE CAN DO A FULL DRESS REHEARSAL!

SORRY, **SEÑOR SENILITY,** BUT I CAN'T BE IN YOUR PLAY.

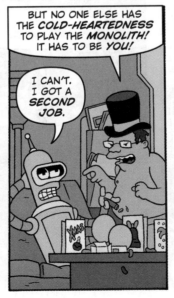

BUT NO ONE ELSE HAS THE **COLD-HEARTEDNESS** TO PLAY THE **MONOLITH!** IT HAS TO BE **YOU!**

I CAN'T. I GOT A **SECOND JOB.**

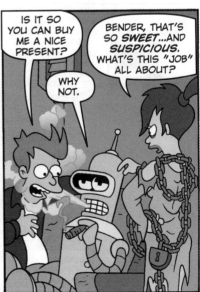

IS IT SO YOU CAN BUY ME A NICE PRESENT?

WHY NOT.

BENDER, THAT'S SO **SWEET**...AND **SUSPICIOUS.** WHAT'S THIS "JOB" ALL ABOUT?

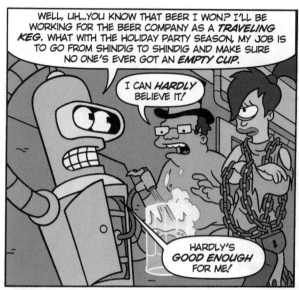

WELL, UH...YOU KNOW THAT BEER I WON? I'LL BE WORKING FOR THE BEER COMPANY AS A *TRAVELING KEG*. WHAT WITH THE HOLIDAY PARTY SEASON, MY JOB IS TO GO FROM SHINDIG TO SHINDIG AND MAKE SURE NO ONE'S EVER GOT AN *EMPTY CUP*.

I CAN *HARDLY* BELIEVE IT!

HARDLY'S *GOOD ENOUGH* FOR ME!

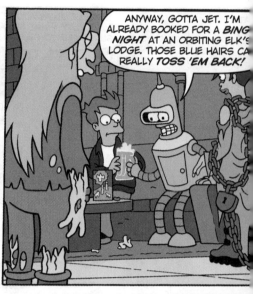

ANYWAY, GOTTA JET. I'M ALREADY BOOKED FOR A *BINGO NIGHT* AT AN ORBITING ELK'S LODGE. THOSE BLUE HAIRS CAN REALLY *TOSS 'EM BACK!*

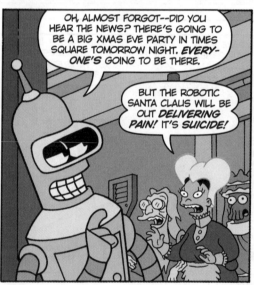

OH, ALMOST FORGOT--DID YOU HEAR THE NEWS? THERE'S GOING TO BE A BIG XMAS EVE PARTY IN TIMES SQUARE TOMORROW NIGHT. *EVERY-ONE'S* GOING TO BE THERE.

BUT THE ROBOTIC SANTA CLAUS WILL BE OUT *DELIVERING PAIN!* IT'S *SUICIDE!*

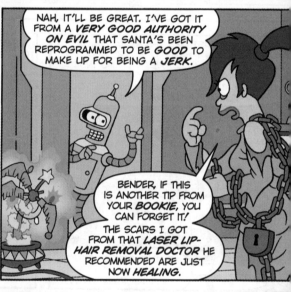

NAH, IT'LL BE GREAT. I'VE GOT IT FROM A *VERY GOOD AUTHORITY ON EVIL* THAT SANTA'S BEEN REPROGRAMMED TO BE *GOOD* TO MAKE UP FOR BEING A *JERK*.

BENDER, IF THIS IS ANOTHER TIP FROM YOUR *BOOKIE*, YOU CAN FORGET IT!

THE SCARS I GOT FROM THAT *LASER LIP-HAIR REMOVAL DOCTOR* HE RECOMMENDED ARE JUST NOW *HEALING*.

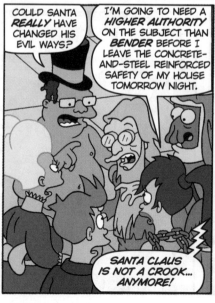

COULD SANTA *REALLY* HAVE CHANGED HIS EVIL WAYS?

I'M GOING TO NEED A *HIGHER AUTHORITY* ON THE SUBJECT THAN *BENDER* BEFORE I LEAVE THE CONCRETE-AND-STEEL REINFORCED SAFETY OF MY HOUSE TOMORROW NIGHT.

SANTA CLAUS IS NOT A CROOK... ANYMORE!

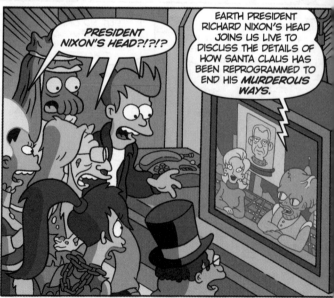

PRESIDENT NIXON'S HEAD?!?!?

EARTH PRESIDENT RICHARD NIXON'S HEAD JOINS US LIVE TO DISCUSS THE DETAILS OF HOW SANTA CLAUS HAS BEEN REPROGRAMMED TO END HIS *MURDEROUS WAYS*.

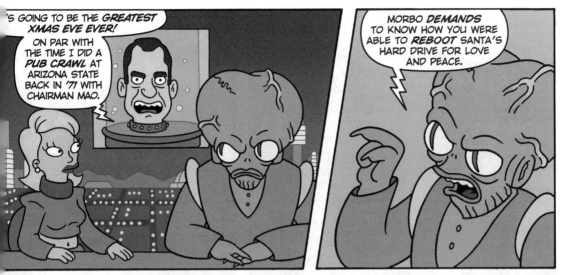

'S GOING TO BE THE *GREATEST XMAS EVE EVER!*

ON PAR WITH THE TIME I DID A *PUB CRAWL* AT ARIZONA STATE BACK IN *'77* WITH CHAIRMAN MAO.

MORBO *DEMANDS* TO KNOW HOW YOU WERE ABLE TO *REBOOT* SANTA'S HARD DRIVE FOR LOVE AND PEACE.

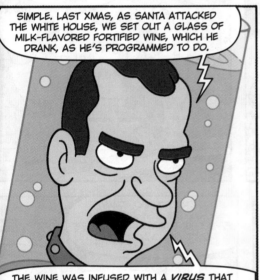

SIMPLE. LAST XMAS, AS SANTA ATTACKED THE WHITE HOUSE, WE SET OUT A GLASS OF MILK-FLAVORED FORTIFIED WINE, WHICH HE DRANK, AS HE'S PROGRAMMED TO DO.

THE WINE WAS INFUSED WITH A *VIRUS* THAT ERASED THE "NAUGHTY" FILE FROM HIS HARD DRIVE, CAUSING SANTA TO JUDGE EVERYONE *"NICE"* FROM NOW ON. MEANING HE WILL REWARD THE WORLD WITH PRESENTS INSTEAD OF DEATH!

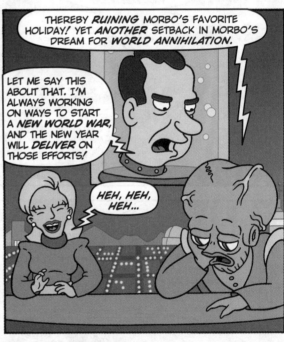

THEREBY *RUINING* MORBO'S FAVORITE HOLIDAY! YET *ANOTHER* SETBACK IN MORBO'S DREAM FOR *WORLD ANNIHILATION.*

LET ME SAY THIS ABOUT THAT. I'M ALWAYS WORKING ON WAYS TO START A *NEW WORLD WAR,* AND THE NEW YEAR WILL *DELIVER* ON THOSE EFFORTS!

HEH, HEH, HEH...

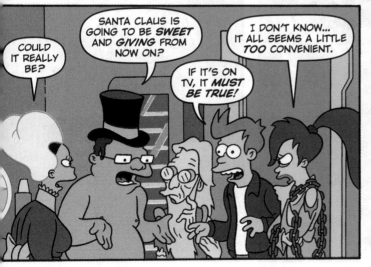

COULD IT REALLY BE?

SANTA CLAUS IS GOING TO BE *SWEET* AND *GIVING* FROM NOW ON?

I DON'T KNOW... IT ALL SEEMS A LITTLE *TOO* CONVENIENT.

IF IT'S ON TV, IT *MUST BE TRUE!*

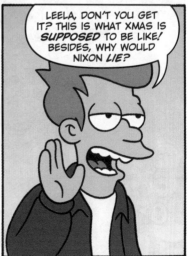

LEELA, DON'T YOU GET IT? THIS IS WHAT XMAS IS *SUPPOSED* TO BE LIKE! BESIDES, WHY WOULD NIXON *LIE?*

ELSEWHERE...
...SO IF YOU REALLY WANT THAT MAIL-ORDER VENUTIAN YOU'VE BEEN ASKING FOR, ALL YOU GOTTA DO IS BE IN TIMES SQUARE TONIGHT, AND SANTA WILL DELIVER!
I'LL USE SOAPS BEFORE I COMES!
REMEMBER TO TELL 'EM BENDER SENT YOU!
YOUS GOTS IT!
TIME TO LUBE THE OLD VOICE BOX!
ZORGNAX'S PUB
A PINT O'OIL, BARKEEP.
YOU GOT IT!
OUT OF ORDER
TIP
THERE YOU GO, TINNY TIM--THE NEW PENTIUM FIVE CHIP FOR YOUR TROUBLES. DON'T DOWNLOAD IT ALL IN ONE PLACE.
THANK YOU, KIND SIR! AND MAY YOU GET KNOBS THAT GO TO ELEVEN THIS XMAS!
HEY, FENDER! IT'S YOUR OLD PAL, BENDER!

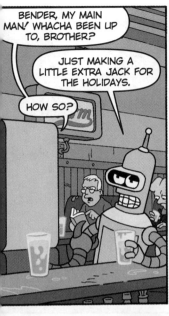

BENDER, MY MAIN MAN! WHACHA BEEN UP TO, BROTHER?

JUST MAKING A LITTLE EXTRA JACK FOR THE HOLIDAYS.

HOW SO?

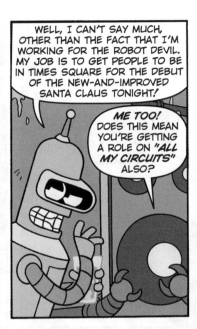

WELL, I CAN'T SAY MUCH, OTHER THAN THE FACT THAT I'M WORKING FOR THE ROBOT DEVIL. MY JOB IS TO GET PEOPLE TO BE IN TIMES SQUARE FOR THE DEBUT OF THE NEW-AND-IMPROVED SANTA CLAUS TONIGHT!

ME TOO! DOES THIS MEAN YOU'RE GETTING A ROLE ON "ALL MY CIRCUITS" ALSO?

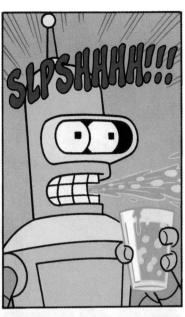

SLPSHHHH!!!

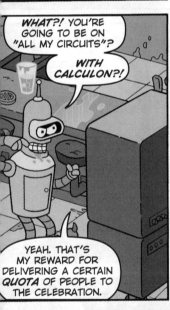

WHAT?! YOU'RE GOING TO BE ON "ALL MY CIRCUITS"?

WITH CALCULON?!

YEAH. THAT'S MY REWARD FOR DELIVERING A CERTAIN QUOTA OF PEOPLE TO THE CELEBRATION.

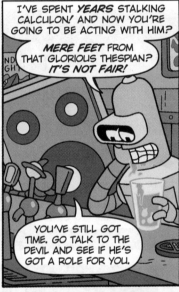

I'VE SPENT YEARS STALKING CALCULON! AND NOW YOU'RE GOING TO BE ACTING WITH HIM?

MERE FEET FROM THAT GLORIOUS THESPIAN? IT'S NOT FAIR!

YOU'VE STILL GOT TIME. GO TALK TO THE DEVIL AND SEE IF HE'S GOT A ROLE FOR YOU.

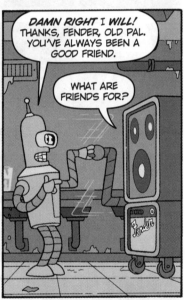

DAMN RIGHT I WILL! THANKS, FENDER, OLD PAL. YOU'VE ALWAYS BEEN A GOOD FRIEND.

WHAT ARE FRIENDS FOR?

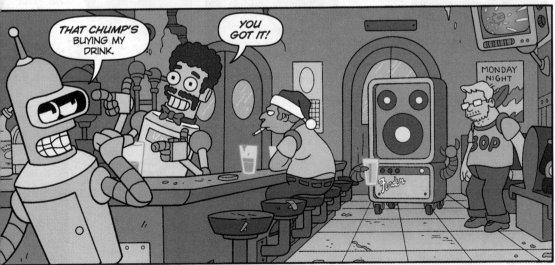

THAT CHUMP'S BUYING MY DRINK.

YOU GOT IT!

MONDAY NIGHT

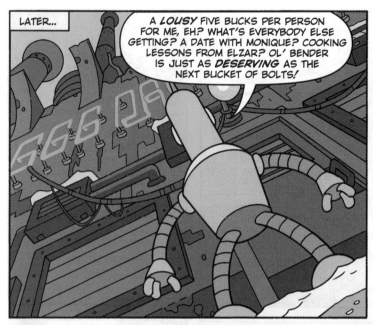

LATER...

A *LOUSY* FIVE BUCKS PER PERSON FOR ME, EH? WHAT'S EVERYBODY ELSE GETTING? A DATE WITH MONIQUE? COOKING LESSONS FROM ELZAR? OL' BENDER IS JUST AS *DESERVING* AS THE NEXT BUCKET OF BOLTS!

GGGDD

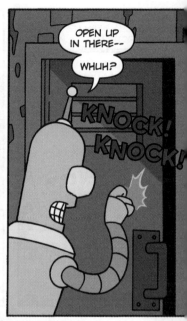

OPEN UP IN THERE--

WHUH?

KNOCK! KNOCK!

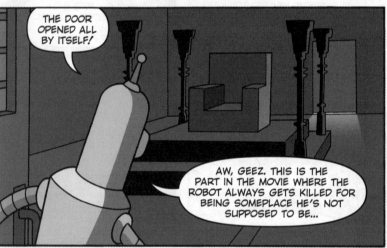

THE DOOR OPENED ALL BY ITSELF!

AW, GEEZ. THIS IS THE PART IN THE MOVIE WHERE THE ROBOT ALWAYS GETS KILLED FOR BEING SOMEPLACE HE'S NOT SUPPOSED TO BE...

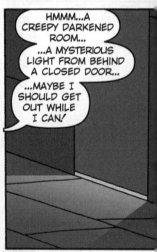

HMMM...A CREEPY DARKENED ROOM...

...A MYSTERIOUS LIGHT FROM BEHIND A CLOSED DOOR...

...MAYBE I SHOULD GET OUT WHILE I CAN!

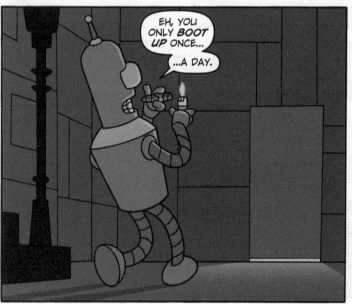

EH, YOU ONLY *BOOT UP* ONCE...

...A DAY.

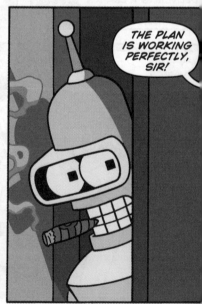

THE PLAN IS WORKING PERFECTLY, SIR!

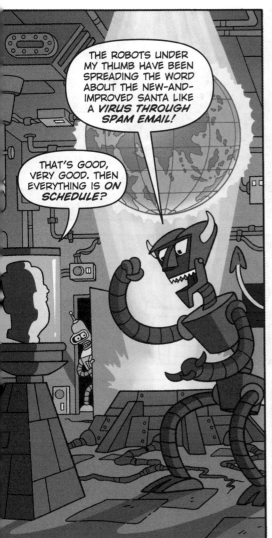

THE ROBOTS UNDER MY THUMB HAVE BEEN SPREADING THE WORD ABOUT THE NEW-AND-IMPROVED SANTA LIKE A *VIRUS THROUGH SPAM EMAIL!*

THAT'S GOOD, VERY GOOD. THEN EVERYTHING IS *ON SCHEDULE?*

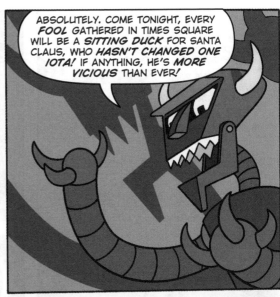

ABSOLUTELY. COME TONIGHT, EVERY *FOOL* GATHERED IN TIMES SQUARE WILL BE A *SITTING DUCK* FOR SANTA CLAUS, WHO *HASN'T CHANGED ONE IOTA!* IF ANYTHING, HE'S *MORE VICIOUS* THAN EVER!

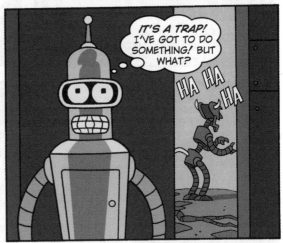

IT'S A TRAP! I'VE GOT TO DO SOMETHING! BUT WHAT?

HA HA HA

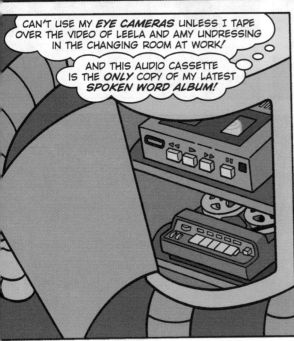

CAN'T USE MY *EYE CAMERAS* UNLESS I TAPE OVER THE VIDEO OF LEELA AND AMY UNDRESSING IN THE CHANGING ROOM AT WORK!

AND THIS AUDIO CASSETTE IS THE *ONLY* COPY OF MY LATEST *SPOKEN WORD ALBUM!*

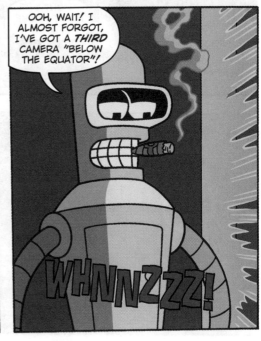

OOH, WAIT! I ALMOST FORGOT, I'VE GOT A *THIRD* CAMERA "BELOW THE EQUATOR"!

WHNNZZZ!

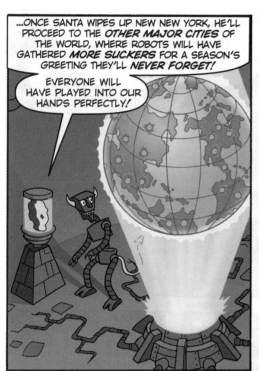

...ONCE SANTA WIPES UP NEW NEW YORK, HE'LL PROCEED TO THE *OTHER MAJOR CITIES* OF THE WORLD, WHERE ROBOTS WILL HAVE GATHERED *MORE SUCKERS* FOR A SEASON'S GREETING THEY'LL *NEVER FORGET!*

EVERYONE WILL HAVE PLAYED INTO OUR HANDS PERFECTLY!

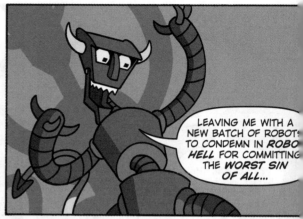

LEAVING ME WITH A NEW BATCH OF ROBOTS TO CONDEMN IN *ROBO HELL* FOR COMMITTING THE *WORST SIN OF ALL...*

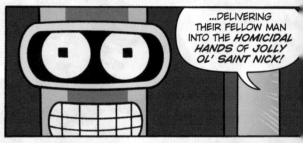

...DELIVERING THEIR FELLOW MAN INTO THE *HOMICIDAL HANDS* OF *JOLLY OL' SAINT NICK!*

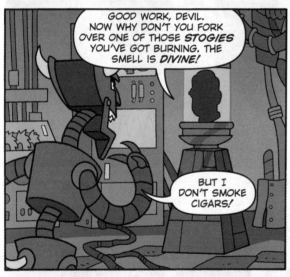

GOOD WORK, DEVIL. NOW WHY DON'T YOU FORK OVER ONE OF THOSE *STOGIES* YOU'VE GOT BURNING. THE SMELL IS *DIVINE!*

BUT I DON'T SMOKE CIGARS!

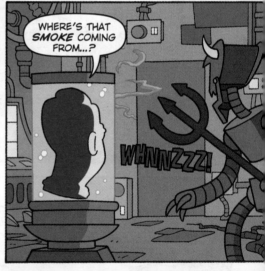

WHERE'S THAT *SMOKE* COMING FROM...?

WHNNNZZZ!

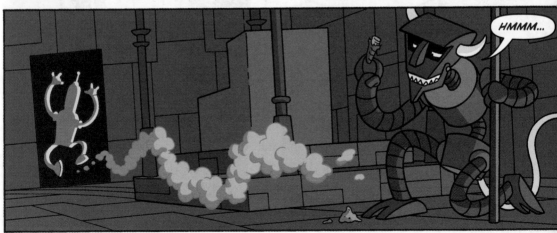

HMMM...

LITTLE LATER...

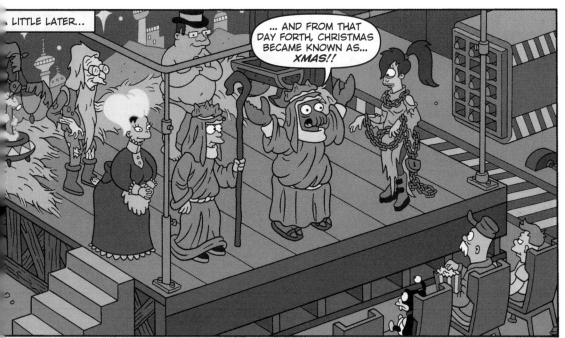

... AND FROM THAT DAY FORTH, CHRISTMAS BECAME KNOWN AS... *XMAS!!*

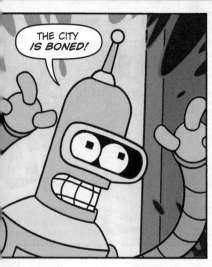

THE CITY *IS BONED!*

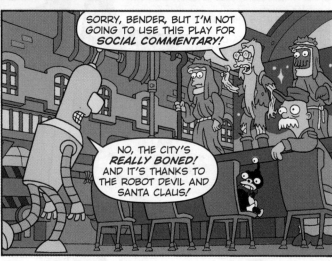

SORRY, BENDER, BUT I'M NOT GOING TO USE THIS PLAY FOR *SOCIAL COMMENTARY!*

NO, THE CITY'S *REALLY BONED!* AND IT'S THANKS TO THE ROBOT DEVIL AND SANTA CLAUS!

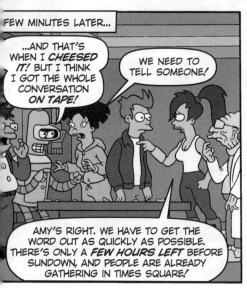

FEW MINUTES LATER...

...AND THAT'S WHEN I *CHEESED IT!* BUT I THINK I GOT THE WHOLE CONVERSATION *ON TAPE!*

WE NEED TO TELL SOMEONE!

AMY'S RIGHT. WE HAVE TO GET THE WORD OUT AS QUICKLY AS POSSIBLE. THERE'S ONLY A *FEW HOURS LEFT* BEFORE SUNDOWN, AND PEOPLE ARE ALREADY GATHERING IN TIMES SQUARE!

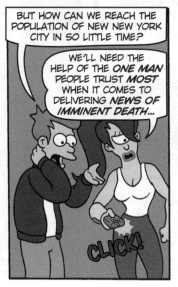

BUT HOW CAN WE REACH THE POPULATION OF NEW NEW YORK CITY IN SO LITTLE TIME?

WE'LL NEED THE HELP OF THE *ONE MAN* PEOPLE TRUST *MOST* WHEN IT COMES TO DELIVERING *NEWS OF IMMINENT DEATH...*

CLICK!

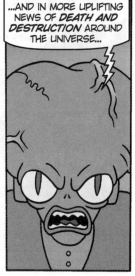

...AND IN MORE UPLIFTING NEWS OF *DEATH AND DESTRUCTION* AROUND THE UNIVERSE...

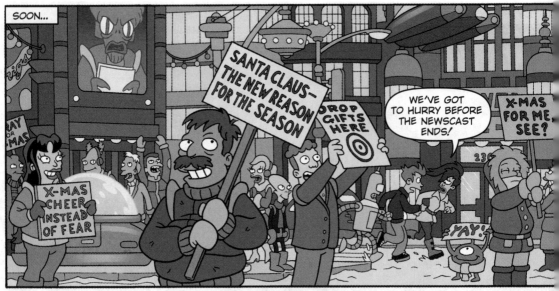

SOON...

SANTA CLAUS— THE NEW REASON FOR THE SEASON

DROP GIFTS HERE

WE'VE GOT TO HURRY BEFORE THE NEWSCAST ENDS!

X-MAS FOR ME, SEE?

X-MAS CHEER INSTEAD OF FEAR

YAY!

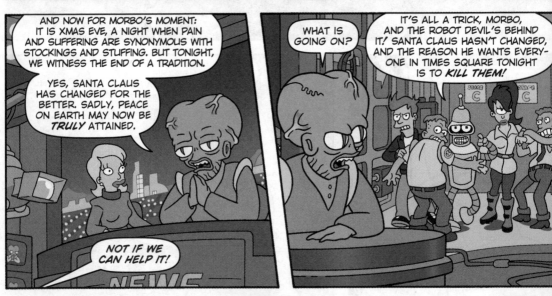

AND NOW FOR MORBO'S MOMENT: IT IS XMAS EVE, A NIGHT WHEN PAIN AND SUFFERING ARE SYNONYMOUS WITH STOCKINGS AND STUFFING. BUT TONIGHT, WE WITNESS THE END OF A TRADITION.

YES, SANTA CLAUS HAS CHANGED FOR THE BETTER. SADLY, PEACE ON EARTH MAY NOW BE *TRULY* ATTAINED.

NOT IF WE CAN HELP IT!

WHAT IS GOING ON?

IT'S ALL A TRICK, MORBO, AND THE ROBOT DEVIL'S BEHIND IT! SANTA CLAUS HASN'T CHANGED, AND THE REASON HE WANTS EVERY-ONE IN TIMES SQUARE TONIGHT IS TO *KILL THEM!*

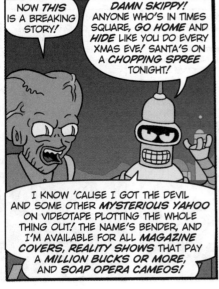

NOW *THIS* IS A BREAKING STORY!

DAMN SKIPPY! ANYONE WHO'S IN TIMES SQUARE, *GO HOME* AND *HIDE* LIKE YOU DO EVERY XMAS EVE! SANTA'S ON A *CHOPPING SPREE* TONIGHT!

I KNOW 'CAUSE I GOT THE DEVIL AND SOME OTHER *MYSTERIOUS YAHOO* ON VIDEOTAPE PLOTTING THE WHOLE THING OUT! THE NAME'S BENDER, AND I'M AVAILABLE FOR ALL *MAGAZINE COVERS, REALITY SHOWS* THAT PAY A *MILLION BUCKS OR MORE,* AND *SOAP OPERA CAMEOS!*

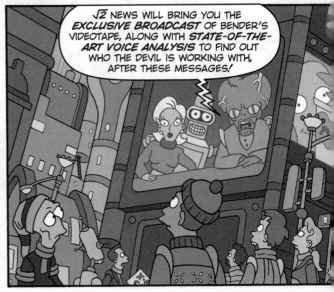

$\sqrt{2}$ NEWS WILL BRING YOU THE *EXCLUSIVE BROADCAST* OF BENDER'S VIDEOTAPE, ALONG WITH *STATE-OF-THE-ART VOICE ANALYSIS* TO FIND OUT WHO THE DEVIL IS WORKING WITH, AFTER THESE MESSAGES!

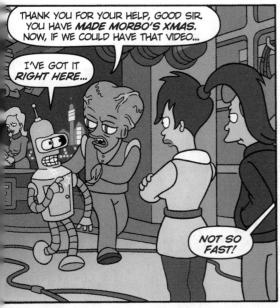

THANK YOU FOR YOUR HELP, GOOD SIR. YOU HAVE **MADE MORBO'S XMAS.** NOW, IF WE COULD HAVE THAT VIDEO...

I'VE GOT IT **RIGHT HERE...**

NOT SO FAST!

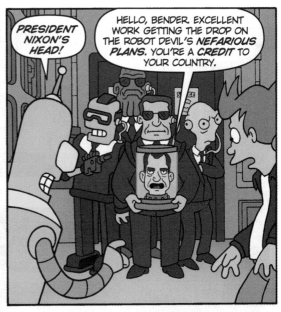

PRESIDENT NIXON'S HEAD!

HELLO, BENDER. EXCELLENT WORK GETTING THE DROP ON THE ROBOT DEVIL'S **NEFARIOUS PLANS.** YOU'RE A **CREDIT** TO YOUR COUNTRY.

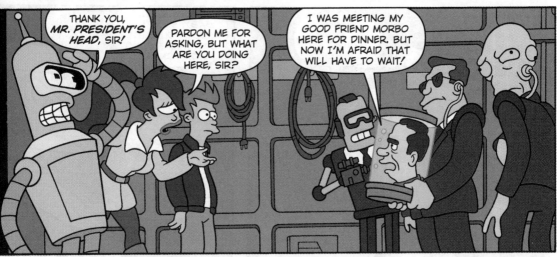

THANK YOU, **MR. PRESIDENT'S HEAD,** SIR!

PARDON ME FOR ASKING, BUT WHAT ARE YOU DOING HERE, SIR?

I WAS MEETING MY GOOD FRIEND MORBO HERE FOR DINNER. BUT NOW I'M AFRAID THAT WILL HAVE TO WAIT!

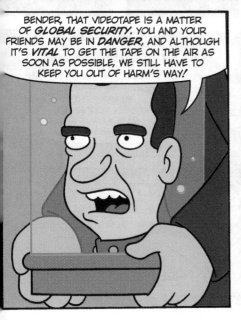

BENDER, THAT VIDEOTAPE IS A MATTER OF **GLOBAL SECURITY.** YOU AND YOUR FRIENDS MAY BE IN **DANGER,** AND ALTHOUGH IT'S **VITAL** TO GET THE TAPE ON THE AIR AS SOON AS POSSIBLE, WE STILL HAVE TO KEEP YOU OUT OF HARM'S WAY!

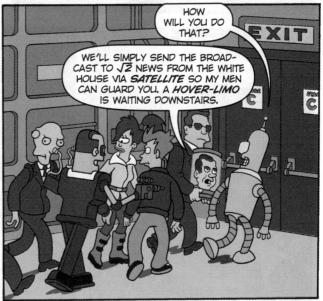

HOW WILL YOU DO THAT?

WE'LL SIMPLY SEND THE BROADCAST TO $\sqrt{2}$ NEWS FROM THE WHITE HOUSE VIA **SATELLITE** SO MY MEN CAN GUARD YOU. A **HOVER-LIMO** IS WAITING DOWNSTAIRS.

EXIT

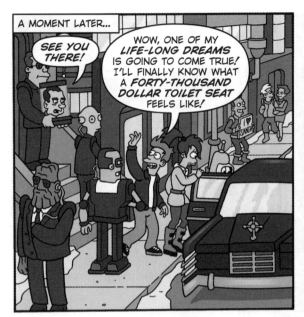

A MOMENT LATER...

SEE YOU THERE!

WOW, ONE OF MY *LIFE-LONG DREAMS* IS GOING TO COME TRUE! I'LL FINALLY KNOW WHAT A *FORTY-THOUSAND DOLLAR TOILET SEAT* FEELS LIKE!

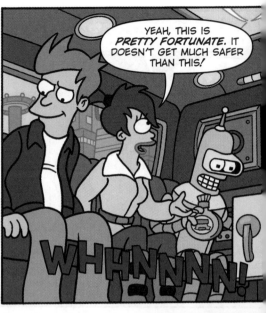

YEAH, THIS IS *PRETTY FORTUNATE.* IT DOESN'T GET MUCH SAFER THAN THIS!

WHHNNNNN!

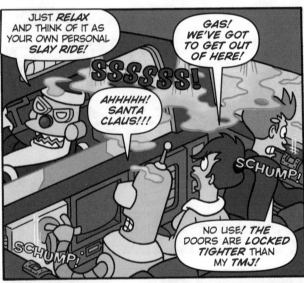

JUST *RELAX* AND THINK OF IT AS YOUR OWN PERSONAL *SLAY RIDE!*

GAS! WE'VE GOT TO GET OUT OF HERE!

SSSSSS!

AHHHHH! SANTA CLAUS!!!

SCHUMP!

SCHUMP!

NO USE! *THE DOORS ARE LOCKED TIGHTER* THAN MY *TMJ!*

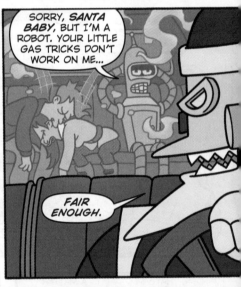

SORRY, *SANTA BABY,* BUT I'M A ROBOT. YOUR LITTLE GAS TRICKS DON'T WORK ON ME...

FAIR ENOUGH.

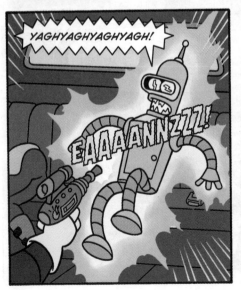

YAGHYAGHYAGHYAGH!

EAAAANNZZZ!

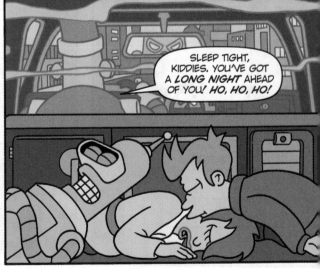

SLEEP TIGHT, KIDDIES. YOU'VE GOT A *LONG NIGHT* AHEAD OF YOU! HO, HO, HO!

LATER THAT EVENING...
WHUH? WH-WHAT HAPPENED? WHERE AM I?
YOU'RE IN THE ***BOWELS OF HELL,*** BENDER!
HAHAHAHAHAHA!!!

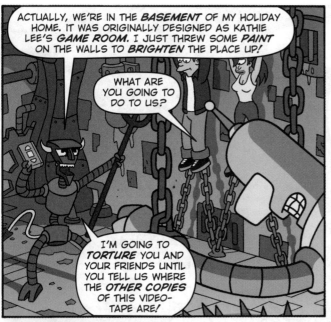

ACTUALLY, WE'RE IN THE *BASEMENT* OF MY HOLIDAY HOME. IT WAS ORIGINALLY DESIGNED AS KATHIE LEE'S *GAME ROOM*. I JUST THREW SOME *PAINT* ON THE WALLS TO *BRIGHTEN* THE PLACE UP!

WHAT ARE YOU GOING TO DO TO US?

I'M GOING TO *TORTURE* YOU AND YOUR FRIENDS UNTIL YOU TELL US WHERE THE *OTHER COPIES* OF THIS VIDEO-TAPE ARE!

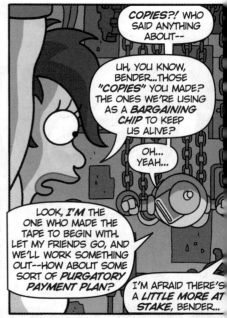

COPIES?! WHO SAID ANYTHING ABOUT--

UH, YOU KNOW, BENDER...THOSE *"COPIES"* YOU MADE? THE ONES WE'RE USING AS A *BARGAINING CHIP* TO KEEP US ALIVE?

OH... YEAH...

LOOK, *I'M* THE ONE WHO MADE THE TAPE TO BEGIN WITH. LET MY FRIENDS GO, AND WE'LL WORK SOMETHING OUT--HOW ABOUT SOME SORT OF *PURGATORY PAYMENT PLAN*?

I'M AFRAID THERE'S A *LITTLE MORE AT STAKE*, BENDER...

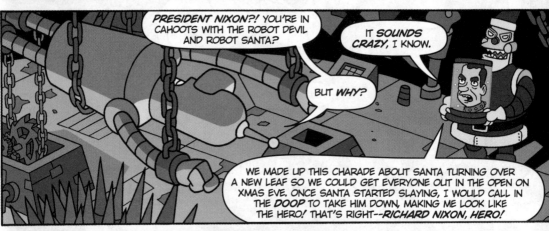

PRESIDENT NIXON?! YOU'RE IN CAHOOTS WITH THE ROBOT DEVIL AND ROBOT SANTA?

IT *SOUNDS CRAZY*, I KNOW.

BUT *WHY*?

WE MADE UP THIS CHARADE ABOUT SANTA TURNING OVER A NEW LEAF SO WE COULD GET EVERYONE OUT IN THE OPEN ON XMAS EVE. ONCE SANTA STARTED SLAYING, I WOULD CALL IN THE *DOOP* TO TAKE HIM DOWN, MAKING ME LOOK LIKE THE HERO! THAT'S RIGHT--*RICHARD NIXON, HERO!*

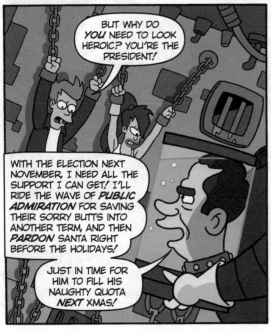

BUT WHY DO *YOU* NEED TO LOOK HEROIC? YOU'RE THE PRESIDENT!

WITH THE ELECTION NEXT NOVEMBER, I NEED ALL THE SUPPORT I CAN GET! I'LL RIDE THE WAVE OF *PUBLIC ADMIRATION* FOR SAVING THEIR SORRY BUTTS INTO ANOTHER TERM, AND THEN *PARDON* SANTA RIGHT BEFORE THE HOLIDAYS!

JUST IN TIME FOR HIM TO FILL HIS *NAUGHTY QUOTA NEXT XMAS!*

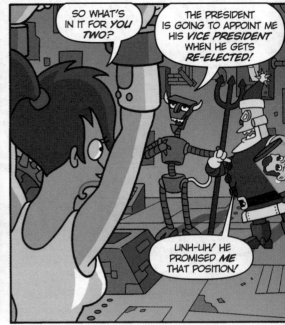

SO WHAT'S IN IT FOR *YOU TWO*?

THE PRESIDENT IS GOING TO APPOINT ME HIS *VICE PRESIDENT* WHEN HE GETS *RE-ELECTED!*

UNH-UH! HE PROMISED *ME* THAT POSITION!

SORRY, BUT IT'S OBVIOUS WHO'S MORE SUITED FOR PUBLIC OFFICE. I WAS THE MASTERMIND BEHIND THIS ENTIRE PLAN. NOW, LET'S GET ON WITH THE TORTURE, SHALL WE?...
WRRRRRR!
NO WAY! I EARNED THAT JOB! ALL YOU DID WAS BRIBE A BUNCH OF STUPID ROBOTS WHO ARE JUST GOING TO END UP WAXING YOUR BUTT IN ROBOT HELL!
OYS, RELAX. I'M SURE THERE'S AN EASY WAY TO SETTLE THIS. A POTATO SACK RACE, OR SOMETHING...
NO WAY! 'E'RE GOING TO NDLE THIS LIKE MENBOTS!
BRING IT ON, FAT BOY!
HOW ABOUT WE LET OLD BENDER DOWN FIRST?
THIS IS A LONG TIME COMING, BEELZEBOT! YOU'VE BEEN AT THE TOP OF MY NAUGHTY LIST FOR YEARS!
SHUK!
LIKE YOU DON'T HAVE YOUR OWN PRIVATE CIRCLE AWAITING YOU IN ROBOT HELL, MORON?
AHHH! THAT ROCKET'S COMING RIGHT AT US, LEELA!
I SEE IT! MY DEPTH PERCEPTION ISN'T THAT BAD!
SHOOOOOOM!
YOWZA!
KERPLOW!
HERE'S A SAMPLE OF MY XMAS WRAPPING TECHNIQUE!
GLAGH!
IT IMPACTED ON OUR CHAINS! WE'RE FREE!

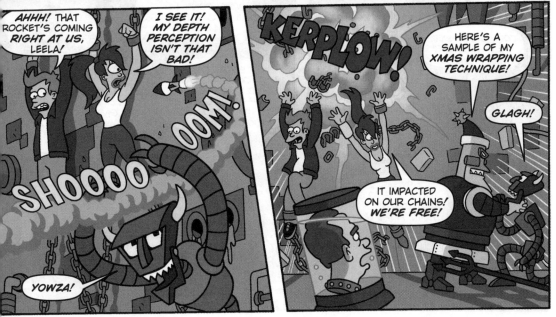

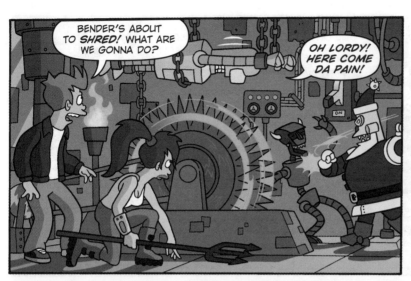

BENDER'S ABOUT TO *SHRED!* WHAT ARE WE GONNA DO?

OH LORDY! HERE COME DA PAIN!

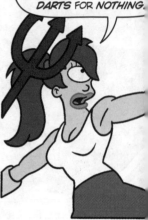

COME ON, LEELA. YOU DIDN'T SPEND ALL THOSE NIGHTS *ALONE* AT O'GLORGNAX'S PUB PLAYING *DARTS* FOR NOTHING.

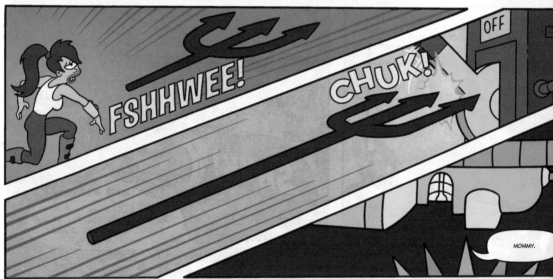

FSHHWEE!

CHUK!

MOMMY.

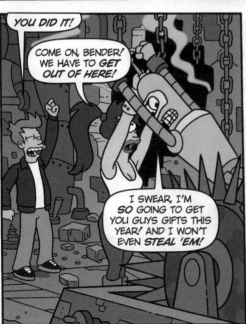

YOU DID IT!

COME ON, BENDER! WE HAVE TO *GET OUT OF HERE!*

I SWEAR, I'M SO GOING TO GET YOU GUYS GIFTS THIS YEAR! AND I WON'T EVEN *STEAL 'EM!*

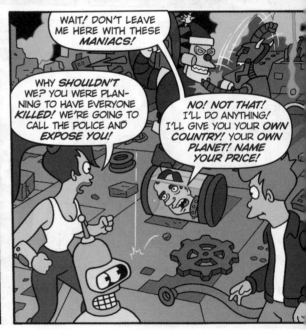

WAIT! DON'T LEAVE ME HERE WITH THESE *MANIACS!*

WHY *SHOULDN'T* WE? YOU WERE PLANNING TO HAVE EVERYONE *KILLED!* WE'RE GOING TO CALL THE POLICE AND *EXPOSE YOU!*

NO! NOT THAT! I'LL DO ANYTHING! I'LL GIVE YOU YOUR *OWN COUNTRY!* YOUR *OWN PLANET!* NAME YOUR PRICE!

I'VE GOT A BETTER IDEA. PICK HIM UP, BENDER. THE PRESIDENT'S SPENDING XMAS EVE WITH *US!*

LATER THAT NIGHT...

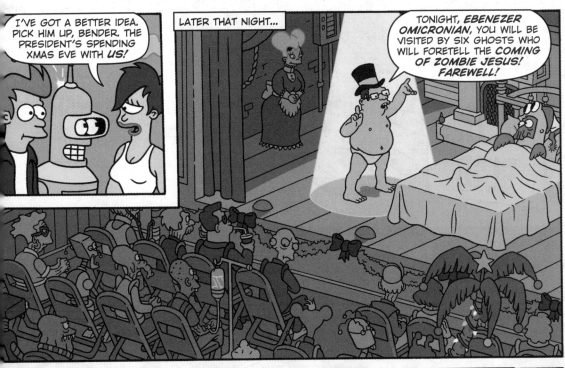

TONIGHT, *EBENEZER OMICRONIAN,* YOU WILL BE VISITED BY SIX GHOSTS WHO WILL FORETELL THE *COMING OF ZOMBIE JESUS!* FAREWELL!

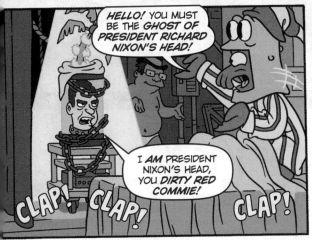

HELLO! YOU MUST BE THE *GHOST OF PRESIDENT RICHARD NIXON'S HEAD!*

I *AM* PRESIDENT NIXON'S HEAD, YOU *DIRTY RED COMMIE!*

CLAP! CLAP! CLAP!

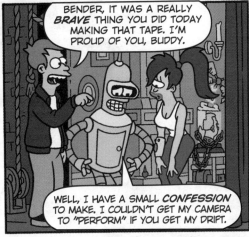

BENDER, IT WAS A REALLY *BRAVE* THING YOU DID TODAY MAKING THAT TAPE. I'M PROUD OF YOU, BUDDY.

WELL, I HAVE A SMALL *CONFESSION* TO MAKE. I COULDN'T GET MY CAMERA TO "PERFORM" IF YOU GET MY DRIFT.

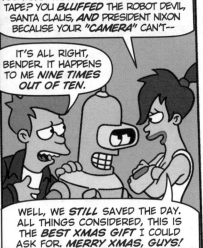

YOU MEAN THERE WAS *NOTHING* ON THE TAPE? YOU *BLUFFED* THE ROBOT DEVIL, SANTA CLAUS, *AND* PRESIDENT NIXON BECAUSE YOUR "CAMERA" CAN'T--

IT'S ALL RIGHT, BENDER. IT HAPPENS TO ME *NINE TIMES OUT OF TEN.*

WELL, WE *STILL* SAVED THE DAY. ALL THINGS CONSIDERED, THIS IS THE *BEST XMAS GIFT* I COULD ASK FOR. *MERRY XMAS, GUYS!*

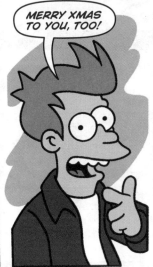

MERRY XMAS TO YOU, TOO!

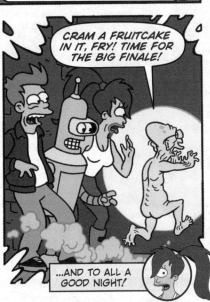

CRAM A FRUITCAKE IN IT, FRY! TIME FOR THE BIG FINALE!

...AND TO ALL A GOOD NIGHT!

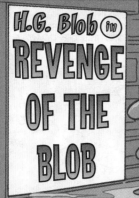

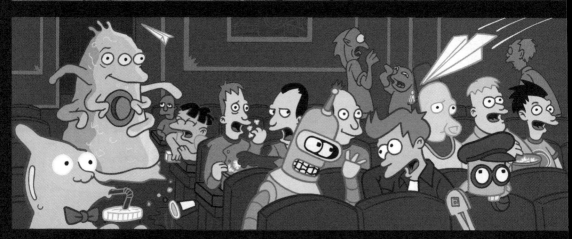

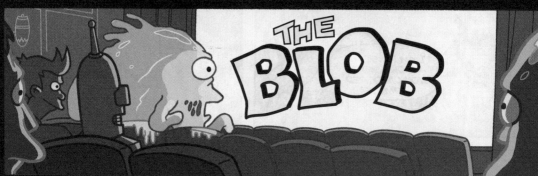

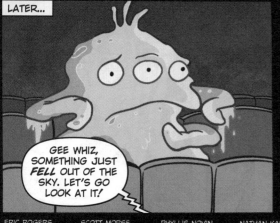

ERIC ROGERS
WRITER

SCOTT MORSE
PENCILS

PHYLLIS NOVIN
INKS

NATHAN KANE
COLORS

KAREN BATES
LETTERS

BILL MORRISON
EDITOR

MATT GROENING
HEAD USHER

LATER STILL...
WOO HOO! YEAH! GET 'EM!
THE BLOB IS EATING THE ENTIRE TOWN! GOLLY GEE, WE'RE DOOMED!
EVEN LATER...
THE BLOB IS DEAD! IT'S SAFE TO SOCK-HOP AND WEAR POODLE SKIRTS AGAIN!
HEY, LOOK AT THIS GUY! OOH, SCARY! "THE BLOB" MUST'VE BEEN THIS GUY'S COUSIN! ANYBODY GOT A JELLO MOLD HANDY SO I CAN DEFEND MYSELF?
THE END?
THAT NIGHT...
HOW COME YOU'RE NOT EATING YOUR DINNER, DEAR?
EHH, I FILLED UP ON JUNK AT THE THEATER.
THE END

NO ANIMATED TV CHARACTERS WERE HARMED IN THE MAKING OF THIS COMIC BOOK!
BONGO COMICS GROUP
APPROVED BY THE COMICS CODE AUTHORITY
US $2.50
CAN $3.50
#7
FUTURAMA
COMICS
HASTA LA VISTA, MEATBAG!
©2002 BONGO ENTERTAINMENT, INC. FUTURAMA ©&TM TWENTIETH CENTURY FOX FILM CORPORATION. ALL RIGHTS RESERVED.
MATT GROENING

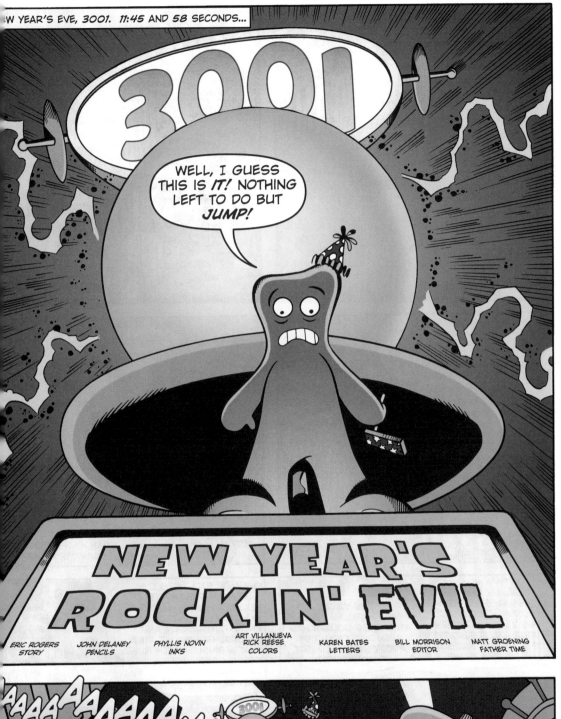

NEW YEAR'S ROCKIN' EVIL

ERIC ROGERS
STORY

JOHN DELANEY
PENCILS

PHYLLIS NOVIN
INKS

ART VILLANUEVA
RICK REESE
COLORS

KAREN BATES
LETTERS

BILL MORRISON
EDITOR

MATT GROENING
FATHER TIME

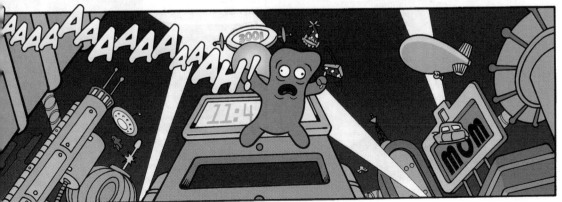

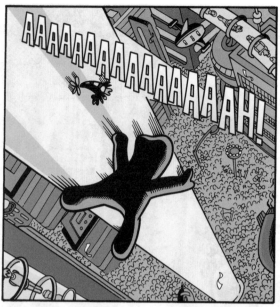

AAAAAAAAAAAAAAAAAAAAH!

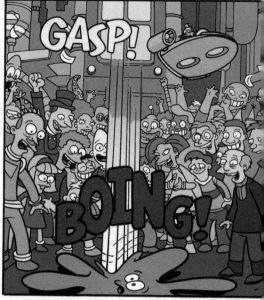

GASP!

BOING!

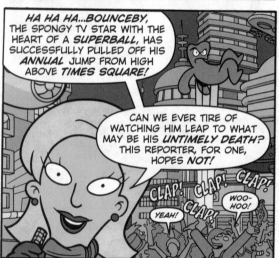

HA HA HA...BOUNCEBY, THE SPONGY TV STAR WITH THE HEART OF A *SUPERBALL*, HAS SUCCESSFULLY PULLED OFF HIS *ANNUAL* JUMP FROM HIGH ABOVE *TIMES SQUARE*!

CAN WE EVER TIRE OF WATCHING HIM LEAP TO WHAT MAY BE HIS *UNTIMELY DEATH*? THIS REPORTER, FOR ONE, HOPES *NOT*!

CLAP! CLAP! CLAP! CLAP!
YEAH!
WOO-HOO!

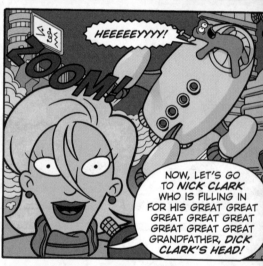

HEEEEEYYYY!

ZOOM!

NOW, LET'S GO TO *NICK CLARK* WHO IS FILLING IN FOR HIS GREAT GREAT GREAT GREAT GREAT GREAT GRANDFATHER, *DICK CLARK'S HEAD*!

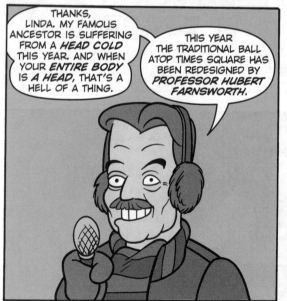

THANKS, LINDA. MY FAMOUS ANCESTOR IS SUFFERING FROM A *HEAD COLD* THIS YEAR. AND WHEN YOUR *ENTIRE BODY* IS *A HEAD*, THAT'S A HELL OF A THING.

THIS YEAR THE TRADITIONAL BALL ATOP TIMES SQUARE HAS BEEN REDESIGNED BY *PROFESSOR HUBERT FARNSWORTH*.

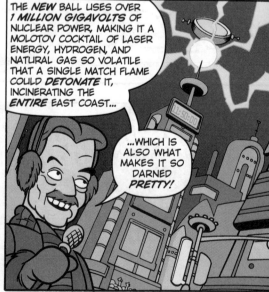

THE *NEW* BALL USES OVER *1 MILLION GIGAVOLTS* OF NUCLEAR POWER, MAKING IT A MOLOTOV COCKTAIL OF LASER ENERGY, HYDROGEN, AND NATURAL GAS SO VOLATILE THAT A SINGLE MATCH FLAME COULD *DETONATE* IT, INCINERATING THE *ENTIRE* EAST COAST...

...WHICH IS ALSO WHAT MAKES IT SO DARNED *PRETTY*!

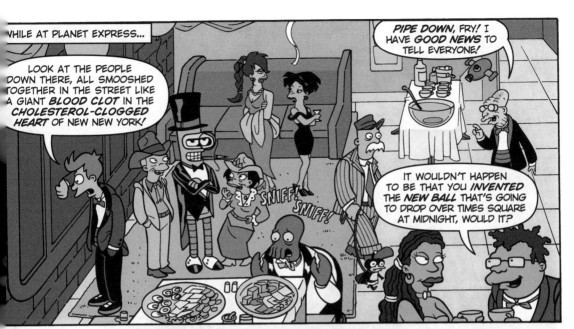

WHILE AT PLANET EXPRESS...

LOOK AT THE PEOPLE DOWN THERE, ALL SMOOSHED TOGETHER IN THE STREET LIKE A GIANT *BLOOD CLOT* IN THE *CHOLESTEROL-CLOGGED HEART* OF NEW NEW YORK!

SNIFF!

SNIFF!

PIPE DOWN, FRY! I HAVE *GOOD NEWS* TO TELL EVERYONE!

IT WOULDN'T HAPPEN TO BE THAT YOU *INVENTED* THE *NEW BALL* THAT'S GOING TO DROP OVER TIMES SQUARE AT MIDNIGHT, WOULD IT?

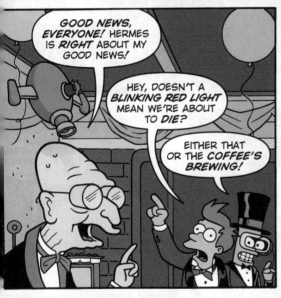

GOOD NEWS, EVERYONE! HERMES IS *RIGHT* ABOUT MY GOOD NEWS!

HEY, DOESN'T A *BLINKING RED LIGHT* MEAN WE'RE ABOUT TO *DIE?*

EITHER THAT OR THE *COFFEE'S BREWING!*

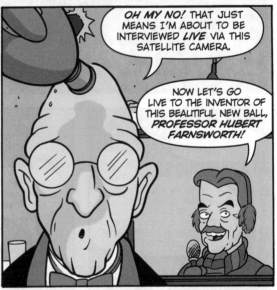

OH MY NO! THAT JUST MEANS I'M ABOUT TO BE INTERVIEWED *LIVE* VIA THIS SATELLITE CAMERA.

NOW LET'S GO LIVE TO THE INVENTOR OF THIS BEAUTIFUL NEW BALL, *PROFESSOR HUBERT FARNSWORTH!*

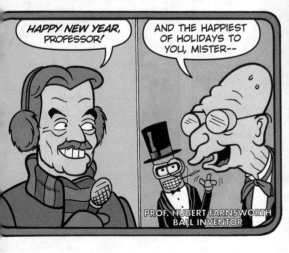

HAPPY NEW YEAR, PROFESSOR!

AND THE HAPPIEST OF HOLIDAYS TO YOU, MISTER--

PROF. HUBERT FARNSWORTH
BALL INVENTOR

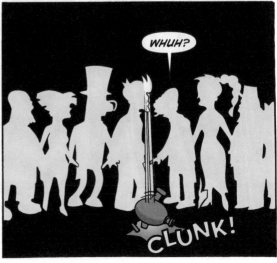

WHUH?

CLUNK!

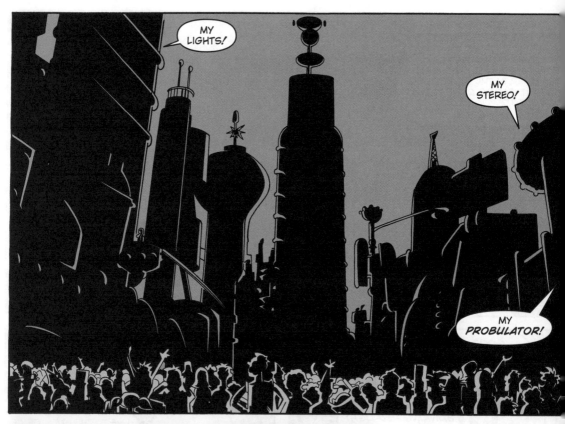

MY LIGHTS!

MY STEREO!

MY PROBULATOR!

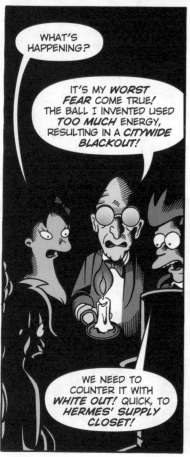

WHAT'S HAPPENING?

IT'S MY *WORST FEAR* COME TRUE! THE BALL I INVENTED USED *TOO MUCH* ENERGY, RESULTING IN A *CITYWIDE BLACKOUT!*

WE NEED TO COUNTER IT WITH *WHITE OUT!* QUICK, TO *HERMES' SUPPLY CLOSET!*

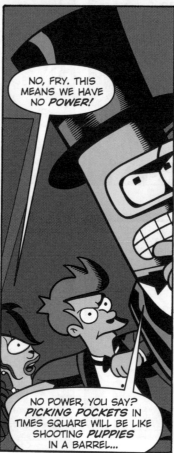

NO, FRY. THIS MEANS WE HAVE NO *POWER!*

NO POWER, YOU SAY? *PICKING POCKETS* IN TIMES SQUARE WILL BE LIKE SHOOTING *PUPPIES* IN A BARREL...

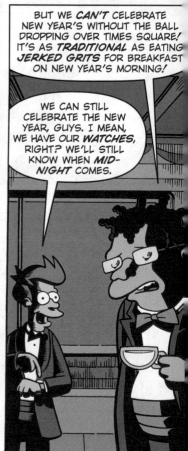

BUT WE *CAN'T* CELEBRATE NEW YEAR'S WITHOUT THE BALL DROPPING OVER TIMES SQUARE! IT'S AS *TRADITIONAL* AS EATING *JERKED GRITS* FOR BREAKFAST ON NEW YEAR'S MORNING!

WE CAN STILL CELEBRATE THE NEW YEAR, GUYS. I MEAN, WE HAVE OUR *WATCHES*, RIGHT? WE'LL STILL KNOW WHEN *MID-NIGHT* COMES.

FRY, A NEW YEAR'S EVE WITHOUT THE DROPPING BALL IS LIKE AN XMAS WITH-OUT FEAR OF DEATH!
LIKE THE MOON WITHOUT FUNNEL CAKES!
LIKE A MAD SCIENTIST WITHOUT AN UNSUSPECTING GREAT UNCLE TO TEST HIS LATEST INNOVATIONS ON WHILE HE SLEEPS!
WE STILL HAVE EACH OTHER! MAYBE WE CAN PLAY A GAME OR SING SONGS! OOH, WHAT ABOUT THAT TIME WE POSED "WHAT IF" QUESTIONS TO THAT TV THINGY THE PROFESSOR INVENTED?
HEY, I'VE GOT ONE--"WHAT IF FRY TOOK A LOOK AROUND AND NOTICED WE DON'T HAVE POWER?" HOW IS THE MACHINE GOING TO WORK WITHOUT ELECTRICITY? NEW YEAR'S EVE IS RUINED! RUINED!
OF COURSE IT IS! BUT WE CAN STILL WATCH THE WHAT-IF MACHINE...
KEEERASH!
HERE IT IS!
HOW IS IT ABLE TO OPERATE?
HHHUUUMMMM!
I DESIGNED IT TO RUN ON ELECTRICITY OR BATTERIES, JUST IN CASE WE EVER NEEDED TO AKE IT TO THE BEACH OR PACK IT IN AN EARTH-QUAKE KIT! NOW WHO WANTS TO GO FIRST?
I GOT A DOOZY! SINCE FRY IS ALWAYS TALKING ABOUT HIS GLORIOUS 20TH CENTURY, I CAN'T HELP BUT WONDER..."WHAT WOULD HAPPEN IF I TRAVELLED BACK TO 1999?"
AAAH!
OOOH!
BRAAAP!

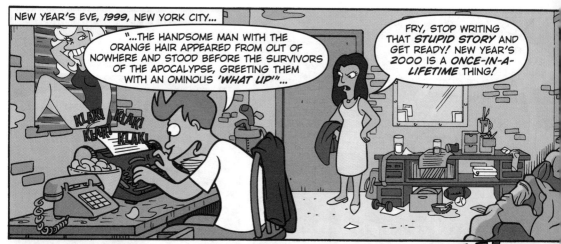

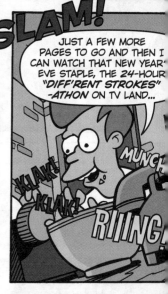

NEW YEAR'S EVE, *1999*, NEW YORK CITY...

"...THE HANDSOME MAN WITH THE ORANGE HAIR APPEARED FROM OUT OF NOWHERE AND STOOD BEFORE THE SURVIVORS OF THE APOCALYPSE, GREETING THEM WITH AN OMINOUS *'WHAT UP'*"...

FRY, STOP WRITING THAT *STUPID STORY* AND GET READY! NEW YEAR'S 2000 IS A *ONCE-IN-A-LIFETIME* THING!

KLAK! KLAK! KLAK! KLAK!

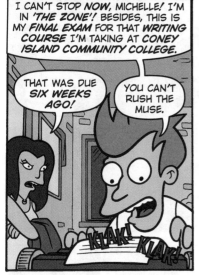

I CAN'T STOP *NOW*, MICHELLE! I'M IN *'THE ZONE'*! BESIDES, THIS IS MY *FINAL EXAM* FOR THAT *WRITING COURSE* I'M TAKING AT *CONEY ISLAND COMMUNITY COLLEGE*.

THAT WAS DUE *SIX WEEKS* AGO!

YOU CAN'T *RUSH* THE MUSE.

KLAK! KLAK!

FINE! IF YOU WANT TO SPEND THE *DAWN OF A NEW MILLENNIUM* WRITING A STUPID STORY, THEN I'LL JUST GO HAVE FUN *SOMEWHERE ELSE!* MAYBE MY *"FRIEND"* JEAN-CLAUDE DOWN THE HALL CAN SHOW ME A *GOOD TIME!*

LOVE YOU, TOO.

SLAM!

JUST A FEW MORE PAGES TO GO AND THEN I CAN WATCH THAT NEW YEAR'S EVE STAPLE, THE 24-HOUR *"DIFF'RENT STROKES"* -ATHON ON TV LAND...

KLAK! KLAK! MUNCH

RIIING!

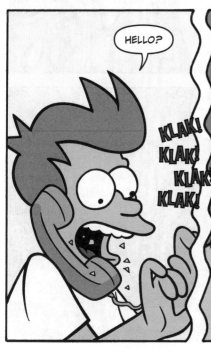

HELLO?

FRY, IT'S YER BOSS, *MR. PANUCCI!* YA GOTTA GET DOWN HERE AND *WORK* 'CAUSE I GOT NOBODY TO DELIVER THESE *PIZZAS!*

KLAK! KLAK! KLAK! KLAK!

BUT I ASKED FOR TONIGHT *OFF!*

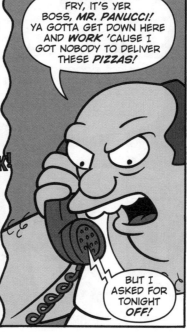

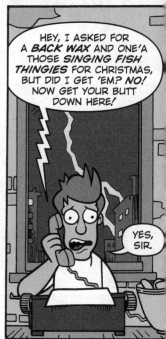

HEY, I ASKED FOR A *BACK WAX* AND ONE'A THOSE *SINGING FISH THINGIES* FOR CHRISTMAS, BUT DID I GET 'EM? *NO!* NOW GET YOUR BUTT DOWN HERE!

YES, SIR.

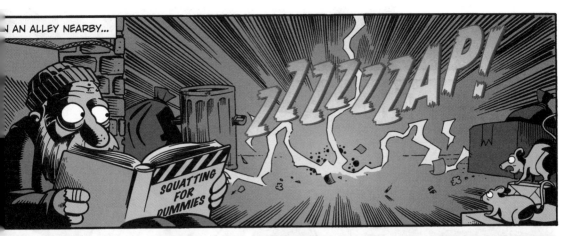

ZZZZZZAP!

SQUATTING FOR DUMMIES

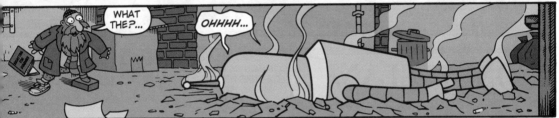

WHAT THE?...

OHHHH...

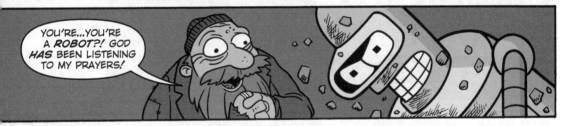

YOU'RE...YOU'RE A *ROBOT*?! GOD *HAS* BEEN LISTENING TO MY PRAYERS!

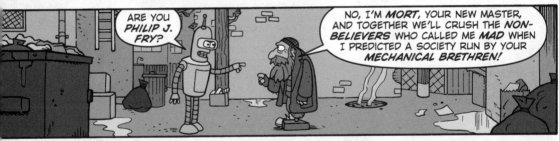

ARE YOU *PHILIP J. FRY*?

NO, I'M *MORT*, YOUR NEW MASTER, AND TOGETHER WE'LL CRUSH THE *NON-BELIEVERS* WHO CALLED ME *MAD* WHEN I PREDICTED A SOCIETY RUN BY YOUR *MECHANICAL BRETHREN!*

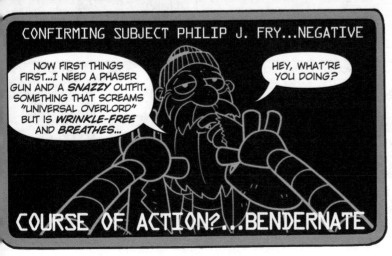

CONFIRMING SUBJECT PHILIP J. FRY...NEGATIVE

NOW FIRST THINGS FIRST...I NEED A PHASER GUN AND A *SNAZZY* OUTFIT. SOMETHING THAT SCREAMS "UNIVERSAL OVERLORD" BUT IS *WRINKLE-FREE* AND *BREATHES*...

HEY, WHAT'RE YOU DOING?

COURSE OF ACTION?...BENDERNATE

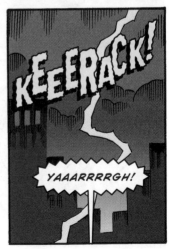

KEEERACK!

YAAARRRRGH!

MEANWHILE, ACROSS TOWN...
ZZZZZZZZZZAP!
CONEY ISLAND COMMUNITY COLLEGE
OHHH... WHERE AM I?
IS THIS THE PAST?
CONEY ISLAND COMMUNITY COLLEGE
CONEY ISLAND COMMUNITY COLLEGE? I MADE IT! THIS IS WHERE FRY GOES TO SCHOOL!
I TOLD YOU, TINA, WE'RE WEARIN' WA TOO MUCH IF WE WANT TO GET A'S AT THIS SCHOOL.
INSIDE THE HALL, LAP DANCING 101...
TODAY WE'LL STUDY THE ROOTS OF OUR RICH STRIPPING HERITAGE, BEGINNING WITH THE VERY FIRST LAP DANCE GIVEN BY POCAHONTAS. OPEN YOUR BOOKS TO CHAPTER TWO...
LAP DANCING 101
UM, EXCUSE ME...?
YOUNG LADY, YOU KNOW THE RULES ABOUT DRESS CODE!
YA HAFTA WEAR A SET OF HEELS AT LEAST FIVE INCHES TALL TO ENTER THIS CLASSROOM!
LAP DANCING 101
NO, I'M NOT A STUDENT. I'M ACTUALLY LOOK-ING FOR ONE OF YOURS--PHILIP J. FRY?

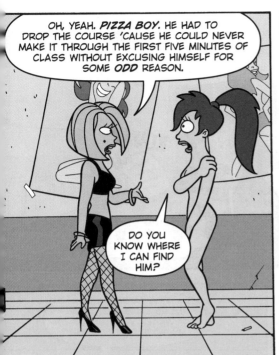

OH, YEAH. *PIZZA BOY.* HE HAD TO DROP THE COURSE 'CAUSE HE COULD NEVER MAKE IT THROUGH THE FIRST FIVE MINUTES OF CLASS WITHOUT EXCUSING HIMSELF FOR SOME *ODD* REASON.

DO YOU KNOW WHERE I CAN FIND HIM?

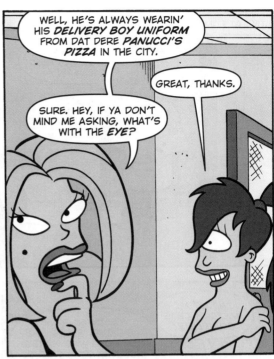

WELL, HE'S ALWAYS WEARIN' HIS *DELIVERY BOY UNIFORM* FROM DAT DERE *PANUCCI'S PIZZA* IN THE CITY.

GREAT, THANKS.

SURE. HEY, IF YA DON'T MIND ME ASKING, WHAT'S WITH THE *EYE?*

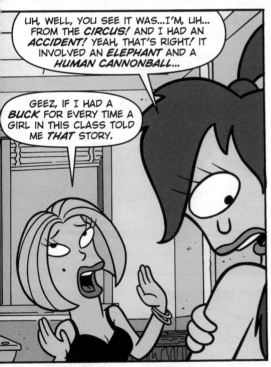

UH, WELL, YOU SEE IT WAS...I'M, UH... FROM THE *CIRCUS!* AND I HAD AN *ACCIDENT!* YEAH, THAT'S RIGHT! IT INVOLVED AN *ELEPHANT* AND A *HUMAN CANNONBALL...*

GEEZ, IF I HAD A *BUCK* FOR EVERY TIME A GIRL IN THIS CLASS TOLD ME *THAT* STORY.

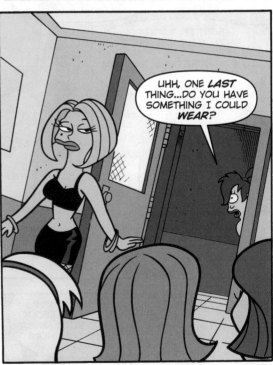

UHH, ONE *LAST* THING...DO YOU HAVE SOMETHING I COULD *WEAR?*

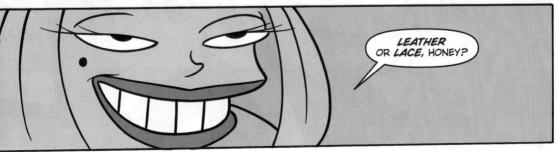

LEATHER OR *LACE,* HONEY?

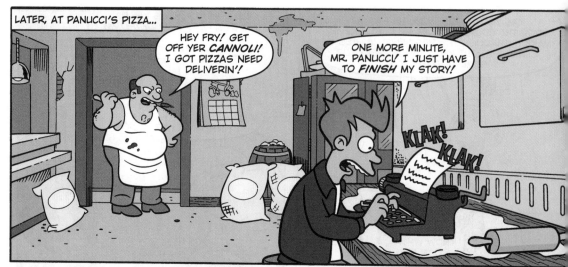

LATER, AT PANUCCI'S PIZZA...

HEY FRY! GET OFF YER CANNOLI! I GOT PIZZAS NEED DELIVERIN'!

ONE MORE MINUTE, MR. PANUCCI! I JUST HAVE TO FINISH MY STORY!

KLAK! KLAK!

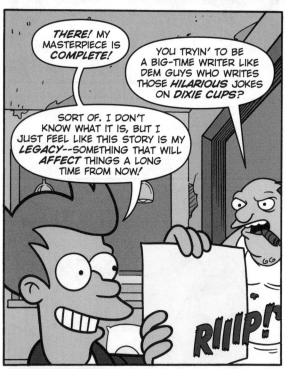

THERE! MY MASTERPIECE IS COMPLETE!

YOU TRYIN' TO BE A BIG-TIME WRITER LIKE DEM GUYS WHO WRITES THOSE HILARIOUS JOKES ON DIXIE CUPS?

SORT OF. I DON'T KNOW WHAT IT IS, BUT I JUST FEEL LIKE THIS STORY IS MY LEGACY--SOMETHING THAT WILL AFFECT THINGS A LONG TIME FROM NOW!

RIIIP!

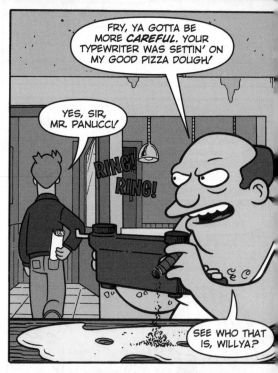

FRY, YA GOTTA BE MORE CAREFUL. YOUR TYPEWRITER WAS SETTIN' ON MY GOOD PIZZA DOUGH!

YES, SIR, MR. PANUCCI!

RING! RING!

SEE WHO THAT IS, WILLYA?

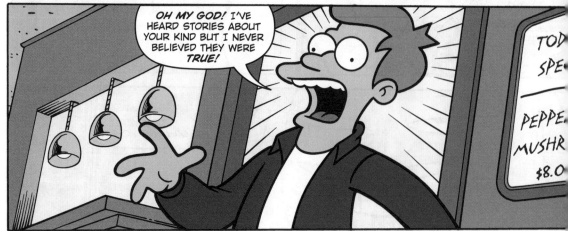

OH MY GOD! I'VE HEARD STORIES ABOUT YOUR KIND BUT I NEVER BELIEVED THEY WERE TRUE!

TOD
SPE

PEPPE
MUSHR
$8.0

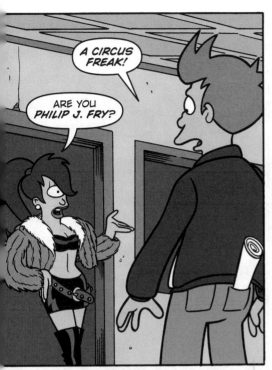

A CIRCUS FREAK!

ARE YOU PHILIP J. FRY?

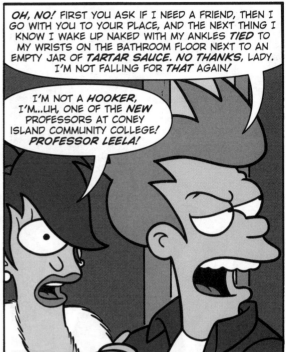

OH, NO! FIRST YOU ASK IF I NEED A FRIEND, THEN I GO WITH YOU TO YOUR PLACE, AND THE NEXT THING I KNOW I WAKE UP NAKED WITH MY ANKLES **TIED** TO MY WRISTS ON THE BATHROOM FLOOR NEXT TO AN EMPTY JAR OF **TARTAR SAUCE. NO THANKS**, LADY. I'M NOT FALLING FOR **THAT** AGAIN!

I'M NOT A **HOOKER**, I'M...UH, ONE OF THE **NEW** PROFESSORS AT CONEY ISLAND COMMUNITY COLLEGE! **PROFESSOR LEELA!**

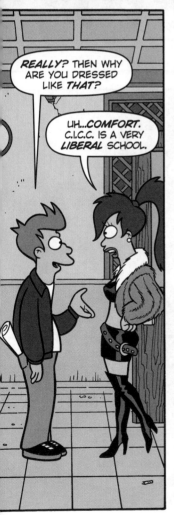

REALLY? THEN WHY ARE YOU DRESSED LIKE **THAT?**

UH...**COMFORT.** C.I.C.C. IS A VERY **LIBERAL** SCHOOL.

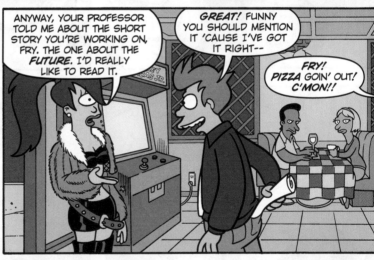

ANYWAY, YOUR PROFESSOR TOLD ME ABOUT THE SHORT STORY YOU'RE WORKING ON, FRY. THE ONE ABOUT THE **FUTURE.** I'D REALLY LIKE TO READ IT.

GREAT! FUNNY YOU SHOULD MENTION IT 'CAUSE I'VE GOT IT RIGHT--

FRY! PIZZA GOIN' OUT! C'MON!!

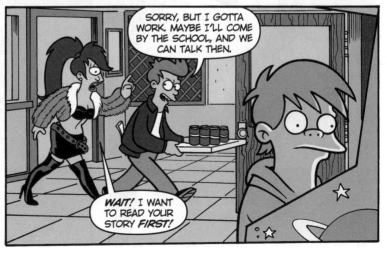

SORRY, BUT I GOTTA WORK. MAYBE I'LL COME BY THE SCHOOL, AND WE CAN TALK THEN.

WAIT! I WANT TO READ YOUR STORY **FIRST!**

PANUCCI'S
PIZZA

LADY, I HAVE TO GO. IF YOU *REALLY* WANT TO TALK, YOU CAN DELIVER THIS PIZZA WITH ME, OKAY?

FRY, I CAN'T LET YOU DO THIS! THE FATE OF MANKIND *DEPENDS* ON YOU!

HEY, I KNOW WHAT THIS IS ABOUT...

YOU DO?

SURE. YOU WANT ME TO BE IN *YOUR* CLASS NEXT SEMESTER, PROFESSOR LEELA. BUT AFTER MY *LAP DANCING 101* AND *BASIC HYGIENE WORKSHOP* CLASSES, I DON'T HAVE ANY FREE TIME. MAYBE NEXT YEAR, THOUGH.

SEE YA!

THE *STORY!* OH, I WISH I HAD MY NIKE *RUNNING PUMPS* FROM THE FUTURE!

SOON, AT APPLIED CRYOGENICS...
FRY, WAIT! DON'T GO IN THERE!
I HAVE TO GET UP TO THE CRYOGENICS LAB BEFORE FRY DOES!
HAPPY NEW YEAR!
STAIRS
♫ A LITTLE BIT ♪ OF BLAH BLAH IN MY LIFE, A LITTLE BIT OF DINGLY DANG BY MY ♪ SIDE... ♫
SKRITCH! SKRITCH!
FRY! STOP!
PIZZA DELIVERY FOR...
I.C. WIENER... OH, NO!
YOU'RE A DEAD MAN, FRY!...

AAAH!
YOU'RE A...A...
A ROBOT! A BENDING ROBOT, TO BE PRECISE! AND I'VE COME FROM THE YEAR 3001 TO FIND YOU!
WHAT? WHY ME? I CAN'T EVEN COUNT TO 3001!
TRUE. AND HOW DO I KNOW THIS, YOU ASK? BECAUSE I AM YOUR BEST FRIEND IN THE FUTURE, FRY. AND YOU WILL BE A DEAD MAN...
...UNLESS YOU COME WITH ME!
DON'T LISTEN TO HIM, FRY!
WHAT THE HELL'S GOING ON?
I'M HERE TO SAVE YOU FROM THE BENDERNATOR, FRY! HE WANTS TO DESTROY YOU AND YOUR STORY SO THAT IT NEVER MAKES IT TO THE FUTURE!
BUT WHAT DOES MY STORY HAVE TO DO WITH THE FUTURE?
"IN THE YEAR 2943, MANKIND IS WIPED OFF THE FACE OF THE EARTH BY A NUCLEAR HOLOCAUST, SAVE FOR A REBELLIOUS AND FORTUNATE FEW WHO HAVE MADE IT UNDERGROUND. ROBOTS TAKE OVER THE WORLD AND BEGIN TO TERMINATE ANY HUMAN BEING THEY FIND. THAT IS UNTIL YOU COME ALONG!"
YOU WERE FROZEN IN ONE OF THESE CRYOGENIC TUBES ON NEW YEAR'S EVE 1999...TONIGHT! WHEN YOU AWOKE 1,000 YEARS LATER, YOU LED THE REBEL HUMANS INTO A WAR AGAINST THE MACHINES. YOU EVEN CONVINCED SOME OF THE ROBOT FORCES TO JOIN YOU!
AND THAT'S WHERE I COME IN! I HAVE BECOME YOUR MOST TRUSTED FRIEND AND CONFIDANT IN REBUILDING A SOCIETY OF HUMANS, ROBOTS, AND ALIENS LIVING HARMONIOUSLY TOGETHER!

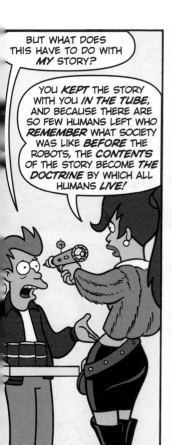

BUT WHAT DOES THIS HAVE TO DO WITH *MY* STORY?

YOU *KEPT* THE STORY WITH YOU *IN THE TUBE*, AND BECAUSE THERE ARE SO FEW HUMANS LEFT WHO *REMEMBER* WHAT SOCIETY WAS LIKE *BEFORE* THE ROBOTS, THE *CONTENTS* OF THE STORY BECOME *THE DOCTRINE* BY WHICH ALL HUMANS *LIVE!*

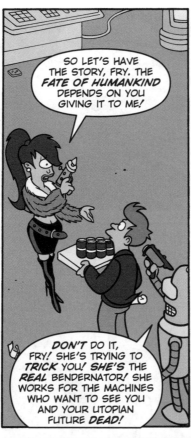

SO LET'S HAVE THE STORY, FRY. THE *FATE OF HUMANKIND* DEPENDS ON YOU GIVING IT TO ME!

DON'T DO IT, FRY! SHE'S TRYING TO *TRICK* YOU! *SHE'S* THE *REAL* BENDERNATOR! SHE WORKS FOR THE MACHINES WHO WANT TO SEE YOU AND YOUR UTOPIAN FUTURE *DEAD!*

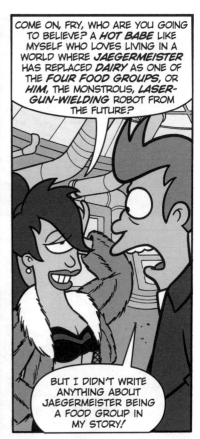

COME ON, FRY, WHO ARE YOU GOING TO BELIEVE? A *HOT BABE* LIKE MYSELF WHO LOVES LIVING IN A WORLD WHERE *JAEGERMEISTER* HAS REPLACED *DAIRY* AS ONE OF THE *FOUR FOOD GROUPS*, OR *HIM*, THE MONSTROUS, *LASER-GUN-WIELDING* ROBOT FROM THE FUTURE?

BUT I DIDN'T WRITE ANYTHING ABOUT JAEGERMEISTER BEING A FOOD GROUP IN MY STORY!

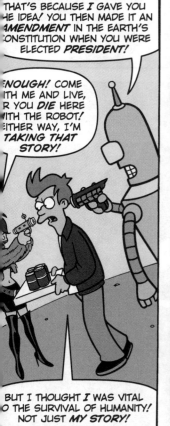

THAT'S BECAUSE *I* GAVE YOU THE IDEA! YOU THEN MADE IT AN *AMENDMENT* IN THE EARTH'S CONSTITUTION WHEN YOU WERE ELECTED *PRESIDENT!*

ENOUGH! COME WITH ME AND LIVE, OR YOU *DIE* HERE WITH THE ROBOT! EITHER WAY, I'M *TAKING THAT STORY!*

BUT I THOUGHT *I* WAS VITAL TO THE SURVIVAL OF HUMANITY! NOT JUST *MY STORY!*

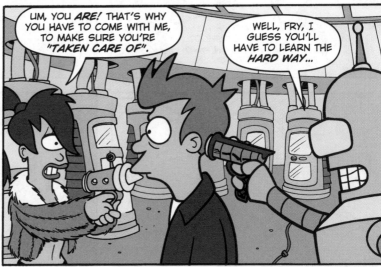

UM, YOU *ARE!* THAT'S WHY YOU HAVE TO COME WITH ME, TO MAKE SURE YOU'RE "*TAKEN CARE OF*".

WELL, FRY, I GUESS YOU'LL HAVE TO LEARN THE *HARD WAY...*

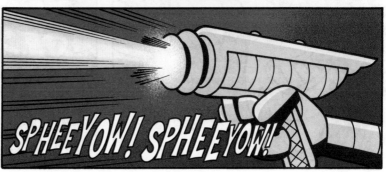

SPHEEYOW! SPHEEYOW!

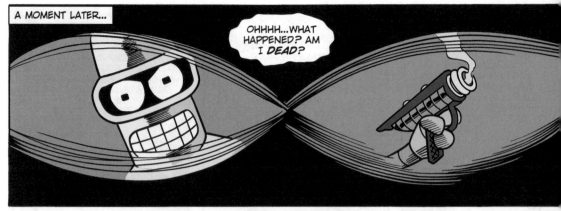

A MOMENT LATER...

OHHHH...WHAT HAPPENED? AM I *DEAD?*

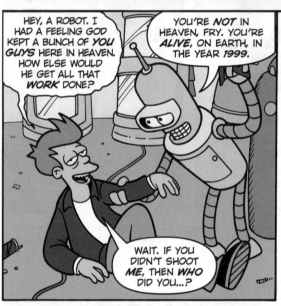

HEY, A ROBOT. I HAD A FEELING GOD KEPT A BUNCH OF *YOU GUYS* HERE IN HEAVEN. HOW ELSE WOULD HE GET ALL THAT *WORK* DONE?

YOU'RE *NOT* IN HEAVEN, FRY. YOU'RE *ALIVE*, ON EARTH, IN THE YEAR *1999.*

WAIT. IF YOU DIDN'T SHOOT *ME*, THEN *WHO* DID YOU...?

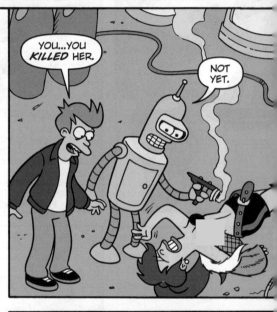

YOU...YOU *KILLED* HER.

NOT YET.

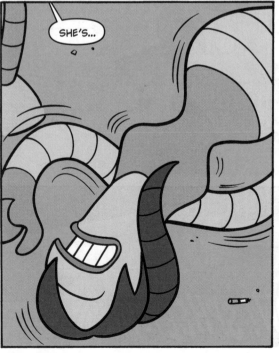

SHE'S...

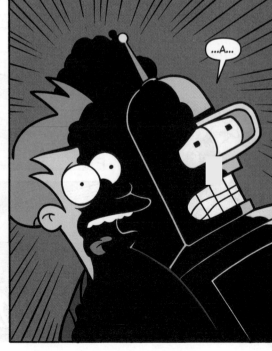

...A...

...BENDERNATOR!
AWESOME!
I MEAN, OH, NO!

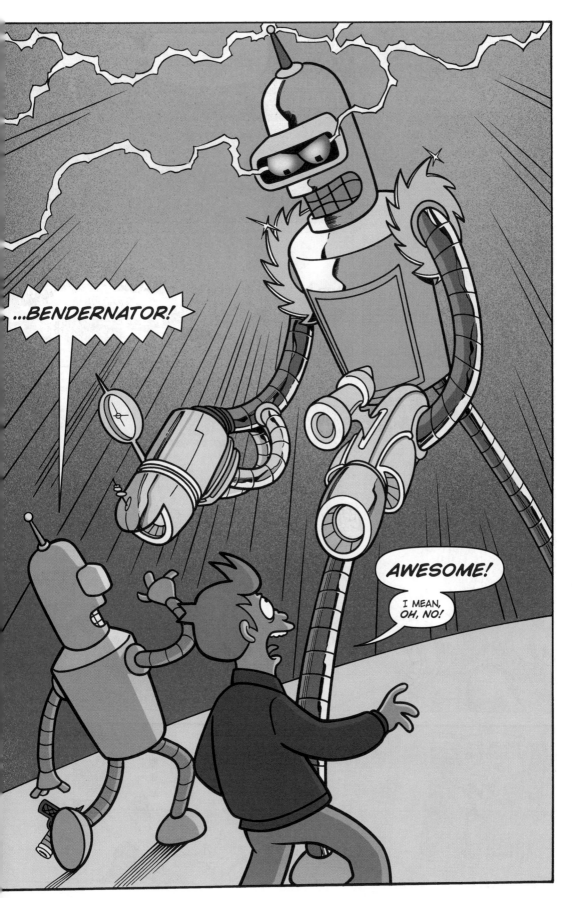

HOW ELSE COULD A WOMAN SPRINT TEN BLOCKS IN *FIVE-INCH HEELS?*
WHAT ARE WE GONNA *DO?* I HAVE TO GET TO THE FUTURE IN ONE OF THESE TUBES, RIGHT?
TARGET ACQUIRED: BENDERNATE AT WILL
I'M AFRAID IT'S *TOO LATE* FOR THAT. SHE'LL NEVER LET YOU DO IT!
BUT THERE'S ALWAYS TIME FOR A *SMOKE!*
KEERASH!
KEERASH!
SPHEEYOW!
SPHEEYOW!
SFFFEEEEEE!
SPHEEYOW!
SPHEEYOW!
SPHEEYOW!
COME ON, FRY! WE HAVE TO GET YOU AND YOUR STORY *OUT OF HERE!*
LET'S GO!
INSIDE THE *ELEVATOR,* FRY!
STAIRS

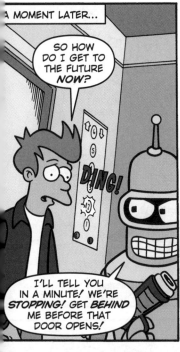

A MOMENT LATER...

SO HOW DO I GET TO THE FUTURE **NOW?**

I'LL TELL YOU IN A MINUTE! WE'RE **STOPPING!** GET **BEHIND** ME BEFORE THAT DOOR OPENS!

DING!

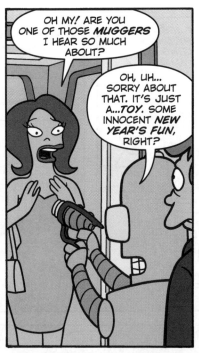

OH MY! ARE YOU ONE OF THOSE **MUGGERS** I HEAR SO MUCH ABOUT?

OH, UH... SORRY ABOUT THAT. IT'S JUST A...**TOY.** SOME INNOCENT **NEW YEAR'S FUN**, RIGHT?

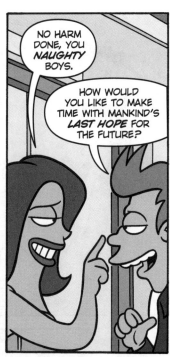

NO HARM DONE, YOU **NAUGHTY** BOYS.

HOW WOULD YOU LIKE TO MAKE TIME WITH MANKIND'S **LAST HOPE** FOR THE FUTURE?

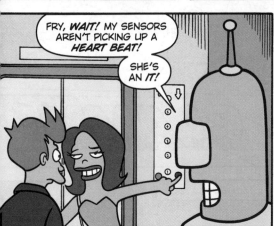

FRY, **WAIT!** MY SENSORS AREN'T PICKING UP A **HEART BEAT!**

SHE'S AN **IT!**

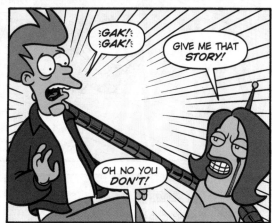

¡GAK! ¡GAK!

GIVE ME THAT **STORY!**

OH NO YOU **DON'T!**

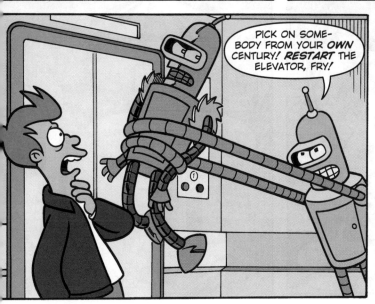

PICK ON SOME-BODY FROM YOUR **OWN** CENTURY! **RESTART** THE ELEVATOR, FRY!

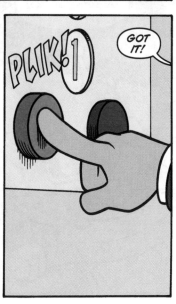

PLIK!

GOT IT!

DING!
SWEET JESUS AND MARY CHAIN! IT'S MELTING OUT OF MY HANDS!
KLANK!
COME ON, BENDER-ROBOT GUY!
IT'S MORPHING AGAIN! OOF!
COMIN' THROUGH!
BLAMM!
OWIE! CURSE MY ARTIFICIAL PAIN SENSOR!
CLANK!
C'MON, LET'S VAMOOSE!
A MOMENT LATER...
11:51:22
SAMSUNG
FOX
COME ON, FRY! THERE'S A TIME PORTAL TO THE FUTURE AT THE TOP OF ONE TIMES SQUARE! WE HAVE TO GET THERE BEFORE IT CLOSES AT MIDNIGHT!

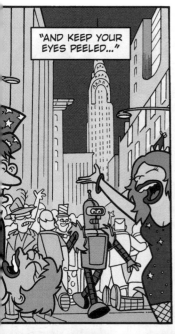

"AND KEEP YOUR EYES PEELED..."

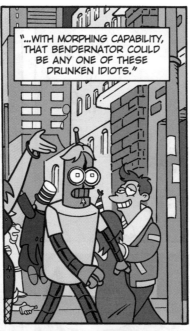

"...WITH MORPHING CAPABILITY, THAT BENDERNATOR COULD BE ANY ONE OF THESE DRUNKEN IDIOTS."

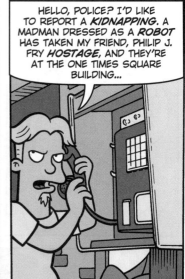

HELLO, POLICE? I'D LIKE TO REPORT A *KIDNAPPING*. A MADMAN DRESSED AS A *ROBOT* HAS TAKEN MY FRIEND, PHILIP J. FRY *HOSTAGE*, AND THEY'RE AT THE ONE TIMES SQUARE BUILDING...

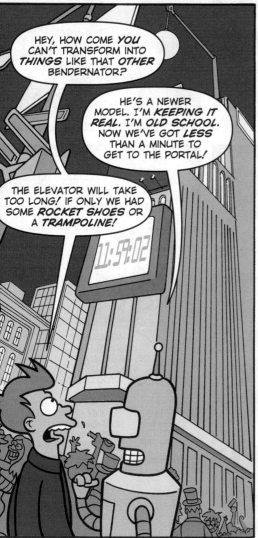

HEY, HOW COME *YOU* CAN'T TRANSFORM INTO *THINGS* LIKE THAT *OTHER* BENDERNATOR?

HE'S A NEWER MODEL. I'M *KEEPING IT REAL*. I'M *OLD SCHOOL*. NOW WE'VE GOT *LESS* THAN A MINUTE TO GET TO THE PORTAL!

THE ELEVATOR WILL TAKE TOO LONG! IF ONLY WE HAD SOME *ROCKET SHOES* OR A *TRAMPOLINE*!

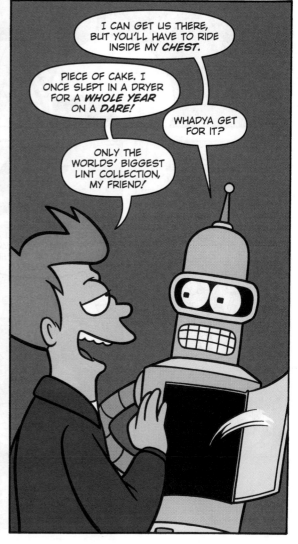

I CAN GET US THERE, BUT YOU'LL HAVE TO RIDE INSIDE MY *CHEST*.

PIECE OF CAKE. I ONCE SLEPT IN A DRYER FOR A *WHOLE YEAR* ON A *DARE*!

WHADYA GET FOR IT?

ONLY THE WORLDS' BIGGEST LINT COLLECTION, MY FRIEND!

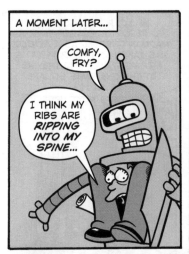

COMFY, FRY?

I THINK MY RIBS ARE *RIPPING* INTO MY *SPINE*...

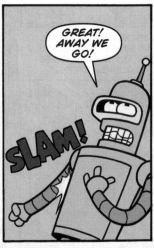

GREAT! AWAY WE GO!

SLAM!

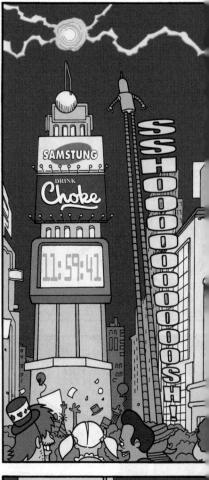

SAMSUNG

DRINK Choke

11:59:41

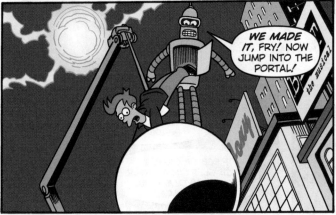

WE MADE IT, FRY! NOW JUMP INTO THE PORTAL!

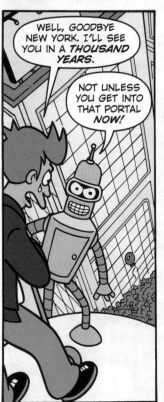

WELL, GOODBYE NEW YORK. I'LL SEE YOU IN A *THOUSAND YEARS.*

NOT UNLESS YOU GET INTO THAT PORTAL *NOW!*

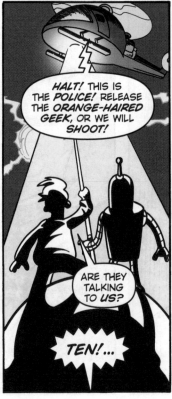

HALT! THIS IS THE *POLICE!* RELEASE THE *ORANGE-HAIRED GEEK*, OR WE WILL *SHOOT!*

ARE THEY TALKING TO *US?*

TEN!...

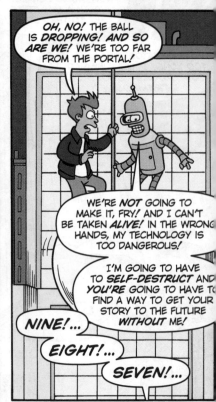

OH, NO! THE BALL IS *DROPPING! AND SO ARE WE!* WE'RE TOO FAR FROM THE PORTAL!

WE'RE *NOT* GOING TO MAKE IT, FRY! AND I CAN'T BE TAKEN *ALIVE!* IN THE WRONG HANDS, MY TECHNOLOGY IS TOO DANGEROUS!

I'M GOING TO HAVE TO *SELF-DESTRUCT* AND *YOU'RE* GOING TO HAVE TO FIND A WAY TO GET YOUR STORY TO THE FUTURE *WITHOUT* ME!

NINE!...

EIGHT!...

SEVEN!...

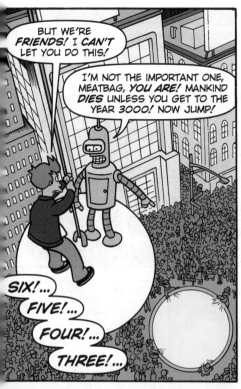

BUT WE'RE *FRIENDS!* I *CAN'T* LET YOU DO THIS!

I'M NOT THE IMPORTANT ONE, MEATBAG, *YOU ARE!* MANKIND *DIES* UNLESS YOU GET TO THE YEAR 3000! NOW JUMP!

SIX!...

FIVE!...

FOUR!...

THREE!...

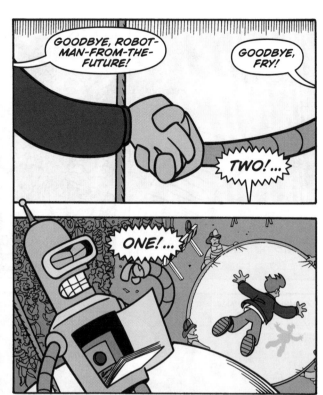

GOODBYE, ROBOT-MAN-FROM-THE-FUTURE!

GOODBYE, FRY!

TWO!...

ONE!...

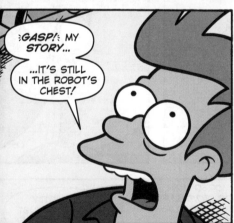

¡GASP!¡ MY STORY...

...IT'S STILL IN THE ROBOT'S CHEST!

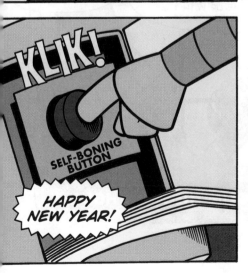

KLIK!

SELF-BONING BUTTON

HAPPY NEW YEAR!

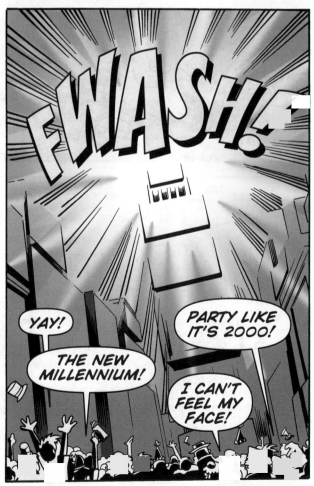

F WASH!

YAY!

THE NEW MILLENNIUM!

PARTY LIKE IT'S 2000!

I CAN'T FEEL MY FACE!

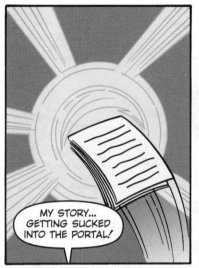

MY STORY... GETTING SUCKED INTO THE PORTAL!

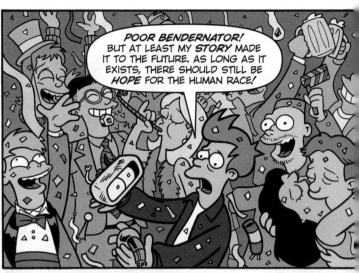

POOR *BENDERNATOR!* BUT AT LEAST MY *STORY* MADE IT TO THE FUTURE. AS LONG AS IT EXISTS, THERE SHOULD STILL BE *HOPE* FOR THE HUMAN RACE!

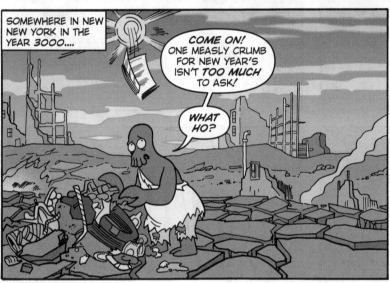

SOMEWHERE IN NEW NEW YORK IN THE YEAR 3000....

COME ON! ONE MEASLY CRUMB FOR NEW YEAR'S ISN'T *TOO MUCH* TO ASK!

WHAT HO?

"*FUTURINO:* WHAT THE WORLD WILL BE LIKE IN *1,000* YEARS BY PHILIP J. FRY." HMMM. MAYBE I CAN TAKE OFF THIS COVER PAGE, PUT *MY NAME* ON THE STORY AND SELL IT FOR *FOOD!*

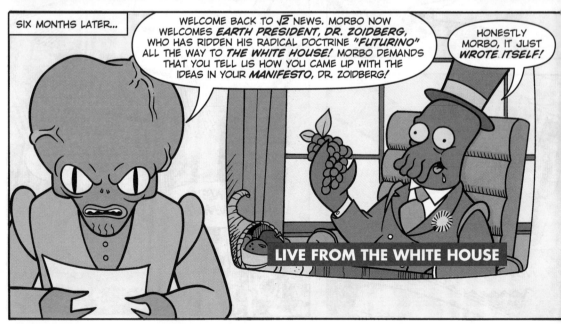

SIX MONTHS LATER...

WELCOME BACK TO √2 NEWS. MORBO NOW WELCOMES *EARTH PRESIDENT, DR. ZOIDBERG,* WHO HAS RIDDEN HIS RADICAL DOCTRINE "*FUTURINO*" ALL THE WAY TO *THE WHITE HOUSE!* MORBO DEMANDS THAT YOU TELL US HOW YOU CAME UP WITH THE IDEAS IN YOUR *MANIFESTO,* DR. ZOIDBERG!

HONESTLY MORBO, IT JUST *WROTE ITSELF!*

LIVE FROM THE WHITE HOUSE

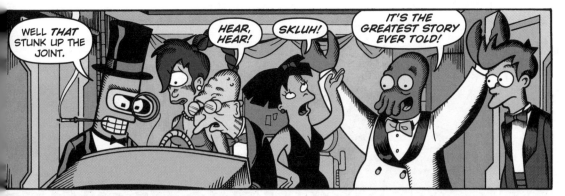

WELL *THAT* STUNK UP THE JOINT.

HEAR, HEAR!

SKLUH!

IT'S THE *GREATEST STORY EVER TOLD!*

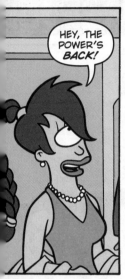

HEY, THE POWER'S *BACK!*

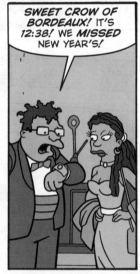

SWEET CROW OF BORDEAUX! IT'S 12:38! WE *MISSED* NEW YEAR'S!

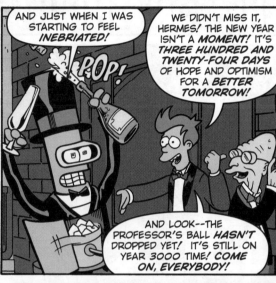

AND JUST WHEN I WAS STARTING TO FEEL *INEBRIATED!*

POP!

WE DIDN'T MISS IT, HERMES! THE NEW YEAR ISN'T A *MOMENT!* IT'S *THREE HUNDRED AND TWENTY-FOUR DAYS* OF HOPE AND OPTIMISM FOR A *BETTER TOMORROW!*

AND LOOK--THE PROFESSOR'S BALL *HASN'T* DROPPED YET! IT'S STILL ON YEAR 3000 TIME! *COME ON, EVERYBODY!*

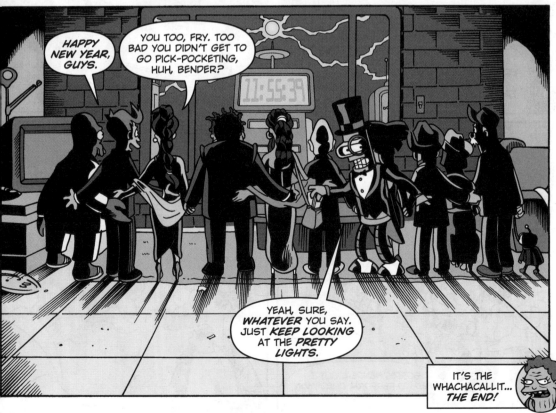

HAPPY NEW YEAR, GUYS.

YOU TOO, FRY. TOO BAD YOU DIDN'T GET TO GO PICK-POCKETING, HUH, BENDER?

YEAH, SURE, *WHATEVER* YOU SAY. JUST *KEEP LOOKING* AT THE *PRETTY LIGHTS.*

IT'S THE *WHACHACALLIT... THE END!*

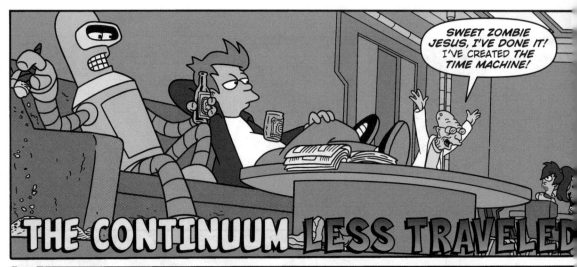

SWEET ZOMBIE JESUS, I'VE DONE IT! I'VE CREATED *THE TIME MACHINE!*

THE CONTINUUM LESS TRAVELED

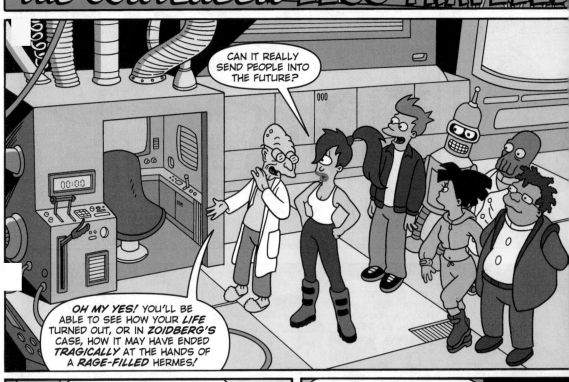

CAN IT REALLY SEND PEOPLE INTO THE FUTURE?

OH MY YES! YOU'LL BE ABLE TO SEE HOW YOUR *LIFE* TURNED OUT, OR IN *ZOIDBERG'S* CASE, HOW IT MAY HAVE ENDED *TRAGICALLY* AT THE HANDS OF A *RAGE-FILLED* HERMES!

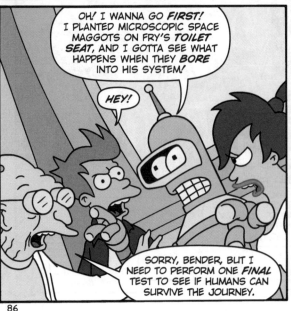

OH! I WANNA GO *FIRST!* I PLANTED MICROSCOPIC SPACE MAGGOTS ON FRY'S *TOILET SEAT,* AND I GOTTA SEE WHAT HAPPENS WHEN THEY *BORE* INTO HIS SYSTEM!

HEY!

SORRY, BENDER, BUT I NEED TO PERFORM ONE *FINAL* TEST TO SEE IF HUMANS CAN SURVIVE THE JOURNEY.

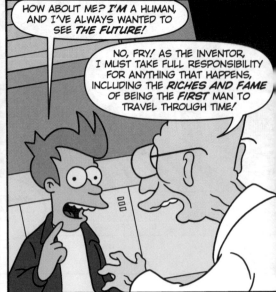

HOW ABOUT ME? *I'M* A HUMAN, AND I'VE ALWAYS WANTED TO SEE *THE FUTURE!*

NO, FRY! AS THE INVENTOR, I MUST TAKE FULL RESPONSIBILITY FOR ANYTHING THAT HAPPENS, INCLUDING THE *RICHES AND FAME* OF BEING THE *FIRST* MAN TO TRAVEL THROUGH TIME!

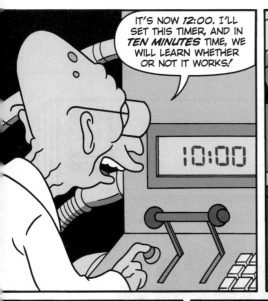

IT'S NOW *12:00.* I'LL SET THIS TIMER, AND IN *TEN MINUTES* TIME, WE WILL LEARN WHETHER OR NOT IT WORKS!

10:00

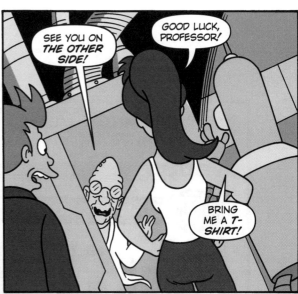

SEE YOU ON *THE OTHER SIDE!*

GOOD LUCK, PROFESSOR!

BRING ME A *T-SHIRT!*

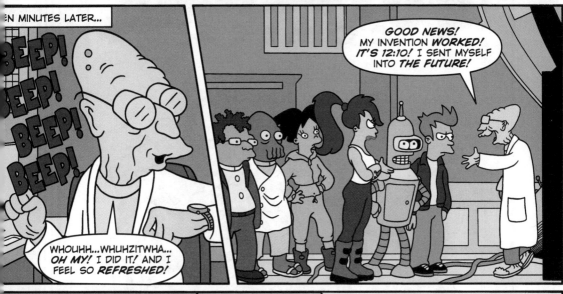

...EN MINUTES LATER...

BEEP! BEEP! BEEP! BEEP!

WHOUHH...WHUHZITWHA... *OH MY!* I DID IT! AND I FEEL SO *REFRESHED!*

GOOD NEWS! MY INVENTION *WORKED!* IT'S *12:10!* I SENT MYSELF INTO *THE FUTURE!*

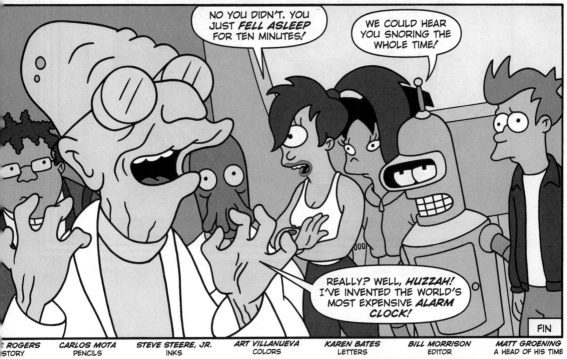

NO YOU DIDN'T. YOU JUST *FELL ASLEEP* FOR TEN MINUTES!

WE COULD HEAR YOU SNORING THE WHOLE TIME!

REALLY? WELL, *HUZZAH!* I'VE INVENTED THE WORLD'S MOST EXPENSIVE *ALARM CLOCK!*

FIN

: ROGERS
STORY

CARLOS MOTA
PENCILS

STEVE STEERE, JR.
INKS

ART VILLANUEVA
COLORS

KAREN BATES
LETTERS

BILL MORRISON
EDITOR

MATT GROENING
A HEAD OF HIS TIME

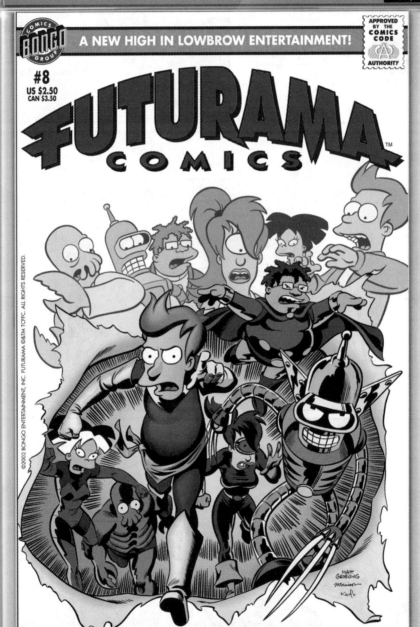

CIC INTERGALACTIC GRADE

Futurama Comics #8
Minty Fresh+ 11.5
Clown White Pages

Bongo Comics Group, 3/02
Death of Flexo
First appearance of Scruffy-Doo
Bill Morrison Cover; Eric Rogers Script; James Lloyd Art

CIC

Comics
Incarceration
Co-op

A NEW HIGH IN LOWBROW ENTERTAINMENT!

APPROVED BY THE COMICS CODE AUTHORITY

#8
US $2.50
CAN $3.50

FUTURAMA COMICS

MATT GROENING PRESENTS
PLANET X-PRESS MEN
JUST...A FEW MORE...FEET. SO... VERY...BONED!
BEHOLD! ANOTHER MIRACULOUS MILESTONE IN THE SENSES-SHATTERING SAGA OF THE GREATEST DELIVERY CREW OF ALL TIME!!
PENNED WITH PRIDE BY: ERIC ROGERS
DRAWN WITH DELIGHT BY: JAMES LLOYD
INKED WITH IRONY BY: STEVE STEERE, JR.
COLORED WITH CHARISMA BY: WICKY WEESE
LETTERED WITH LOVE BY: KAREN BATES
EDITED WITH A BIG RED SHARPIE BY: BILL MORRISON

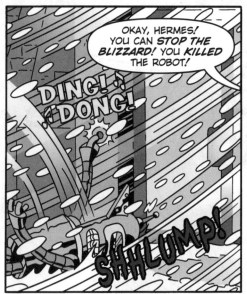

OKAY, HERMES! YOU CAN *STOP THE BLIZZARD!* YOU *KILLED THE ROBOT!*

DING! DONG!

SHHLUMP!

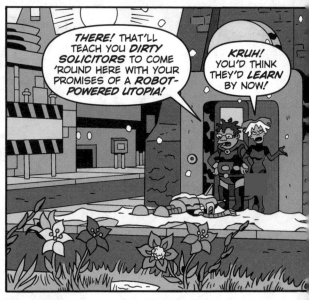

THERE! THAT'LL TEACH YOU *DIRTY SOLICITORS* TO COME 'ROUND HERE WITH YOUR PROMISES OF A *ROBOT-POWERED UTOPIA!*

KRUH! YOU'D THINK THEY'D *LEARN* BY NOW!

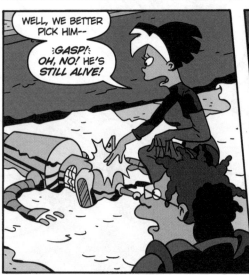

WELL, WE BETTER PICK HIM--

:GASP!: OH, *NO!* HE'S *STILL ALIVE!*

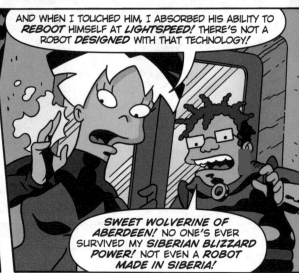

AND WHEN I TOUCHED HIM, I ABSORBED HIS ABILITY TO *REBOOT* HIMSELF AT *LIGHTSPEED!* THERE'S NOT A ROBOT *DESIGNED* WITH THAT TECHNOLOGY!

SWEET WOLVERINE OF ABERDEEN! NO ONE'S EVER SURVIVED MY *SIBERIAN BLIZZARD POWER!* NOT EVEN A *ROBOT MADE IN SIBERIA!*

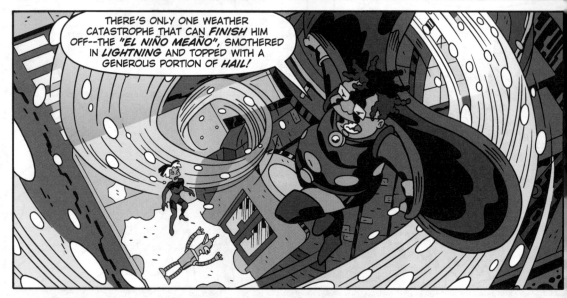

THERE'S ONLY ONE WEATHER CATASTROPHE THAT CAN *FINISH* HIM OFF--THE *"EL NIÑO MEAÑO"*, SMOTHERED IN *LIGHTNING* AND TOPPED WITH A GENEROUS PORTION OF *HAIL!*

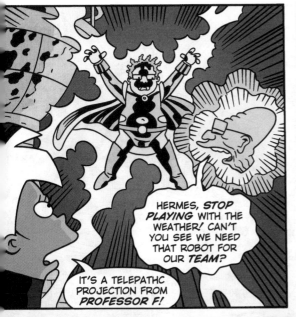

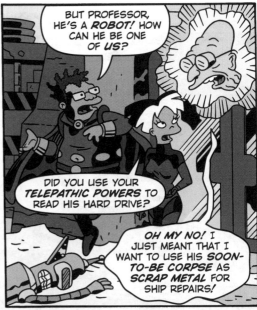

HERMES, *STOP PLAYING* WITH THE WEATHER! CAN'T YOU SEE WE NEED THAT ROBOT FOR OUR *TEAM?*

IT'S A TELEPATHC PROJECTION FROM *PROFESSOR F!*

BUT PROFESSOR, HE'S A *ROBOT!* HOW CAN HE BE ONE OF *US?*

DID YOU USE YOUR *TELEPATHIC POWERS* TO READ HIS HARD DRIVE?

OH MY NO! I JUST MEANT THAT I WANT TO USE HIS *SOON-TO-BE CORPSE* AS *SCRAP METAL* FOR SHIP REPAIRS!

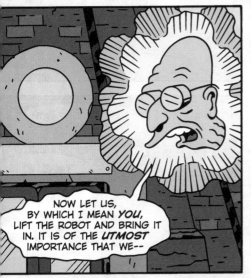

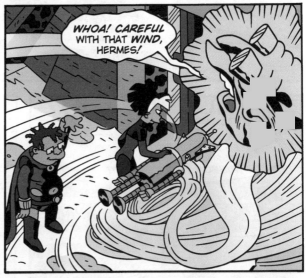

NOW LET US, BY WHICH I MEAN *YOU*, LIFT THE ROBOT AND BRING IT IN. IT IS OF THE *UTMOST* IMPORTANCE THAT WE--

WHOA! CAREFUL WITH THAT *WIND*, HERMES!

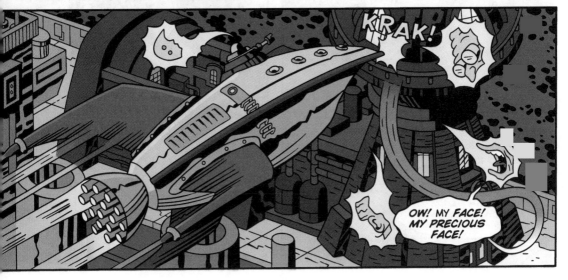

KRAK!

OW! MY *FACE!* MY *PRECIOUS FACE!*

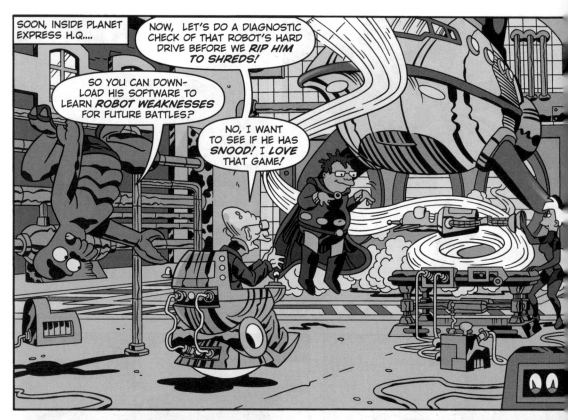

SOON, INSIDE PLANET EXPRESS H.Q....

NOW, LET'S DO A DIAGNOSTIC CHECK OF THAT ROBOT'S HARD DRIVE BEFORE WE *RIP HIM TO SHREDS!*

SO YOU CAN DOWN-LOAD HIS SOFTWARE TO LEARN *ROBOT WEAKNESSES* FOR FUTURE BATTLES?

NO, I WANT TO SEE IF HE HAS *SNOOD!* I *LOVE* THAT GAME!

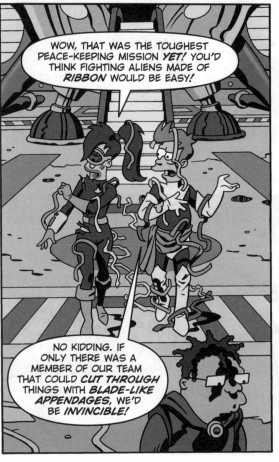

WOW, THAT WAS THE TOUGHEST PEACE-KEEPING MISSION *YET!* YOU'D THINK FIGHTING ALIENS MADE OF *RIBBON* WOULD BE EASY!

NO KIDDING. IF ONLY THERE WAS A MEMBER OF OUR TEAM THAT COULD *CUT THROUGH* THINGS WITH *BLADE-LIKE APPENDAGES,* WE'D BE *INVINCIBLE!*

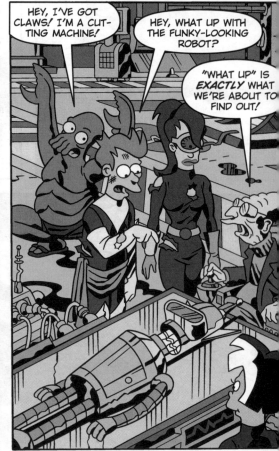

HEY, I'VE GOT *CLAWS!* I'M A CUT-TING MACHINE!

HEY, WHAT UP WITH THE FUNKY-LOOKING ROBOT?

"WHAT UP" IS *EXACTLY* WHAT WE'RE ABOUT TO FIND OUT!

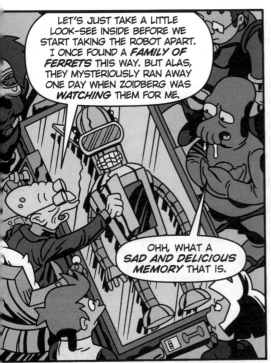

LET'S JUST TAKE A LITTLE LOOK-SEE INSIDE BEFORE WE START TAKING THE ROBOT APART. I ONCE FOUND A *FAMILY OF FERRETS* THIS WAY. BUT ALAS, THEY MYSTERIOUSLY RAN AWAY ONE DAY WHEN ZOIDBERG WAS *WATCHING* THEM FOR ME.

OHH, WHAT A *SAD AND DELICIOUS MEMORY* THAT IS.

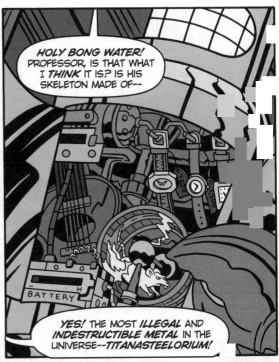

HOLY *BONG WATER!* PROFESSOR, IS THAT WHAT I *THINK* IT IS? IS HIS SKELETON MADE OF--

BATTERY

YES! THE MOST *ILLEGAL* AND *INDESTRUCTIBLE METAL* IN THE UNIVERSE--*TITANASTEELORIUM!*

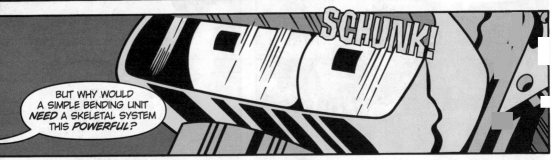

SCHUNK!

BUT WHY WOULD A SIMPLE BENDING UNIT *NEED* A SKELETAL SYSTEM THIS *POWERFUL?*

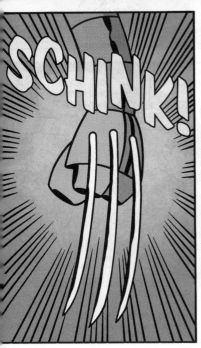

SCHINK!

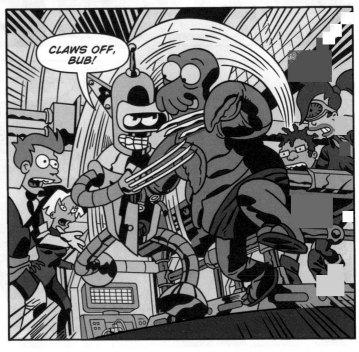

CLAWS OFF, BUB!

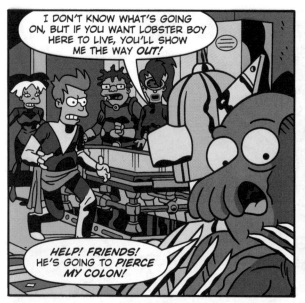

I DON'T KNOW WHAT'S GOING ON, BUT IF YOU WANT LOBSTER BOY HERE TO LIVE, YOU'LL SHOW ME THE WAY *OUT!*

HELP! FRIENDS! HE'S GOING TO *PIERCE MY COLON!*

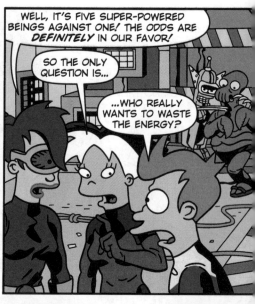

WELL, IT'S FIVE SUPER-POWERED BEINGS AGAINST ONE! THE ODDS ARE *DEFINITELY* IN OUR FAVOR!

SO THE ONLY QUESTION IS...

...WHO REALLY WANTS TO WASTE THE ENERGY?

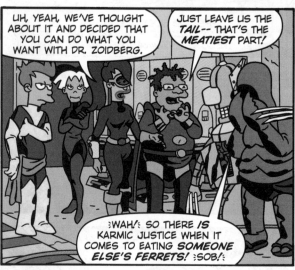

UH, YEAH, WE'VE THOUGHT ABOUT IT AND DECIDED THAT YOU CAN DO WHAT YOU WANT WITH DR. ZOIDBERG.

JUST LEAVE US THE *TAIL--* THAT'S THE *MEATIEST* PART!

:WAH!: SO THERE *IS* KARMIC JUSTICE WHEN IT COMES TO EATING *SOMEONE ELSE'S FERRETS!* :SOB!:

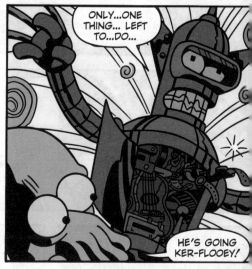

ONLY...ONE THING... LEFT TO...DO...

HE'S GOING KER-FLOOEY!

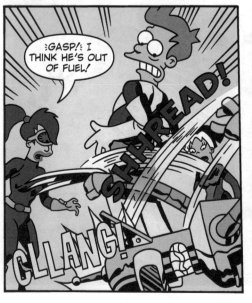

:GASP!: I THINK HE'S OUT OF FUEL!

SSSPREAD!

CLLANG!

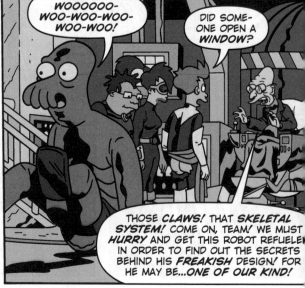

WOOOOOO-WOO-WOO-WOO-WOO-WOO!

DID SOME-ONE OPEN A *WINDOW?*

THOSE *CLAWS!* THAT *SKELETAL SYSTEM!* COME ON, TEAM! WE MUST *HURRY* AND GET THIS ROBOT REFUELED IN ORDER TO FIND OUT THE SECRETS BEHIND HIS *FREAKISH* DESIGN! FOR HE MAY BE...*ONE OF OUR KIND!*

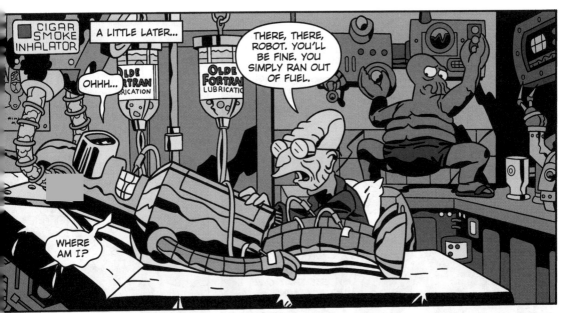

CIGAR SMOKE INHALATOR

A LITTLE LATER...

OHHH...

THERE, THERE, ROBOT. YOU'LL BE FINE. YOU SIMPLY RAN OUT OF FUEL.

OLDE FORTRAN LUBRICATION

OLDE FORTRAN LUBRICATION

WHERE AM I?

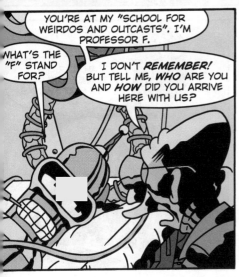

YOU'RE AT MY "SCHOOL FOR WEIRDOS AND OUTCASTS". I'M PROFESSOR F.

WHAT'S THE "F" STAND FOR?

I DON'T REMEMBER! BUT TELL ME, WHO ARE YOU AND HOW DID YOU ARRIVE HERE WITH US?

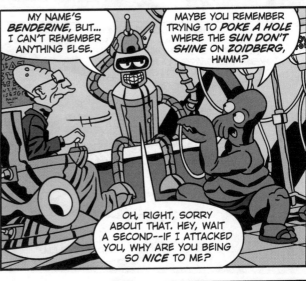

MY NAME'S BENDERINE, BUT... I CAN'T REMEMBER ANYTHING ELSE.

MAYBE YOU REMEMBER TRYING TO POKE A HOLE WHERE THE SUN DON'T SHINE ON ZOIDBERG, HMMM?

OH, RIGHT, SORRY ABOUT THAT. HEY, WAIT A SECOND--IF I ATTACKED YOU, WHY ARE YOU BEING SO NICE TO ME?

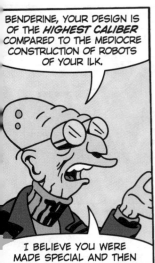

BENDERINE, YOUR DESIGN IS OF THE HIGHEST CALIBER COMPARED TO THE MEDIOCRE CONSTRUCTION OF ROBOTS OF YOUR ILK.

I BELIEVE YOU WERE MADE SPECIAL AND THEN ABANDONED, LIKE MY SUPER-POWERED TEAM OF MISFITS.

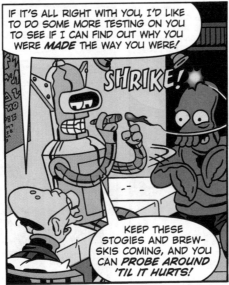

IF IT'S ALL RIGHT WITH YOU, I'D LIKE TO DO SOME MORE TESTING ON YOU TO SEE IF I CAN FIND OUT WHY YOU WERE MADE THE WAY YOU WERE!

SHRIKE!

KEEP THESE STOGIES AND BREW-SKIS COMING, AND YOU CAN PROBE AROUND 'TIL IT HURTS!

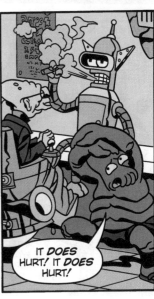

IT DOES HURT! IT DOES HURT!

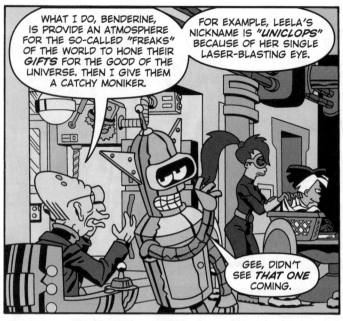

WHAT I DO, BENDERINE, IS PROVIDE AN ATMOSPHERE FOR THE SO-CALLED "FREAKS" OF THE WORLD TO HONE THEIR *GIFTS* FOR THE GOOD OF THE UNIVERSE. THEN I GIVE THEM A CATCHY MONIKER.

FOR EXAMPLE, LEELA'S NICKNAME IS *"UNICLOPS"* BECAUSE OF HER SINGLE LASER-BLASTING EYE.

GEE, DIDN'T SEE *THAT ONE* COMING.

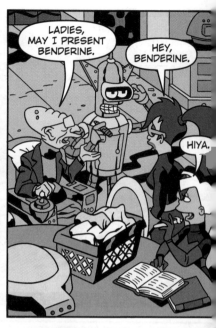

LADIES, MAY I PRESENT BENDERINE.

HEY, BENDERINE.

HIYA.

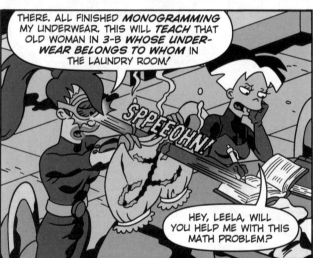

THERE. ALL FINISHED *MONOGRAMMING* MY UNDERWEAR. THIS WILL *TEACH* THAT OLD WOMAN IN 3-B *WHOSE UNDER-WEAR BELONGS TO WHOM* IN THE LAUNDRY ROOM!

SPPEEOHN!

HEY, LEELA, WILL YOU HELP ME WITH THIS MATH PROBLEM?

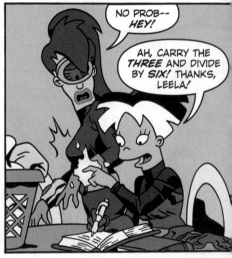

NO PROB-- HEY!

AH, CARRY THE *THREE* AND DIVIDE BY *SIX!* THANKS, LEELA!

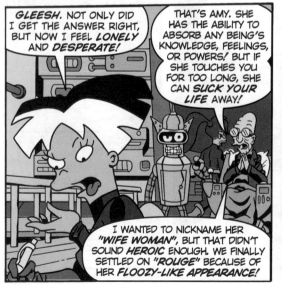

GLEESH. NOT ONLY DID I GET THE ANSWER RIGHT, BUT NOW I FEEL *LONELY* AND *DESPERATE!*

THAT'S AMY. SHE HAS THE ABILITY TO ABSORB ANY BEING'S KNOWLEDGE, FEELINGS, OR POWERS! BUT IF SHE TOUCHES YOU FOR TOO LONG, SHE CAN *SUCK YOUR LIFE* AWAY!

I WANTED TO NICKNAME HER *"WIFE WOMAN"*, BUT THAT DIDN'T SOUND *HEROIC* ENOUGH. WE FINALLY SETTLED ON *"ROUGE"* BECAUSE OF HER *FLOOZY-LIKE APPEARANCE!*

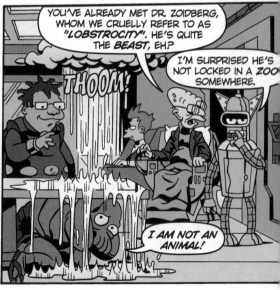

YOU'VE ALREADY MET DR. ZOIDBERG, WHOM WE CRUELLY REFER TO AS *"LOBSTROCITY"*. HE'S QUITE THE *BEAST*, EH?

I'M SURPRISED HE'S NOT LOCKED IN A *ZOO* SOMEWHERE.

THOOM!

I AM NOT AN ANIMAL!

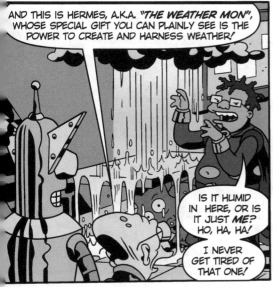

AND THIS IS HERMES, A.K.A. *"THE WEATHER MON"*, WHOSE SPECIAL GIFT YOU CAN PLAINLY SEE IS THE POWER TO CREATE AND HARNESS WEATHER!

IS IT HUMID IN HERE, OR IS IT JUST *ME*? HO, HA, HA!

I NEVER GET TIRED OF THAT ONE!

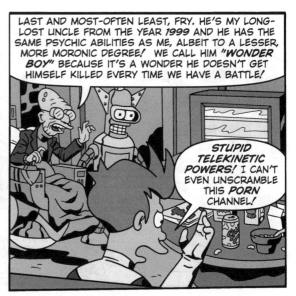

LAST AND MOST-OFTEN LEAST, FRY. HE'S MY LONG-LOST UNCLE FROM THE YEAR *1999* AND HE HAS THE SAME PSYCHIC ABILITIES AS ME, ALBEIT TO A LESSER, MORE MORONIC DEGREE! WE CALL HIM *"WONDER BOY"* BECAUSE IT'S A WONDER HE DOESN'T GET HIMSELF KILLED EVERY TIME WE HAVE A BATTLE!

STUPID TELEKINETIC POWERS! I CAN'T EVEN UNSCRAMBLE THIS *PORN* CHANNEL!

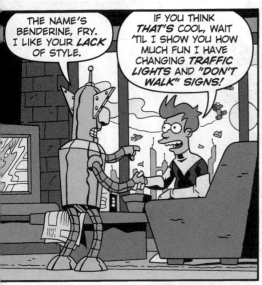

THE NAME'S BENDERINE, FRY. I LIKE YOUR *LACK* OF STYLE.

IF YOU THINK *THAT'S* COOL, WAIT 'TIL I SHOW YOU HOW MUCH FUN I HAVE CHANGING *TRAFFIC LIGHTS* AND *"DON'T WALK"* SIGNS!

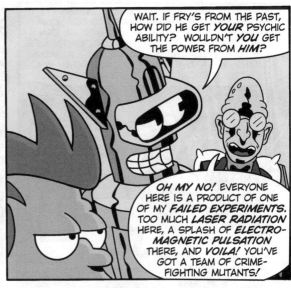

WAIT. IF FRY'S FROM THE PAST, HOW DID HE GET *YOUR* PSYCHIC ABILITY? WOULDN'T *YOU* GET THE POWER FROM *HIM*?

OH MY NO! EVERYONE HERE IS A PRODUCT OF ONE OF MY *FAILED EXPERIMENTS.* TOO MUCH *LASER RADIATION* HERE, A SPLASH OF *ELECTRO-MAGNETIC PULSATION* THERE, AND *VOILA!* YOU'VE GOT A TEAM OF CRIME-FIGHTING MUTANTS!

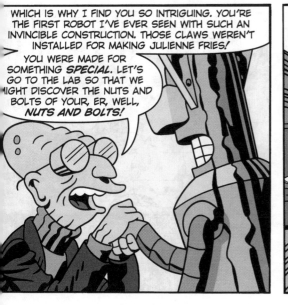

WHICH IS WHY I FIND YOU SO INTRIGUING. YOU'RE THE FIRST ROBOT I'VE EVER SEEN WITH SUCH AN INVINCIBLE CONSTRUCTION. THOSE CLAWS WEREN'T INSTALLED FOR MAKING JULIENNE FRIES!

YOU WERE MADE FOR SOMETHING *SPECIAL.* LET'S GO TO THE LAB SO THAT WE MIGHT DISCOVER THE NUTS AND BOLTS OF YOUR, ER, WELL, *NUTS AND BOLTS!*

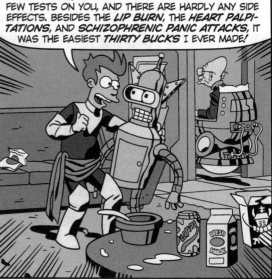

DON'T WORRY, BENDERINE. HE JUST WANTS TO RUN A FEW TESTS ON YOU, AND THERE ARE HARDLY ANY SIDE EFFECTS. BESIDES THE *LIP BURN,* THE *HEART PALPI-TATIONS,* AND *SCHIZOPHRENIC PANIC ATTACKS,* IT WAS THE EASIEST *THIRTY BUCKS* I EVER MADE!

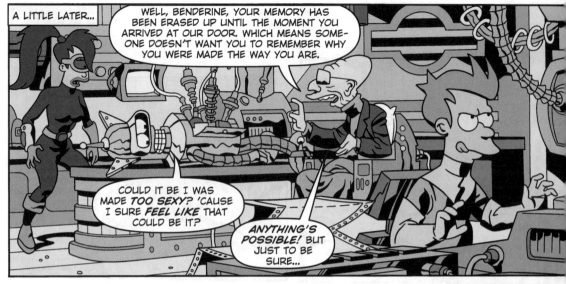

A LITTLE LATER...

WELL, BENDERINE, YOUR MEMORY HAS BEEN ERASED UP UNTIL THE MOMENT YOU ARRIVED AT OUR DOOR. WHICH MEANS SOMEONE DOESN'T WANT YOU TO REMEMBER WHY YOU WERE MADE THE WAY YOU ARE.

COULD IT BE I WAS MADE *TOO SEXY*? 'CAUSE I SURE *FEEL LIKE* THAT COULD BE IT?

ANYTHING'S *POSSIBLE!* BUT JUST TO BE SURE...

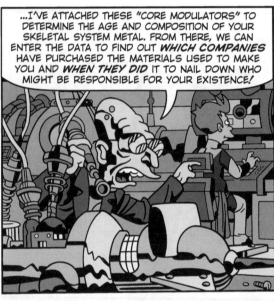

...I'VE ATTACHED THESE "CORE MODULATORS" TO DETERMINE THE AGE AND COMPOSITION OF YOUR SKELETAL SYSTEM METAL. FROM THERE, WE CAN ENTER THE DATA TO FIND OUT *WHICH COMPANIES* HAVE PURCHASED THE MATERIALS USED TO MAKE YOU AND *WHEN THEY DID* IT TO NAIL DOWN WHO MIGHT BE RESPONSIBLE FOR YOUR EXISTENCE!

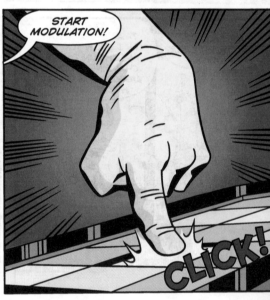

START MODULATION!

CLICK!

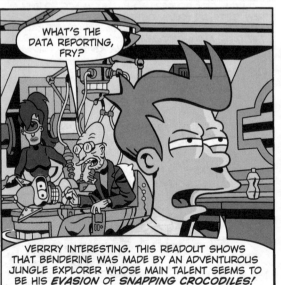

WHAT'S THE DATA REPORTING, FRY?

VERRRY INTERESTING. THIS READOUT SHOWS THAT BENDERINE WAS MADE BY AN ADVENTUROUS JUNGLE EXPLORER WHOSE MAIN TALENT SEEMS TO BE HIS *EVASION* OF *SNAPPING CROCODILES!*

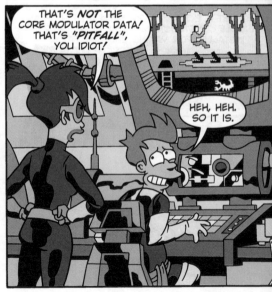

THAT'S *NOT* THE CORE MODULATOR DATA! THAT'S *"PITFALL"*, YOU IDIOT!

HEH, HEH. SO IT IS.

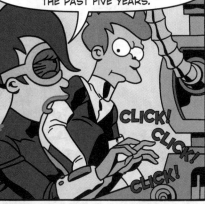

HERE WE GO, PROFESSOR. A LIST OF ALL OF THE ELEMENTS THAT MAKE UP BENDERINE'S TITANASTEELORIUM FRAME, THE AGE OF THE MATERIAL, AND THE RECORDS OF WHO'S PURCHASED THOSE MATERIALS IN BULK OVER THE PAST FIVE YEARS.

CLICK! CLICK! CLICK!

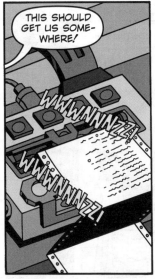

THIS SHOULD GET US SOME- WHERE!

WWWNNNZZZ WWWNNNZZZ

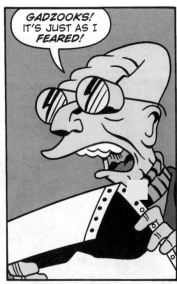

GADZOOKS! IT'S JUST AS I **FEARED!**

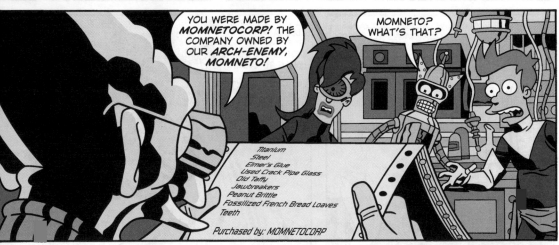

YOU WERE MADE BY **MOMNETOCORP!** THE COMPANY OWNED BY OUR **ARCH-ENEMY, MOMNETO!**

MOMNETO? WHAT'S THAT?

Titanium
Steel
Elmer's Glue
Used Crack Pipe Glass
Old Taffy
Jawbreakers
Peanut Brittle
Fossilized French Bread Loaves
Teeth

Purchased by: MOMNETOCORP

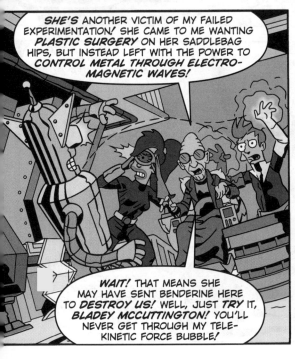

SHE'S ANOTHER VICTIM OF MY FAILED EXPERIMENTATION! SHE CAME TO ME WANTING **PLASTIC SURGERY** ON HER SADDLEBAG HIPS, BUT INSTEAD LEFT WITH THE POWER TO **CONTROL METAL THROUGH ELECTRO-MAGNETIC WAVES!**

WAIT! THAT MEANS SHE MAY HAVE SENT BENDERINE HERE TO **DESTROY US!** WELL, JUST **TRY** IT, **BLADEY MCCUTTINGTON!** YOU'LL NEVER GET THROUGH MY TELE-KINETIC FORCE BUBBLE!

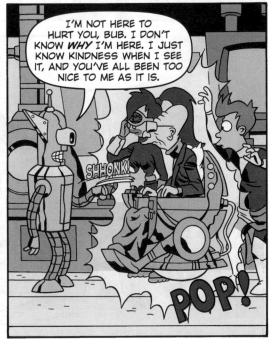

I'M NOT HERE TO HURT YOU, BUB. I DON'T KNOW **WHY** I'M HERE. I JUST KNOW KINDNESS WHEN I SEE IT, AND YOU'VE ALL BEEN TOO NICE TO ME AS IT IS.

SHHONK!

POP!

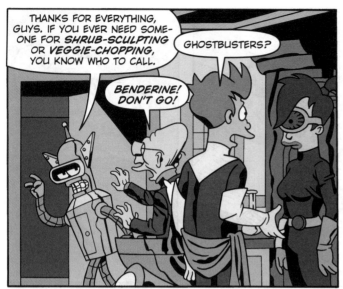

THANKS FOR EVERYTHING, GUYS. IF YOU EVER NEED SOMEONE FOR *SHRUB-SCULPTING* OR *VEGGIE-CHOPPING*, YOU KNOW WHO TO CALL.

GHOSTBUSTERS?

BENDERINE! DON'T GO!

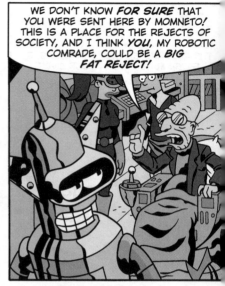

WE DON'T KNOW *FOR SURE* THAT YOU WERE SENT HERE BY MOMNETO! THIS IS A PLACE FOR THE REJECTS OF SOCIETY, AND I THINK *YOU*, MY ROBOTIC COMRADE, COULD BE A *BIG FAT REJECT!*

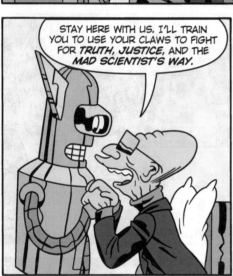

STAY HERE WITH US. I'LL TRAIN YOU TO USE YOUR CLAWS TO FIGHT FOR *TRUTH, JUSTICE,* AND THE *MAD SCIENTIST'S WAY.*

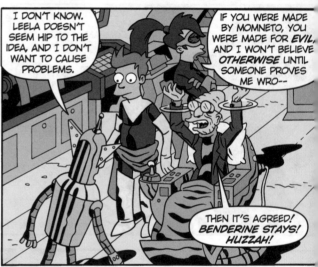

I DON'T KNOW. LEELA DOESN'T SEEM HIP TO THE IDEA, AND I DON'T WANT TO CAUSE PROBLEMS.

IF YOU WERE MADE BY MOMNETO, YOU WERE MADE FOR *EVIL,* AND I WON'T BELIEVE *OTHERWISE* UNTIL SOMEONE PROVES ME WRO--

THEN IT'S AGREED! *BENDERINE STAYS!* HUZZAH!

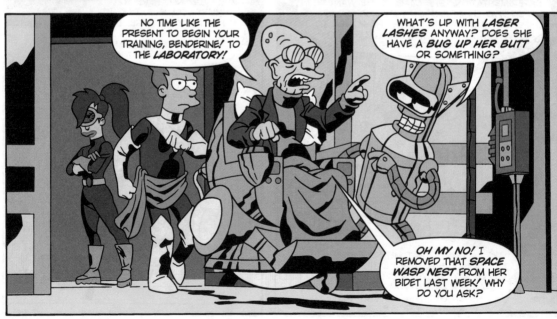

NO TIME LIKE THE PRESENT TO BEGIN YOUR TRAINING, *BENDERINE!* TO THE *LABORATORY!*

WHAT'S UP WITH *LASER LASHES* ANYWAY? DOES SHE HAVE A *BUG UP HER BUTT* OR SOMETHING?

OH MY NO! I REMOVED THAT *SPACE WASP NEST* FROM HER BIDET LAST WEEK! WHY DO YOU ASK?

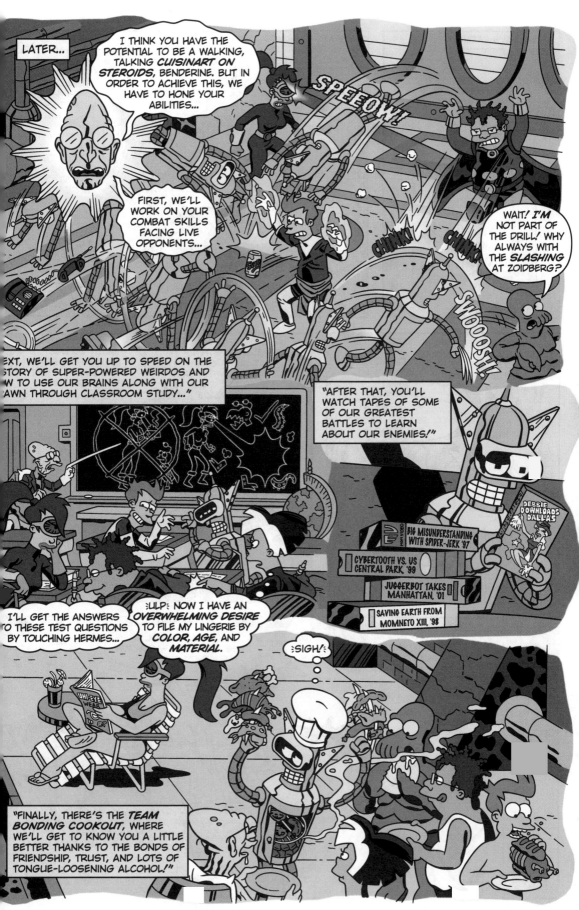

LATER...

I THINK YOU HAVE THE POTENTIAL TO BE A WALKING, TALKING *CUISINART ON STEROIDS,* BENDERINE. BUT IN ORDER TO ACHIEVE THIS, WE HAVE TO HONE YOUR ABILITIES...

SPEEOW!

FIRST, WE'LL WORK ON YOUR COMBAT SKILLS FACING LIVE OPPONENTS...

CHINK!

CHINK!

WAIT! *I'M* NOT PART OF THE DRILL! WHY ALWAYS WITH THE *SLASHING* AT ZOIDBERG?

SWOOOSH!

EXT, WE'LL GET YOU UP TO SPEED ON THE STORY OF SUPER-POWERED WEIRDOS AND W TO USE OUR BRAINS ALONG WITH OUR AWN THROUGH CLASSROOM STUDY..."

"AFTER THAT, YOU'LL WATCH TAPES OF SOME OF OUR GREATEST BATTLES TO LEARN ABOUT OUR ENEMIES!"

DEBBIE DOWNLOADS DALLAS

BIG MISUNDERSTANDING WITH SPIDER-JERK '97

CYBERTOOTH VS. US CENTRAL PARK '99

JUGGERBOT TAKES MANHATTAN, '01

SAVING EARTH FROM MOMNETO XIII, '98

I'LL GET THE ANSWERS TO THESE TEST QUESTIONS BY TOUCHING HERMES...

:ULP: NOW I HAVE AN *OVERWHELMING DESIRE* TO FILE MY LINGERIE BY *COLOR, AGE,* AND *MATERIAL.*

:SIGH!:

UNI-EYE WEAR

"FINALLY, THERE'S THE *TEAM BONDING COOKOUT,* WHERE WE'LL GET TO KNOW YOU A LITTLE BETTER THANKS TO THE BONDS OF FRIENDSHIP, TRUST, AND LOTS OF TONGUE-LOOSENING ALCOHOL!"

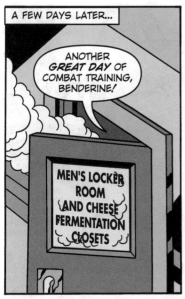

A FEW DAYS LATER...

ANOTHER *GREAT DAY* OF COMBAT TRAINING, BENDERINE!

MEN'S LOCKER ROOM AND CHEESE FERMENTATION CLOSETS

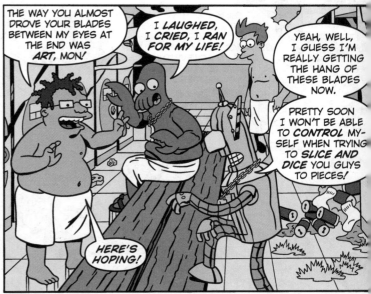

THE WAY YOU ALMOST DROVE YOUR BLADES BETWEEN MY EYES AT THE END WAS *ART*, MON!

I *LAUGHED*, I *CRIED*, I *RAN* FOR MY LIFE!

YEAH, WELL, I GUESS I'M REALLY GETTING THE HANG OF THESE BLADES NOW.

PRETTY SOON I WON'T BE ABLE TO *CONTROL* MY-SELF WHEN TRYING TO *SLICE AND DICE* YOU GUYS TO PIECES!

HERE'S HOPING!

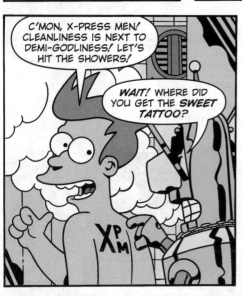

C'MON, X-PRESS MEN! CLEANLINESS IS NEXT TO DEMI-GODLINESS! LET'S HIT THE SHOWERS!

WAIT! WHERE DID YOU GET THE *SWEET TATTOO?*

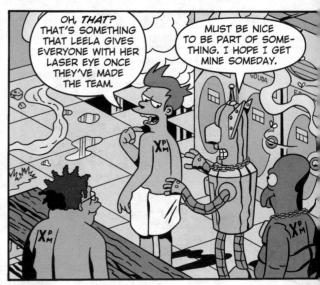

OH, *THAT?* THAT'S SOMETHING THAT LEELA GIVES EVERYONE WITH HER LASER EYE ONCE THEY'VE MADE THE TEAM.

MUST BE NICE TO BE PART OF SOME-THING. I HOPE I GET MINE SOMEDAY.

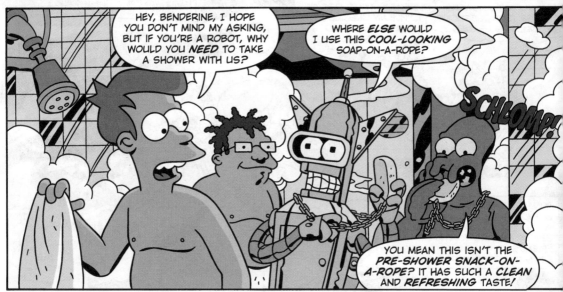

HEY, BENDERINE, I HOPE YOU DON'T MIND MY ASKING, BUT IF YOU'RE A ROBOT, WHY WOULD YOU *NEED* TO TAKE A SHOWER WITH US?

WHERE *ELSE* WOULD I USE THIS *COOL-LOOKING* SOAP-ON-A-ROPE?

SCHLOMP!

YOU MEAN THIS ISN'T THE *PRE-SHOWER SNACK-ON-A-ROPE?* IT HAS SUCH A *CLEAN* AND *REFRESHING* TASTE!

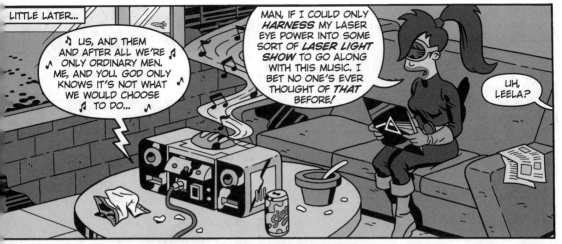

LITTLE LATER...

♪ US, AND THEM AND AFTER ALL WE'RE ONLY ORDINARY MEN. ME, AND YOU. GOD ONLY KNOWS IT'S NOT WHAT WE WOULD CHOOSE ♪ TO DO...

MAN, IF I COULD ONLY *HARNESS* MY LASER EYE POWER INTO SOME SORT OF *LASER LIGHT SHOW* TO GO ALONG WITH THIS MUSIC. I BET NO ONE'S EVER THOUGHT OF *THAT* BEFORE!

UH, LEELA?

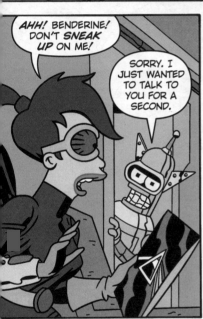

AHH! BENDERINE! DON'T *SNEAK UP* ON ME!

SORRY. I JUST WANTED TO TALK TO YOU FOR A SECOND.

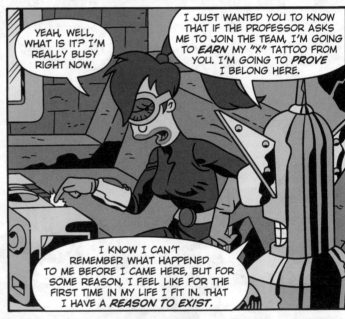

YEAH, WELL, WHAT IS IT? I'M REALLY BUSY RIGHT NOW.

I JUST WANTED YOU TO KNOW THAT IF THE PROFESSOR ASKS ME TO JOIN THE TEAM, I'M GOING TO *EARN* MY "X" TATTOO FROM YOU. I'M GOING TO *PROVE* I BELONG HERE.

I KNOW I CAN'T REMEMBER WHAT HAPPENED TO ME BEFORE I CAME HERE, BUT FOR SOME REASON, I FEEL LIKE FOR THE FIRST TIME IN MY LIFE I FIT IN. THAT I HAVE A *REASON TO EXIST.*

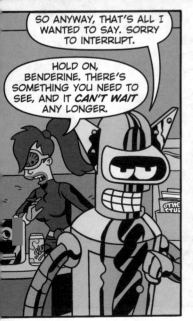

SO ANYWAY, THAT'S ALL I WANTED TO SAY. SORRY TO INTERRUPT.

HOLD ON, BENDERINE. THERE'S SOMETHING YOU NEED TO SEE, AND IT *CAN'T WAIT* ANY LONGER.

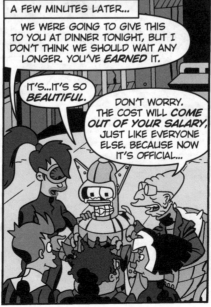

A FEW MINUTES LATER...

WE WERE GOING TO GIVE THIS TO YOU AT DINNER TONIGHT, BUT I DON'T THINK WE SHOULD WAIT ANY LONGER. YOU'VE *EARNED* IT.

IT'S...IT'S SO *BEAUTIFUL.*

DON'T WORRY. THE COST WILL *COME OUT OF YOUR SALARY,* JUST LIKE EVERYONE ELSE. BECAUSE NOW IT'S OFFICIAL...

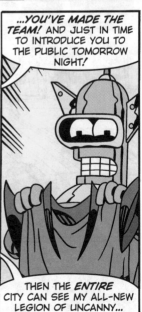

...*YOU'VE MADE THE TEAM!* AND JUST IN TIME TO INTRODUCE YOU TO THE PUBLIC TOMORROW NIGHT!

THEN THE *ENTIRE* CITY CAN SEE MY ALL-NEW LEGION OF UNCANNY...

...PLANET X-PRESS MEN!
C'MON MESS WITH US...MAKE OUR DAY, MON!
WELCOME TO THE X-PRESS MEN, BENDERINE...HOPE YOU SURVIVE THE EXPERIENCE!
THANKS! UH, WHY ARE WE RUNNING?
BIG SPANDEX SALE AT MACY'S! GLUH!
WHITE MEAT
Tuna Safe!

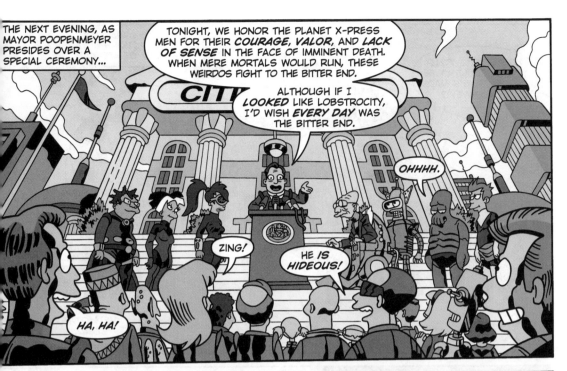

THE NEXT EVENING, AS MAYOR POOPENMEYER PRESIDES OVER A SPECIAL CEREMONY...

TONIGHT, WE HONOR THE PLANET X-PRESS MEN FOR THEIR *COURAGE, VALOR,* AND *LACK OF SENSE* IN THE FACE OF IMMINENT DEATH. WHEN MERE MORTALS WOULD RUN, THESE WEIRDOS FIGHT TO THE BITTER END.

ALTHOUGH IF I *LOOKED* LIKE LOBSTROCITY, I'D WISH *EVERY DAY* WAS THE BITTER END.

OHHHH.

ZING!

HE *IS* HIDEOUS!

HA, HA!

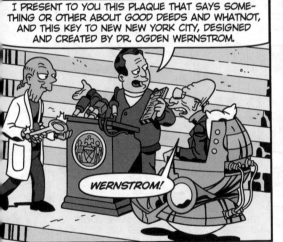

I PRESENT TO YOU THIS PLAQUE THAT SAYS SOMETHING OR OTHER ABOUT GOOD DEEDS AND WHATNOT, AND THIS KEY TO NEW NEW YORK CITY, DESIGNED AND CREATED BY DR. OGDEN WERNSTROM.

WERNSTROM!

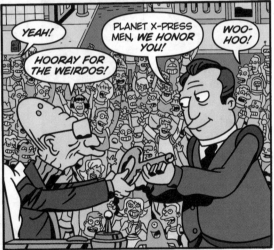

YEAH!

HOORAY FOR THE WEIRDOS!

PLANET X-PRESS MEN, *WE HONOR YOU!*

WOO-HOO!

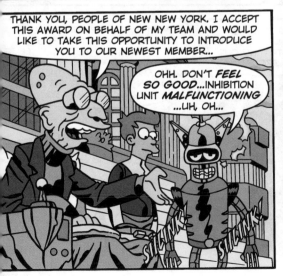

THANK YOU, PEOPLE OF NEW NEW YORK. I ACCEPT THIS AWARD ON BEHALF OF MY TEAM AND WOULD LIKE TO TAKE THIS OPPORTUNITY TO INTRODUCE YOU TO OUR NEWEST MEMBER...

OHH. DON'T *FEEL SO GOOD*...INHIBITION UNIT *MALFUNCTIONING* ...UH, OH...

SHUNK! SHUNK!

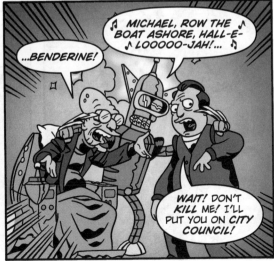

...BENDERINE!

♪ MICHAEL, ROW THE BOAT ASHORE, HALL-E-LOOOOO-JAH!... ♪

WAIT! DON'T *KILL* ME! I'LL PUT YOU ON *CITY COUNCIL!*

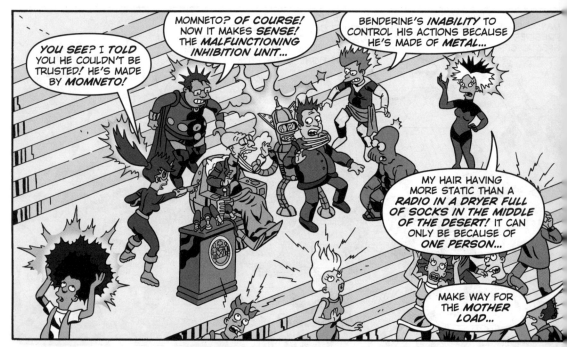

YOU SEE? I TOLD YOU HE COULDN'T BE TRUSTED! HE'S MADE BY MOMNETO!

MOMNETO? OF COURSE! NOW IT MAKES SENSE! THE MALFUNCTIONING INHIBITION UNIT...

BENDERINE'S INABILITY TO CONTROL HIS ACTIONS BECAUSE HE'S MADE OF METAL...

MY HAIR HAVING MORE STATIC THAN A RADIO IN A DRYER FULL OF SOCKS IN THE MIDDLE OF THE DESERT! IT CAN ONLY BE BECAUSE OF ONE PERSON...

MAKE WAY FOR THE MOTHER LOAD...

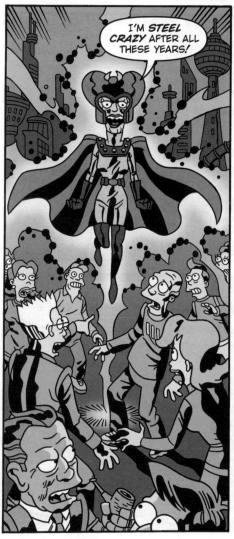

I'M STEEL CRAZY AFTER ALL THESE YEARS!

SO YOU ARE BEHIND BENDERINE INFILTRATING OUR GROUP!

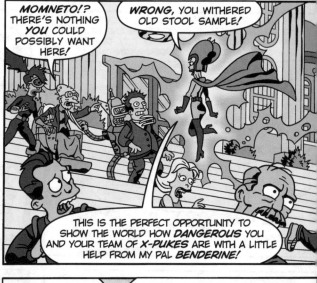

MOMNETO!? THERE'S NOTHING YOU COULD POSSIBLY WANT HERE!

WRONG, YOU WITHERED OLD STOOL SAMPLE!

THIS IS THE PERFECT OPPORTUNITY TO SHOW THE WORLD HOW DANGEROUS YOU AND YOUR TEAM OF X-PUKES ARE WITH A LITTLE HELP FROM MY PAL BENDERINE!

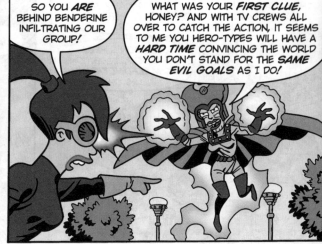

WHAT WAS YOUR FIRST CLUE, HONEY? AND WITH TV CREWS ALL OVER TO CATCH THE ACTION, IT SEEMS TO ME YOU HERO-TYPES WILL HAVE A HARD TIME CONVINCING THE WORLD YOU DON'T STAND FOR THE SAME EVIL GOALS AS I DO!

NOT IF WE JUST KICK YOUR BUTT LIKE USUAL! READY, X-PRESS MEN?
BRING IT ON!
LOOKS LIKE STORMY WEATHER!
AND THE QUICKER WE'RE DONE, THE QUICKER WE'LL GET TO CELEBRATE OUR VICTORY WITH A NICE DINNER!
X-PRESS MEN, ATTACK!
SPLEEEOW!
OH, I DON'T LIKE TO RECEIVE...
...I GIVE 'TIL IT HURTS!
BEE-OOON!
UGGGH!
AND JUST IN CASE YOU GET ANYMORE BRIGHT IDEAS...
KING AVENUE
SHUK!
WHAT THE--?
KING

NOW YOU TWO BE GOOD AND SIT TIGHT FOR ME...
SCHLICK! I'M ABSORBING LOBSTROCITY'S POWERS! AND OH MY GOD, AM I STARVING!
IT'S NOT JUST AN ACT, PEOPLE.
HOW 'BOUT A TASTE OF WHAT YOU'RE DISHIN' OUT, WOMAN?
I THINK YOU NEED TO LIGHTEN UP!
AHH! NOT ONLY IS SHE KICKING OUR BUTTS, BUT HER PUNS ARE SO APPROPRIATE!
OH YEAH? WE'RE NOT BEATEN YET!
OH, NOW I HAVE TO DEAL WITH THE RED-HEADED STEP-CHILD OF THE BUNCH...
SWOOSH! SWOOSH!
SWOOSH!
SPLLSSHH!
GLAGH! GLUGH!

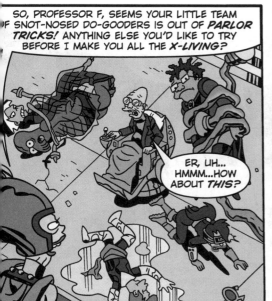

SO, PROFESSOR F, SEEMS YOUR LITTLE TEAM OF SNOT-NOSED DO-GOODERS IS OUT OF *PARLOR TRICKS!* ANYTHING ELSE YOU'D LIKE TO TRY BEFORE I MAKE YOU ALL THE *X-LIVING?*

ER, UH... HMMM...HOW ABOUT *THIS?*

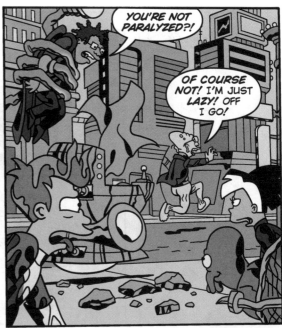

YOU'RE NOT *PARALYZED?!*

OF COURSE *NOT!* I'M JUST *LAZY!* OFF I GO!

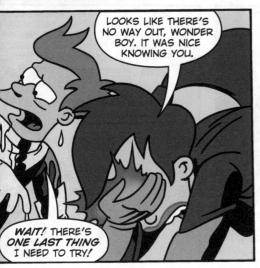

LOOKS LIKE THERE'S NO WAY OUT, WONDER BOY. IT WAS NICE KNOWING YOU.

WAIT! THERE'S *ONE LAST THING* I NEED TO TRY!

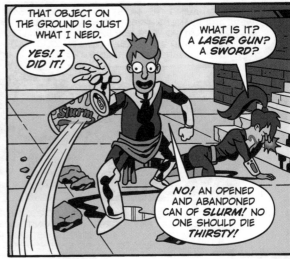

THAT OBJECT ON THE GROUND IS JUST WHAT I NEED.

YES! I DID IT!

WHAT IS IT? A *LASER GUN?* A *SWORD?*

NO! AN OPENED AND ABANDONED CAN OF *SLURM!* NO ONE SHOULD DIE *THIRSTY!*

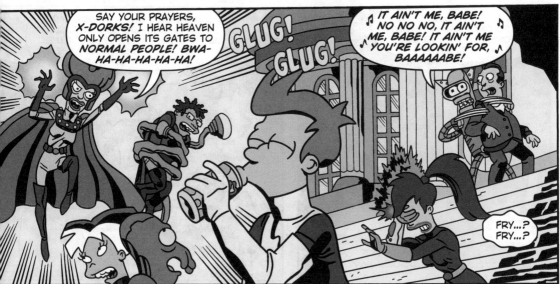

SAY YOUR PRAYERS, *X-DORKS!* I HEAR HEAVEN ONLY OPENS ITS GATES TO *NORMAL PEOPLE!* BWA-HA-HA-HA-HA-HA!

GLUG! GLUG!

♪ IT AIN'T ME, BABE! NO NO NO, IT AIN'T ME, BABE! IT AIN'T YOU'RE LOOKIN' FOR, BAAAAAABE! ♪

FRY...? FRY...?

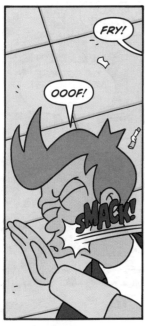

FRY!

OOOF!

SMACK!

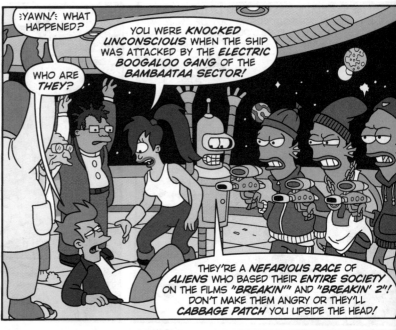

¡YAWN!¿ WHAT HAPPENED?

WHO ARE THEY?

YOU WERE KNOCKED UNCONSCIOUS WHEN THE SHIP WAS ATTACKED BY THE ELECTRIC BOOGALOO GANG OF THE BAMBAATAA SECTOR!

THEY'RE A NEFARIOUS RACE OF ALIENS WHO BASED THEIR ENTIRE SOCIETY ON THE FILMS "BREAKIN'" AND "BREAKIN' 2"! DON'T MAKE THEM ANGRY OR THEY'LL CABBAGE PATCH YOU UPSIDE THE HEAD!

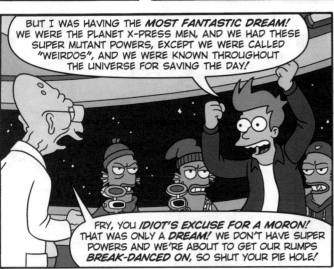

BUT I WAS HAVING THE MOST FANTASTIC DREAM! WE WERE THE PLANET X-PRESS MEN, AND WE HAD THESE SUPER MUTANT POWERS, EXCEPT WE WERE CALLED "WEIRDOS", AND WE WERE KNOWN THROUGHOUT THE UNIVERSE FOR SAVING THE DAY!

FRY, YOU IDIOT'S EXCUSE FOR A MORON! THAT WAS ONLY A DREAM! WE DON'T HAVE SUPER POWERS AND WE'RE ABOUT TO GET OUR RUMPS BREAK-DANCED ON, SO SHUT YOUR PIE HOLE!

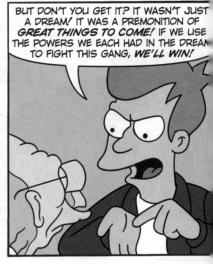

BUT DON'T YOU GET IT? IT WASN'T JUST A DREAM! IT WAS A PREMONITION OF GREAT THINGS TO COME! IF WE USE THE POWERS WE EACH HAD IN THE DREAM TO FIGHT THIS GANG, WE'LL WIN!

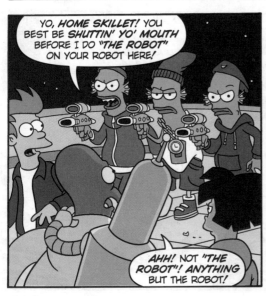

YO, HOME SKILLET! YOU BEST BE SHUTTIN' YO' MOUTH BEFORE I DO "THE ROBOT" ON YOUR ROBOT HERE!

AHH! NOT "THE ROBOT"! ANYTHING BUT THE ROBOT!

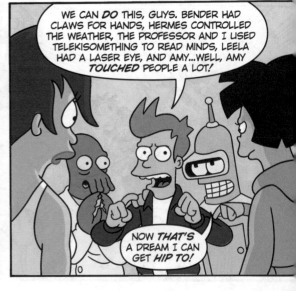

WE CAN DO THIS, GUYS. BENDER HAD CLAWS FOR HANDS, HERMES CONTROLLED THE WEATHER, THE PROFESSOR AND I USED TELEKISOMETHING TO READ MINDS, LEELA HAD A LASER EYE, AND AMY...WELL, AMY TOUCHED PEOPLE A LOT!

NOW THAT'S A DREAM I CAN GET HIP TO!

I'LL FIGHT THEM MYSELF IF I HAVE TO! COME ON, MIND POWERS!
YO, MAN, IS THIS FOOL TRIPPIN' OR WHAT?
I'M ABOUT TO SPIN ON HIS HEAD, G!
DON'T FRONT ON DA ELECTRIC BOOGALOO POSSE!
OOOF! OUCH! UGGH!
BAM!
CRASH!
HEY! HERMES' WIND POWER...IT'S WORKING!
FLOMP!
PRESSURE HATCH
YEAH, FRY, "IT'S" WORKING ALL RIGHT!
TIME FOR ME TO DO "THE CENTIPEDE" ON YOU, FOOL! WHAT THE--?
SMACK!
ONE MOVE AND YOU'RE LASER TOAST, "G".

I WOULDN'T REACH FOR THAT PISTOL, SNOOP!
I'LL FILE YOUR EYES INTO SILICON, SWISS ARMY STYLE, PAL!
AND LAST BUT NOT LEAST...
ZOIDBERG! FETCH!
GO, ZOIDBERG, GO!
WHAT A BEAST!
LEFTOVERS! SCHLOMPGLOMPH! SLLRPGLOOM!
AIIIEE!
I WANNA GO BACK TO THE 'HOOD!
THIS AIN'T PHAT NO MORE!

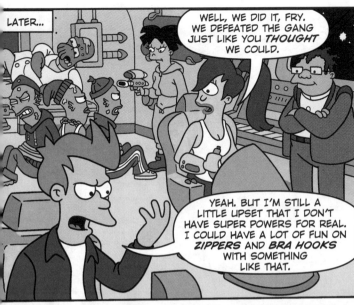

LATER...

WELL, WE DID IT, FRY. WE DEFEATED THE GANG JUST LIKE YOU *THOUGHT* WE COULD.

YEAH. BUT I'M STILL A LITTLE UPSET THAT I DON'T HAVE SUPER POWERS FOR REAL. I COULD HAVE A LOT OF FUN ON *ZIPPERS* AND *BRA HOOKS* WITH SOMETHING LIKE THAT.

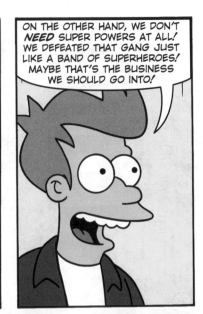

ON THE OTHER HAND, WE DON'T *NEED* SUPER POWERS AT ALL! WE DEFEATED THAT GANG JUST LIKE A BAND OF SUPERHEROES! MAYBE THAT'S THE BUSINESS WE SHOULD GO INTO!

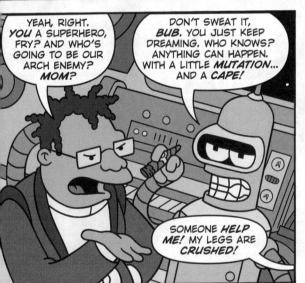

YEAH, RIGHT. *YOU* A SUPERHERO, FRY? AND WHO'S GOING TO BE OUR ARCH ENEMY? *MOM*?

DON'T SWEAT IT, *BUB*. YOU JUST KEEP DREAMING. WHO KNOWS? ANYTHING CAN HAPPEN. WITH A LITTLE *MUTATION*... AND A *CAPE*!

SOMEONE *HELP ME*! MY LEGS ARE *CRUSHED*!

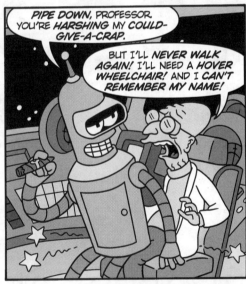

PIPE DOWN, PROFESSOR. YOU'RE *HARSHING* MY *COULD-GIVE-A-CRAP*.

BUT I'LL *NEVER WALK AGAIN*! I'LL NEED A *HOVER WHEELCHAIR*! AND I *CAN'T REMEMBER MY NAME*!

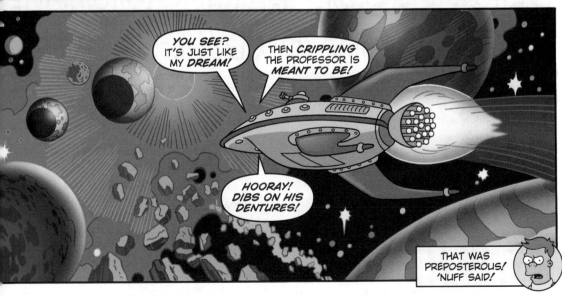

YOU SEE? IT'S JUST LIKE MY *DREAM!*

THEN *CRIPPLING* THE PROFESSOR IS *MEANT TO BE!*

HOORAY! DIBS ON HIS *DENTURES!*

THAT WAS PREPOSTEROUS! 'NUFF SAID!

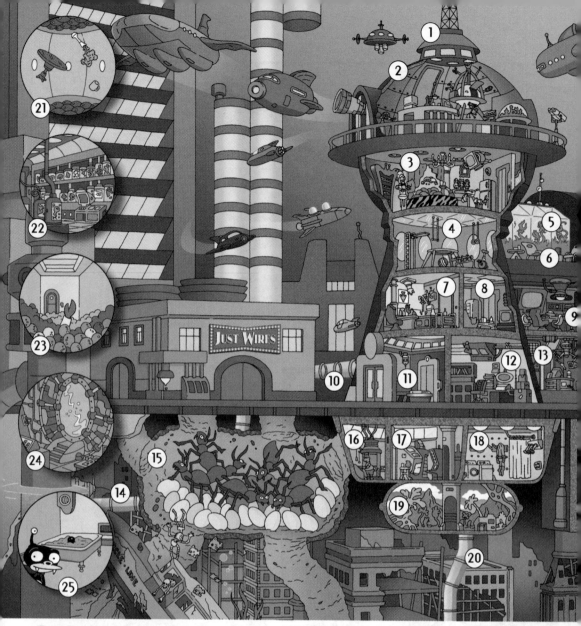

PROFESSOR FARNSWORTH BUILDS HIS DREAM HOUSE

Nestled on a refuse-ridden, mutant lamprey-infested river over the ruined city of Old New York, Pro Farnsworth tirelessly labors to complete the house of his dreams which is already in progress: The Plan Express Building.

Featuring (but not limited to):

1) Powerful AM Radio Antenna to pick-up hilarious drive-time shows

2) Upstairs Laboratory with smelloscope, moon roof, time machine (work in progress), shrunken city under glass

3) Master Bedroom with entertainment module, refreshment storage, Hummel figurines, butler bot w/restorative tonic, dog bot with slippers

4) Ultimate Room of Erotic Pleasure with hanging rings, unicycle, row of circus horns, big balance ball, trapeze, trampoline, high dive

5) Greenhouse for exotic half-plant half-monkey breeding experiments (i.e. chimpadendrons and chrysanthemonkeys)

6) Rooftop deck for nude sunbathing with rotisserie lounge chair

7) Zoidberg's Office and Sick Bay with probes, restraints and very sharp whirling instruments

8) Employee Lounge and Griping Chamber

9) Conference Room with holographic projector

10) Secret Emergency Transport Tube to "Just Wires" store

11) Lobby and/or Antechamber

12) Hermes Conrad's Office

13) Downstairs Laboratory with work stool, table and drawer containing different lengths of amazing wire

14) Secret Transport Tube to County Morgue (for retrieval and disposal)

15) Giant Mutant Ant Farm

16) Cloning Room

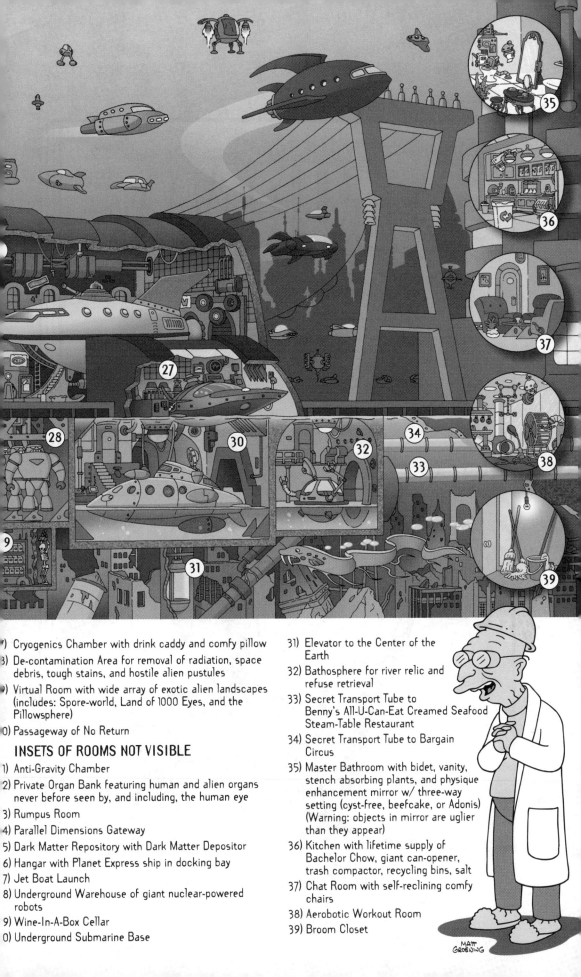

INSETS OF ROOMS NOT VISIBLE

7) Cryogenics Chamber with drink caddy and comfy pillow

8) De-contamination Area for removal of radiation, space debris, tough stains, and hostile alien pustules

9) Virtual Room with wide array of exotic alien landscapes (includes: Spore-world, Land of 1000 Eyes, and the Pillowsphere)

10) Passageway of No Return

1) Anti-Gravity Chamber

2) Private Organ Bank featuring human and alien organs never before seen by, and including, the human eye

3) Rumpus Room

4) Parallel Dimensions Gateway

5) Dark Matter Repository with Dark Matter Depositor

6) Hangar with Planet Express ship in docking bay

7) Jet Boat Launch

8) Underground Warehouse of giant nuclear-powered robots

9) Wine-In-A-Box Cellar

0) Underground Submarine Base

31) Elevator to the Center of the Earth

32) Bathosphere for river relic and refuse retrieval

33) Secret Transport Tube to Benny's All-U-Can-Eat Creamed Seafood Steam-Table Restaurant

34) Secret Transport Tube to Bargain Circus

35) Master Bathroom with bidet, vanity, stench absorbing plants, and physique enhancement mirror w/ three-way setting (cyst-free, beefcake, or Adonis) (Warning: objects in mirror are uglier than they appear)

36) Kitchen with lifetime supply of Bachelor Chow, giant can-opener, trash compactor, recycling bins, salt

37) Chat Room with self-reclining comfy chairs

38) Aerobotic Workout Room

39) Broom Closet

MATT GROENING

BONGO COMICS GROUP
MADE IN THE U.S.A.! (PRINTED IN CANADA)
#9
US $2.50
CAN $3.50
FUTURAMA™
COMICS
©2002 BONGO ENTERTAINMENT, INC. FUTURAMA ©&TM TWENTIETH CENTURY FOX FILM CORPORATION. ALL RIGHTS RESERVED.
MATT GROENING

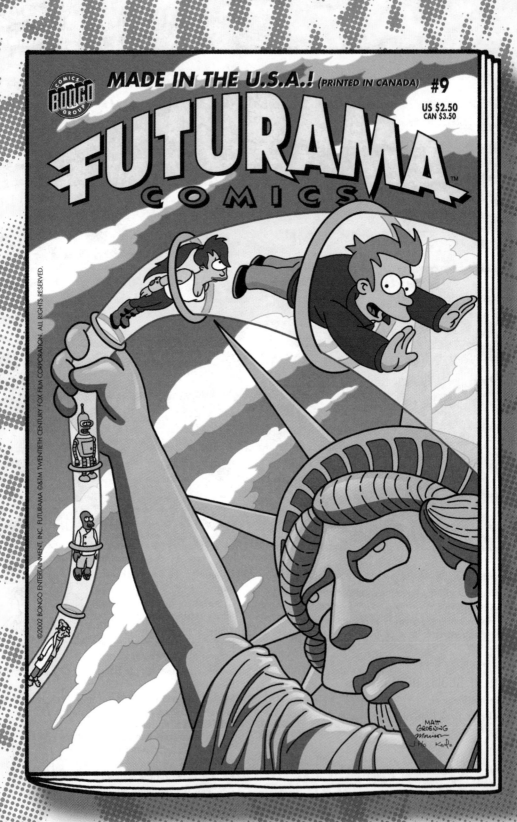

THIS IS THE GREATEST DAY OF MY LIFE!!!
FREAKY FRY-DAY

ERIC ROGERS SCRIPT | TOM KING JOHN DELANEY PENCILS | PHYLLIS NOVIN INKS | RICK REESE COLORS | KAREN BATES LETTERS | BILL MORRISON EDITOR | MATT GROENING MYSTERIOUS STRANGER

Mid-Galaxy Spaceship and Robot BiKini Wash Co.
WE'LL GET YOU ALL WET BEHIND THE GEARS!
WE'LL MAKE YOUR CHASSIS CLASSY!
STOP FOR A SHINY METAL ASS AND GAS!
OOOHH YEAH! SOAP ME UP, BABY! I'M A DIRTY 'BOT, A DIRTY 'BOT!
WOULD YOU LIKES THE FORCE FIELD WAX COATING FOR ONLYS $9.95 MORES...?

...IT GIVES YOUR SHIP THAT STILLS-NEW LOOK FOR UPS TO FORTY DIRECT HITS FROM ENEMY ALIEN FIRE!
JUST A REGULAR WASH PLEASE.

COME ON, FRY. I WANT TO GET A PERM AND LEARN ORIGAMI INSIDE THE SERVICE MART WHILE WE WAIT FOR THE SHIP.
SPLLSSH!
GEEZ, WHAT HAPPENED TO THE GOOD OLD DAYS WHEN ALL THERE WAS TO DO AT THE CAR WASH WAS GET A MASSAGE OR SING KARAOKE OR GET A LOAN?

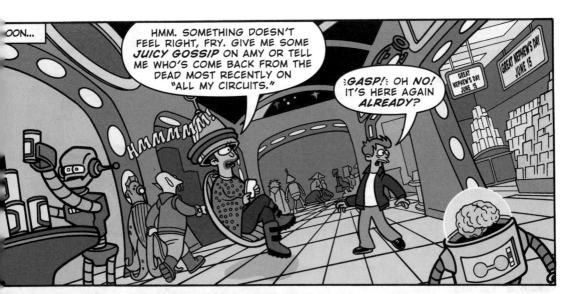

...OON...

HMM. SOMETHING DOESN'T FEEL RIGHT, FRY. GIVE ME SOME *JUICY GOSSIP* ON AMY OR TELL ME WHO'S COME BACK FROM THE DEAD MOST RECENTLY ON "ALL MY CIRCUITS."

¡GASP!; OH *NO!* IT'S HERE AGAIN *ALREADY?*

GREAT NEPHEW'S DAY JUNE 15

GREAT NEPHEW'S DAY JUNE 15

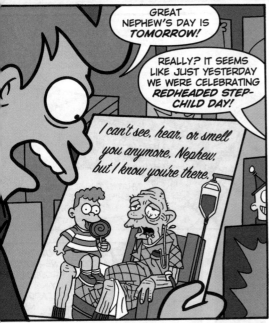

GREAT NEPHEW'S DAY IS *TOMORROW!*

REALLY? IT SEEMS LIKE JUST YESTERDAY WE WERE CELEBRATING *REDHEADED STEP-CHILD DAY!*

I can't see, hear, or smell you anymore, Nephew, but I know you're there.

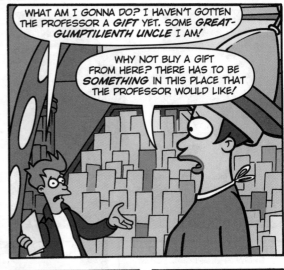

WHAT AM I GONNA DO? I HAVEN'T GOTTEN THE PROFESSOR A *GIFT* YET. SOME *GREAT-GUMPTILIENTH UNCLE* I AM!

WHY NOT BUY A GIFT FROM HERE? THERE HAS TO BE *SOMETHING* IN THIS PLACE THAT THE PROFESSOR WOULD LIKE!

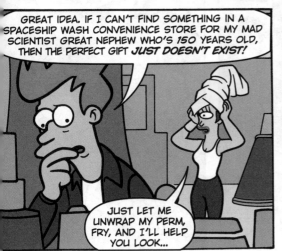

GREAT IDEA. IF I CAN'T FIND SOMETHING IN A SPACESHIP WASH CONVENIENCE STORE FOR MY MAD SCIENTIST GREAT NEPHEW WHO'S 150 YEARS OLD, THEN THE PERFECT GIFT *JUST DOESN'T EXIST!*

JUST LET ME UNWRAP MY PERM, FRY, AND I'LL HELP YOU LOOK...

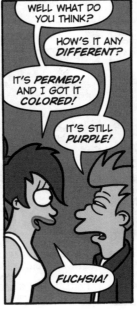

WELL WHAT DO YOU THINK?

HOW'S IT ANY *DIFFERENT?*

IT'S *PERMED!* AND I GOT IT *COLORED!*

IT'S STILL *PURPLE!*

FUCHSIA!

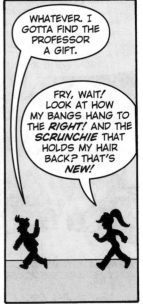

WHATEVER. I GOTTA FIND THE PROFESSOR A GIFT.

FRY, WAIT! LOOK AT HOW MY BANGS HANG TO THE *RIGHT!* AND THE *SCRUNCHIE* THAT HOLDS MY HAIR BACK? THAT'S *NEW!*

119

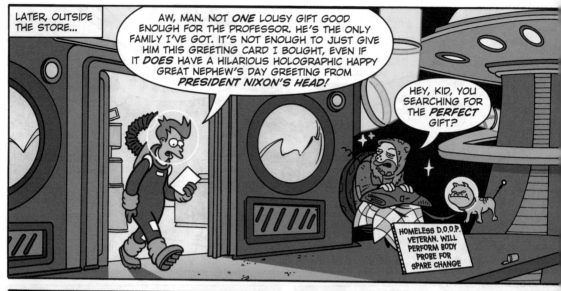

AW, MAN. NOT *ONE* LOUSY GIFT GOOD ENOUGH FOR THE PROFESSOR. HE'S THE ONLY FAMILY I'VE GOT. IT'S NOT ENOUGH TO JUST GIVE HIM THIS GREETING CARD I BOUGHT, EVEN IF IT *DOES* HAVE A HILARIOUS HOLOGRAPHIC HAPPY GREAT NEPHEW'S DAY GREETING FROM *PRESIDENT NIXON'S HEAD!*

HEY, KID, YOU SEARCHING FOR THE *PERFECT* GIFT?

HOMELESS D.O.O.P. VETERAN. WILL PERFORM BODY PROBE FOR SPARE CHANGE

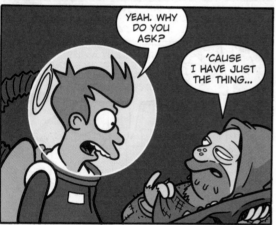

YEAH. WHY DO YOU ASK?

'CAUSE I HAVE JUST THE THING...

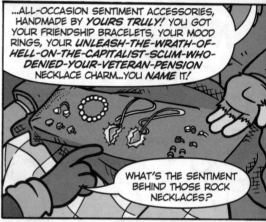

...ALL-OCCASION SENTIMENT ACCESSORIES, HANDMADE BY *YOURS TRULY!* YOU GOT YOUR FRIENDSHIP BRACELETS, YOUR MOOD RINGS, YOUR *UNLEASH-THE-WRATH-OF-HELL-ON-THE-CAPITALIST-SCUM-WHO-DENIED-YOUR-VETERAN-PENSION* NECKLACE CHARM...YOU *NAME* IT!

WHAT'S THE SENTIMENT BEHIND THOSE ROCK NECKLACES?

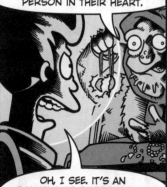

THIS CHARM IS DESIGNED TO SHOW THE SPECIAL BOND BETWEEN TWO PEOPLE--THAT WHEREVER ONE MAY GO OR WHAT HE MAY DO, THERE'S ALWAYS ANOTHER PERSON OUT IN THE UNIVERSE WHO IS KEEPING A SPECIAL PLACE FOR THAT PERSON IN THEIR HEART.

OH, I SEE. IT'S AN EXAMPLE OF *CHEESE-BALL MERCHANDISING*, TAILOR-MADE FOR *DESPERATE SUCKERS ON A BUDGET.* WELL, ALL I CAN SAY IS...*I'LL TAKE IT!*

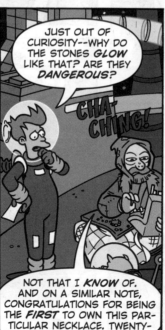

JUST OUT OF CURIOSITY--WHY DO THE STONES *GLOW* LIKE THAT? ARE THEY *DANGEROUS?*

CHA-CHING!

NOT THAT I *KNOW* OF. AND ON A SIMILAR NOTE, CONGRATULATIONS FOR BEING THE *FIRST* TO OWN THIS PARTICULAR NECKLACE. TWENTY-FIVE DOLLARS, PLEASE.

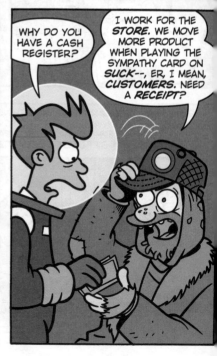

WHY DO YOU HAVE A CASH REGISTER?

I WORK FOR THE *STORE.* WE MOVE MORE PRODUCT WHEN PLAYING THE SYMPATHY CARD ON *SUCK--*, ER, I MEAN, *CUSTOMERS.* NEED A *RECEIPT?*

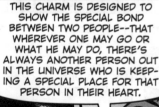

COME ON, FRY. THE SHIP'S READY TO GO, BUT I CAN'T FIND BENDER. DO YOU THINK HE DOESN'T RECOGNIZE ME BECAUSE OF MY HAIR?
WOW! I NEVER KNEW MY ASS COULD GET THAT SHINY! I HOPE NO ONE EVER BITES IT NOW!
MR. BENDER, DO YOU WANT THE "EXTRA SERVICE"?
DO I EVER, DOLL FACE!
OKAY!
SHHUNK!
AHHH! CRUSHINATOR! IT'S YOU!
BENDER. IT HAS BEEN SO LONG. WHY HAVEN'T YOU CALLED? I HAVE A SURPRISE FOR YOU...
SHHHHNNNN!
HE IS THE FRUIT OF YOUR SOFTWARE. I CALL HIM "JUNIOR."
DADDY.
wheeeenn!
NOOO!
FIRE UP THE ENGINES! GO FOR LAUNCH! GET ME THE HELL OUT OF HEEEERE!
BY THE WAY, SASSY NEW 'DO, LEELA!

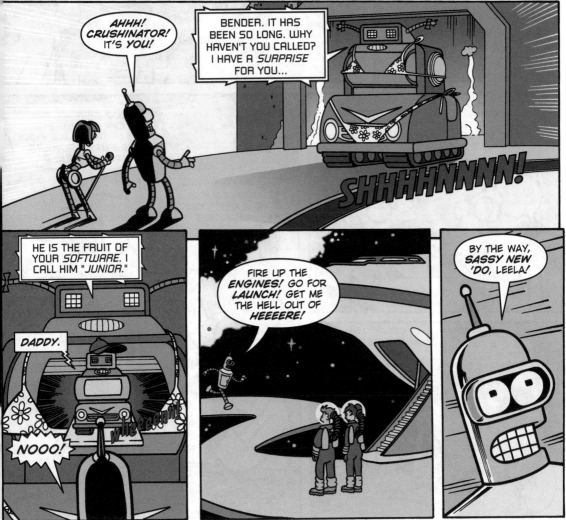

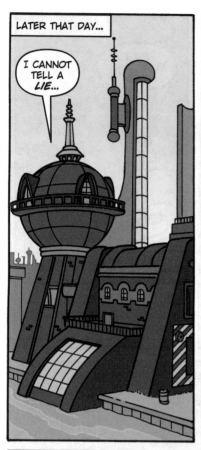

LATER THAT DAY...

I CANNOT TELL A *LIE*...

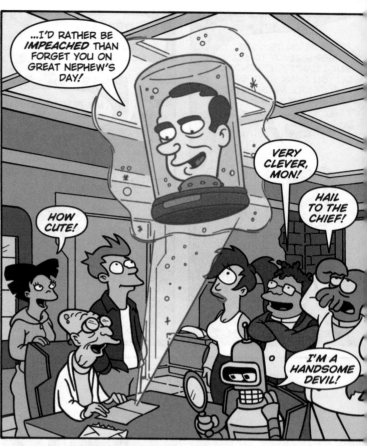

...I'D RATHER BE *IMPEACHED* THAN FORGET YOU ON GREAT NEPHEW'S DAY!

VERY CLEVER, MON!

HAIL TO THE CHIEF!

HOW CUTE!

I'M A HANDSOME DEVIL!

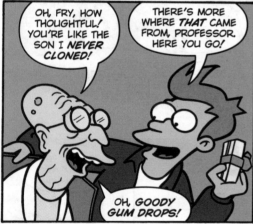

OH, FRY, HOW THOUGHTFUL! YOU'RE LIKE THE SON I *NEVER CLONED!*

THERE'S MORE WHERE *THAT* CAME FROM, PROFESSOR. HERE YOU GO!

OH, GOODY GUM DROPS!

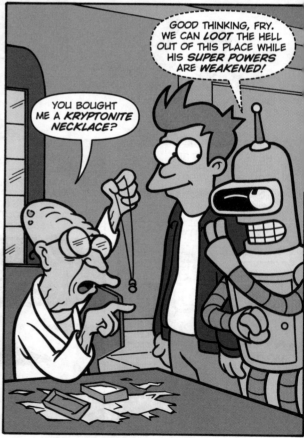

GOOD THINKING, FRY. WE CAN *LOOT* THE HELL OUT OF THIS PLACE WHILE HIS *SUPER POWERS* ARE *WEAKENED!*

YOU BOUGHT ME A *KRYPTONITE* NECKLACE?

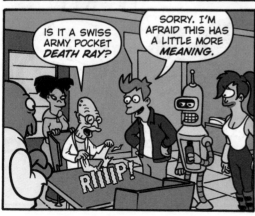

IS IT A SWISS ARMY POCKET *DEATH RAY?*

SORRY. I'M AFRAID THIS HAS A LITTLE MORE *MEANING.*

RIIIIP!

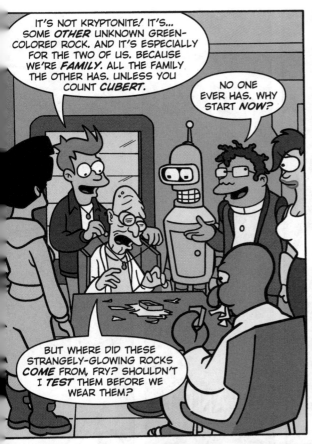

IT'S NOT KRYPTONITE! IT'S... SOME *OTHER* UNKNOWN GREEN-COLORED ROCK. AND IT'S ESPECIALLY FOR THE TWO OF US. BECAUSE WE'RE *FAMILY.* ALL THE FAMILY THE OTHER HAS. UNLESS YOU COUNT *CUBERT.*

NO ONE EVER HAS. WHY START *NOW?*

BUT WHERE DID THESE STRANGELY-GLOWING ROCKS *COME* FROM, FRY? SHOULDN'T I *TEST* THEM BEFORE WE WEAR THEM?

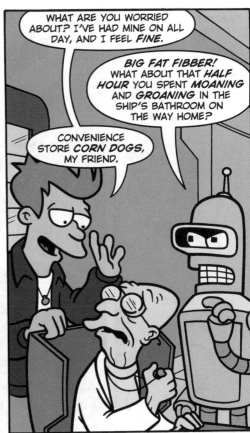

WHAT ARE YOU WORRIED ABOUT? I'VE HAD MINE ON ALL DAY, AND I FEEL *FINE.*

BIG FAT FIBBER! WHAT ABOUT THAT *HALF HOUR* YOU SPENT *MOANING* AND *GROANING* IN THE SHIP'S BATHROOM ON THE WAY HOME?

CONVENIENCE STORE *CORN DOGS,* MY FRIEND.

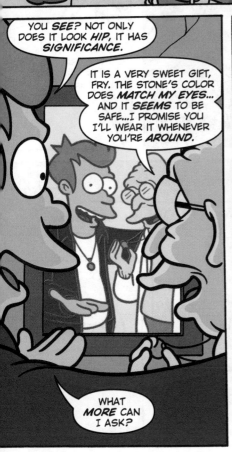

YOU *SEE?* NOT ONLY DOES IT LOOK *HIP,* IT HAS *SIGNIFICANCE.*

IT IS A VERY SWEET GIFT, FRY. THE STONE'S COLOR DOES *MATCH MY EYES...* AND IT *SEEMS* TO BE SAFE...I PROMISE YOU I'LL WEAR IT WHENEVER YOU'RE *AROUND.*

WHAT *MORE* CAN I ASK?

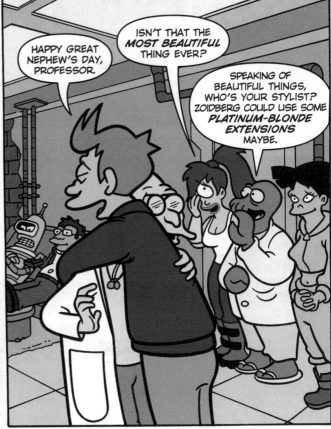

HAPPY GREAT NEPHEW'S DAY, PROFESSOR.

ISN'T THAT THE *MOST BEAUTIFUL* THING EVER?

SPEAKING OF BEAUTIFUL THINGS, WHO'S YOUR STYLIST? ZOIDBERG COULD USE SOME *PLATINUM-BLONDE EXTENSIONS* MAYBE.

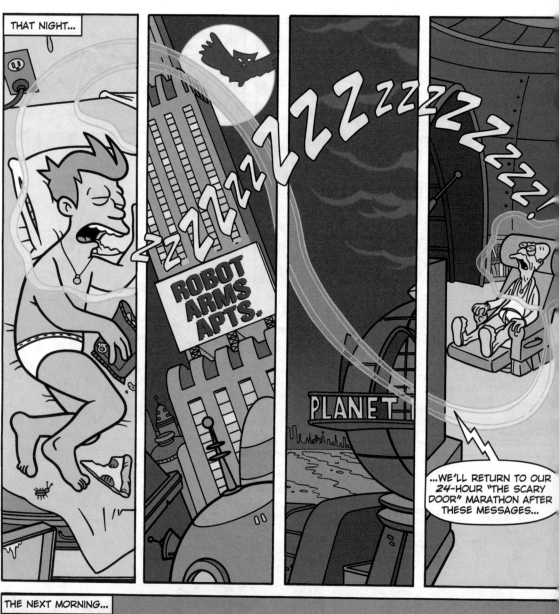

THAT NIGHT...

ROBOT ARMS APTS.

PLANET

...WE'LL RETURN TO OUR 24-HOUR "THE SCARY DOOR" MARATHON AFTER THESE MESSAGES...

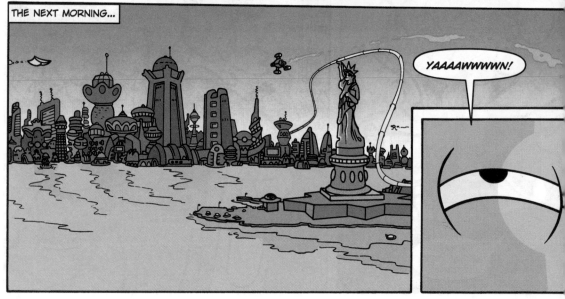

THE NEXT MORNING...

YAAAAWWWWN!

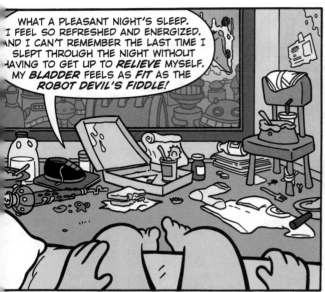

WHAT A PLEASANT NIGHT'S SLEEP. I FEEL SO REFRESHED AND ENERGIZED. AND I CAN'T REMEMBER THE LAST TIME I SLEPT THROUGH THE NIGHT WITHOUT HAVING TO GET UP TO *RELIEVE* MYSELF. MY *BLADDER* FEELS AS *FIT* AS THE *ROBOT DEVIL'S FIDDLE!*

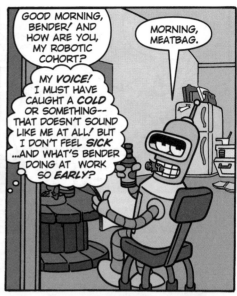

GOOD MORNING, BENDER! AND HOW ARE YOU, MY ROBOTIC COHORT?

MORNING, MEATBAG.

MY *VOICE!* I MUST HAVE CAUGHT A *COLD* OR SOMETHING-- THAT DOESN'T SOUND LIKE ME AT ALL! BUT I DON'T FEEL *SICK* ...AND WHAT'S BENDER DOING AT WORK SO *EARLY?*

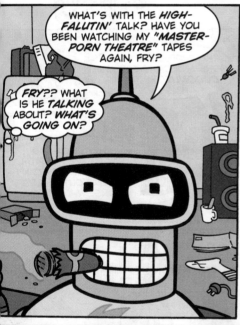

WHAT'S WITH THE *HIGH-FALUTIN'* TALK? HAVE YOU BEEN WATCHING MY *"MASTER-PORN THEATRE"* TAPES AGAIN, FRY?

FRY?? WHAT IS HE *TALKING* ABOUT? *WHAT'S GOING ON?*

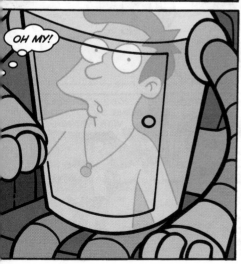

OH MY!

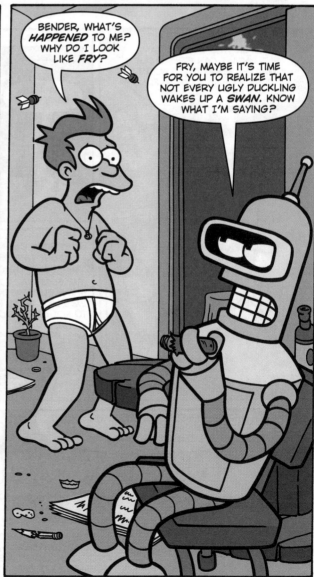

BENDER, WHAT'S *HAPPENED* TO ME? WHY DO I LOOK LIKE *FRY?*

FRY, MAYBE IT'S TIME FOR YOU TO REALIZE THAT NOT EVERY UGLY DUCKLING WAKES UP A *SWAN.* KNOW WHAT I'M SAYING?

YOU MEAN TO SAY...I AM FRY?! THIS IS FRY'S BODY?!?!
SAD BUT TRUE. THAT DIET OF CHIMICHANGAS AND STRAWBERRY QUIK JUST AIN'T DOING YOU ANY FAVORS, PAL.
I'M FRY! I...AM... FRRRRYYYY!
OH, GLORIOUS DAY. NOW, IF YOU'RE DONE STATING THE OBVIOUS, YOU BETTER GET READY FOR WORK, OR YOU'RE GONNA BE LATE.
OH MY YES!
TIME FOR WORK! AS A DELIVERY BOY!
BECAUSE THAT'S WHAT FRY, BY WHICH I MEAN ME, DOES!
OFF I GO!
SEE YA A THE OFFIC PAL.
NO SENSE IN TELLING BENDER WHO I REALLY AM. BUT UNTIL I CAN FIGURE OUT WHAT'S GOING ON, I WON'T DENY MYSELF A BIT OF FUN AT FRY'S EXPENSE!
THAT MORNING...
WHAT'S HAPPENING?
THE PROFESSOR DONE GONE AND CRACKED HIS COCONUT! HE THINKS HE'S FRY!
THEY'RE TAKING HIM TO THE HOSPITAL TO SEE IF THEY CAN FIGURE OUT WHAT'S WRONG. WHERE'S FRY? WE NEED TO GO WITH THE PROFESSOR!
HE'S RIGHT BEHIND ME. I'LL JUST STAY BEHIND AND LET HIM KNOW WHAT'S GOING ON.
BESIDES, I FIND THE BEST WAY TO SHOW SUPPORT IN TIMES LIKE THESE IS TO NOT CARE TOO MUCH...OR AT ALL.
SORRY, BENDER, BUT WE'RE ALL GOING. WE'LL JUST HAVE TO CALL FRY FROM THE HOSPITAL LATER TO FILL HIM IN.
YAY! ZOIDBERG IS GOING ON A FIELD TRIP WITH FRIENDS!
WATCH YOUR GRUBBY MITTS! MY JUST-OFF-THE-ASSEMBLY LINE SHEEN HASN'T WORN OFF YET!

FEW MINUTES LATER...

WHAT'S *THIS*? WHERE *IS* EVERYONE? WHY ISN'T ANYONE *WORKING*?

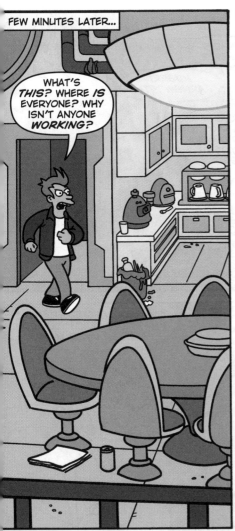

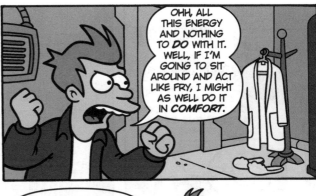

OHH, ALL THIS ENERGY AND NOTHING TO *DO* WITH IT. WELL, IF I'M GOING TO SIT AROUND AND ACT LIKE FRY, I MIGHT AS WELL DO IT IN *COMFORT*.

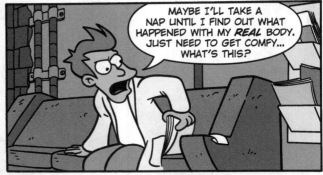

AHHH, *MUCH* BETTER. LET'S SEE...WHAT WOULD FRY DO NOW? *PICK* HIS NOSE? PRODUCE *BODILY NOISES*? *ANNOY* EVERYONE?

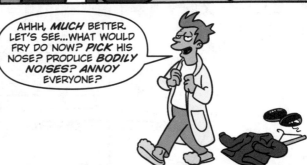

MAYBE I'LL TAKE A NAP UNTIL I FIND OUT WHAT HAPPENED WITH MY *REAL* BODY. JUST NEED TO GET COMFY... WHAT'S THIS?

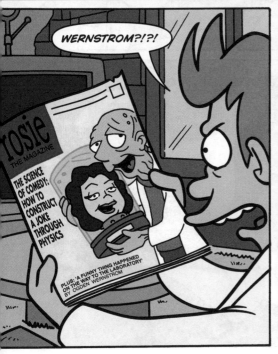

WERNSTROM?!?!

rosie THE MAGAZINE

THE SCIENCE OF COMEDY: HOW TO CONSTRUCT A JOKE THROUGH PHYSICS

PLUS: 'A FUNNY THING HAPPENED ON THE WAY TO THE LABORATORY' BY OGDEN WERNSTROM

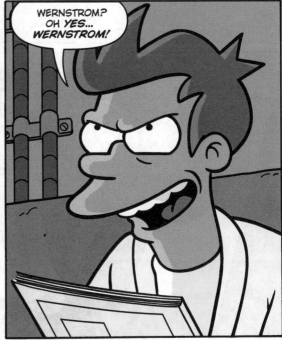

WERNSTROM? OH *YES*... *WERNSTROM!*

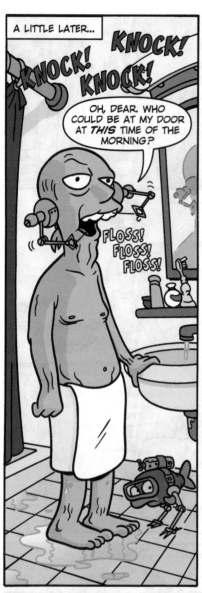

A LITTLE LATER...

KNOCK! KNOCK! KNOCK! KNOCK!

OH, DEAR. WHO COULD BE AT MY DOOR AT *THIS* TIME OF THE MORNING?

FLOSS! FLOSS! FLOSS!

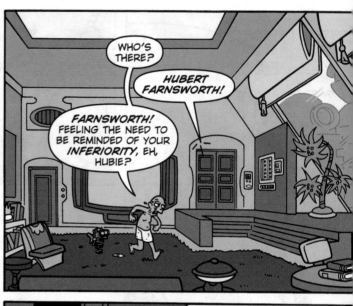

WHO'S THERE?

HUBERT FARNSWORTH!

FARNSWORTH! FEELING THE NEED TO BE REMINDED OF YOUR *INFERIORITY*, EH, HUBIE?

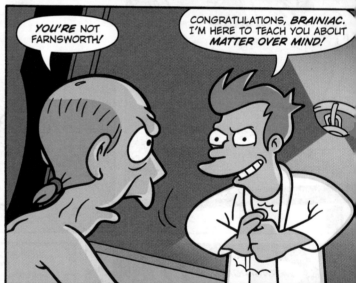

YOU'RE NOT FARNSWORTH!

CONGRATULATIONS, *BRAINIAC*. I'M HERE TO TEACH YOU ABOUT *MATTER OVER MIND!*

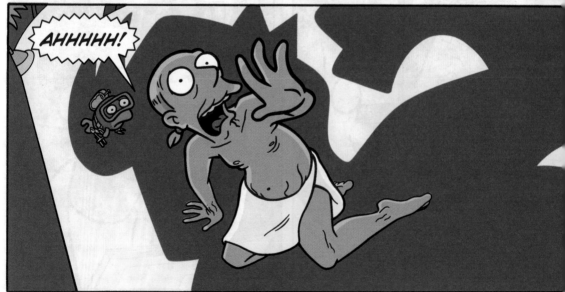

AHHHHH!

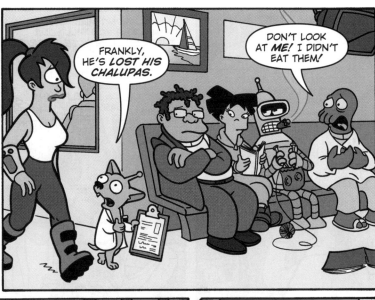

MEANWHILE...

SO WHAT'S **WRONG** WITH THE PROFESSOR, DOCTOR?

TACO BELLEVUE HOSPITAL

FRANKLY, HE'S **LOST HIS CHALUPAS.**

DON'T LOOK AT **ME!** I DIDN'T EAT THEM!

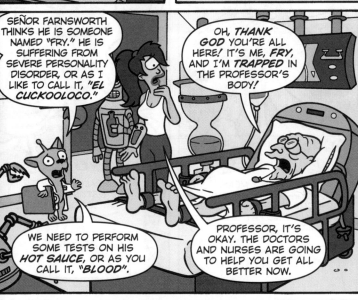

SEÑOR FARNSWORTH THINKS HE IS SOMEONE NAMED "FRY." HE IS SUFFERING FROM SEVERE PERSONALITY DISORDER, OR AS I LIKE TO CALL IT, "**EL CUCKOOLOCO.**"

OH, **THANK GOD** YOU'RE ALL HERE! IT'S ME, **FRY,** AND I'M **TRAPPED** IN THE PROFESSOR'S BODY!

WE NEED TO PERFORM SOME TESTS ON HIS **HOT SAUCE,** OR AS YOU CALL IT, "**BLOOD**".

PROFESSOR, IT'S OKAY. THE DOCTORS AND NURSES ARE GOING TO HELP YOU GET ALL BETTER NOW.

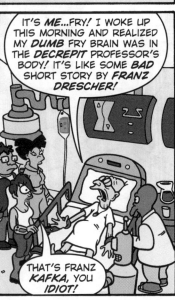

IT'S **ME**...FRY! I WOKE UP THIS MORNING AND REALIZED MY **DUMB** FRY BRAIN WAS IN THE **DECREPIT** PROFESSOR'S BODY! IT'S LIKE SOME **BAD** SHORT STORY BY **FRANZ DRESCHER!**

THAT'S FRANZ **KAFKA,** YOU **IDIOT!**

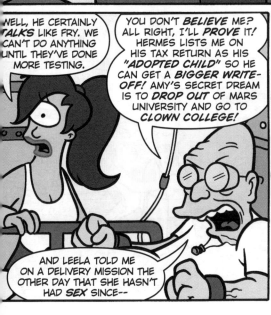

WELL, HE CERTAINLY **TALKS** LIKE FRY. WE CAN'T DO ANYTHING UNTIL THEY'VE DONE MORE TESTING.

YOU DON'T **BELIEVE** ME? ALL RIGHT, I'LL **PROVE** IT! HERMES LISTS ME ON HIS TAX RETURN AS HIS "**ADOPTED CHILD**" SO HE CAN GET A **BIGGER WRITE-OFF!** AMY'S SECRET DREAM IS TO **DROP OUT** OF MARS UNIVERSITY AND GO TO **CLOWN COLLEGE!**

AND LEELA TOLD ME ON A DELIVERY MISSION THE OTHER DAY THAT SHE HASN'T HAD **SEX** SINCE--

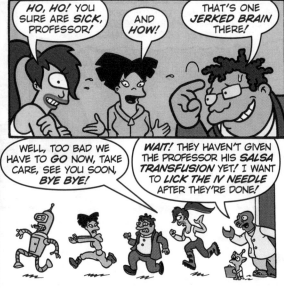

HO, HO! YOU SURE ARE **SICK,** PROFESSOR!

AND **HOW!**

THAT'S ONE **JERKED BRAIN** THERE!

WELL, TOO BAD WE HAVE TO **GO** NOW, TAKE CARE, SEE YOU SOON, **BYE BYE!**

WAIT! THEY HAVEN'T GIVEN THE PROFESSOR HIS **SALSA TRANSFUSION** YET! I WANT TO **LICK THE IV NEEDLE** AFTER THEY'RE DONE!

129

ACROSS TOWN...

ONE MORE FOR THE ROAD, BARKEEP. I HAVEN'T HAD THIS MUCH FUN CONTROLLING MY BLADDER SINCE I HAD MY *REAL ONE* REPLACED!

YOU *GOT IT!*

MIND IF I *JOIN* YOU?

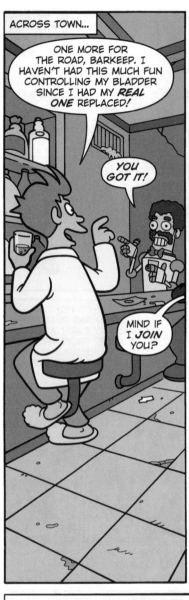

I COULDN'T HELP OVER-HEARING YOU TELL YOUR THEORY OF *PARTICLE HYBRID COMBUSTION REPRODUCTION* TO THE BARTENDER. I THOUGHT TO MYSELF, "LOOKS *AND* BRAINS". I JUST *HAD* TO INTRODUCE MYSELF. LANA LABIANCA.

HUBER--UH, I MEAN, *FRY!* PHILIP J. FRY, BUT FOR SOME REASON EVERYONE JUST CALLS ME FRY. I REALLY SHOULD *FIGURE OUT* WHY THAT IS ONE DAY.

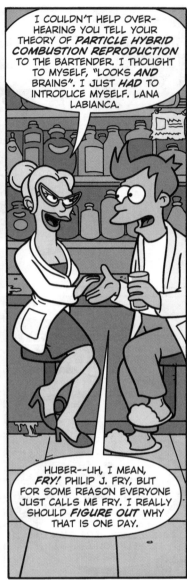

YOU KNOW, FRY, MY APARTMENT IS RIGHT AROUND THE CORNER. AND I JUST *LOVE* LONG-WINDED SCIENTIFIC EXPLANATIONS.

I REALLY *SHOULD* BE GETTING BACK TO MY LABORATORY...

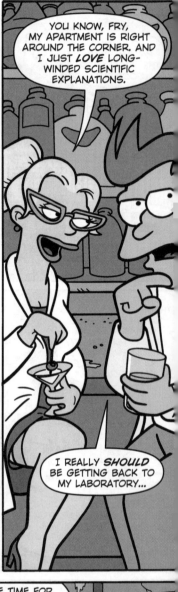

THIS IS YOUR CHANCE TO HAVE *SEX* WITH A WOMAN WHOSE HIPS *HAVEN'T* BEEN *REPLACED*, HUBERT! YOU'LL *NEVER* GET THIS CHANCE AGAIN!

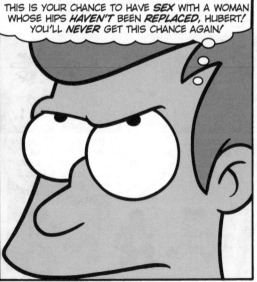

...BUT I *DO* HAVE TIME FOR AT LEAST ONE *MONOTONOUS* AND *BORING* LECTURE ON *GUPPIE CLONING* AND HOW IT RELATES TO THE *BIG BANG THEORY*.

TAKE ME HOME, YOU *SPIKY-HAIRED NERD!*

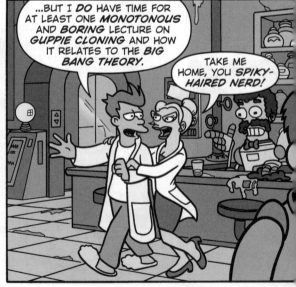

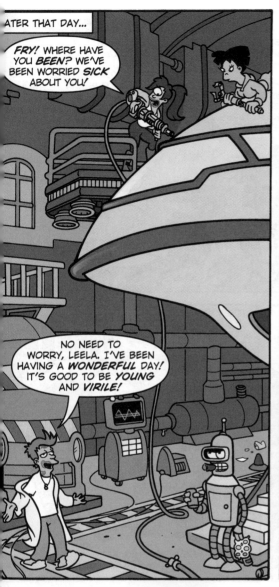

LATER THAT DAY...

FRY! WHERE HAVE YOU *BEEN*? WE'VE BEEN WORRIED *SICK* ABOUT YOU!

NO NEED TO WORRY, LEELA. I'VE BEEN HAVING A *WONDERFUL* DAY! IT'S GOOD TO BE *YOUNG* AND *VIRILE*!

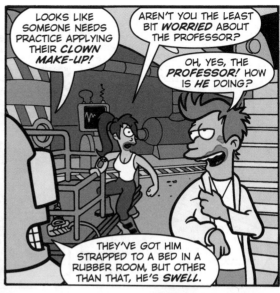

LOOKS LIKE SOMEONE NEEDS PRACTICE APPLYING THEIR *CLOWN MAKE-UP*!

AREN'T YOU THE LEAST BIT *WORRIED* ABOUT THE PROFESSOR?

OH, YES, THE *PROFESSOR*! HOW IS *HE* DOING?

THEY'VE GOT HIM STRAPPED TO A BED IN A RUBBER ROOM, BUT OTHER THAN THAT, HE'S *SWELL*.

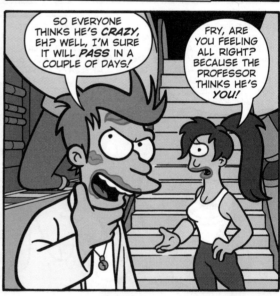

SO EVERYONE THINKS HE'S *CRAZY*, EH? WELL, I'M SURE IT WILL *PASS* IN A COUPLE OF DAYS!

FRY, ARE YOU FEELING ALL RIGHT? BECAUSE THE PROFESSOR THINKS HE'S *YOU*!

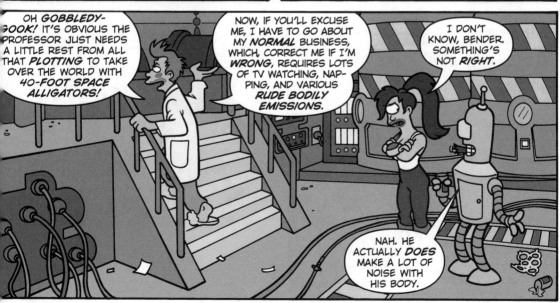

OH *GOBBLEDY-GOOK*! IT'S OBVIOUS THE PROFESSOR JUST NEEDS A LITTLE REST FROM ALL THAT *PLOTTING* TO TAKE OVER THE WORLD WITH *40-FOOT SPACE ALLIGATORS*!

NOW, IF YOU'LL EXCUSE ME, I HAVE TO GO ABOUT MY *NORMAL* BUSINESS, WHICH, CORRECT ME IF I'M *WRONG*, REQUIRES LOTS OF TV WATCHING, NAP-PING, AND VARIOUS *RUDE BODILY EMISSIONS*.

I DON'T KNOW, BENDER. SOMETHING'S NOT *RIGHT*.

NAH. HE ACTUALLY *DOES* MAKE A LOT OF NOISE WITH HIS BODY.

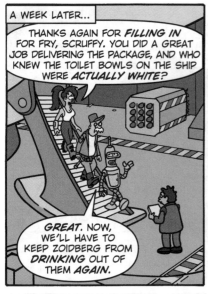

A WEEK LATER...

THANKS AGAIN FOR *FILLING IN* FOR FRY, SCRUFFY. YOU DID A GREAT JOB DELIVERING THE PACKAGE, AND WHO KNEW THE TOILET BOWLS ON THE SHIP WERE *ACTUALLY WHITE?*

GREAT. NOW, WE'LL HAVE TO KEEP ZOIDBERG FROM *DRINKING* OUT OF THEM *AGAIN.*

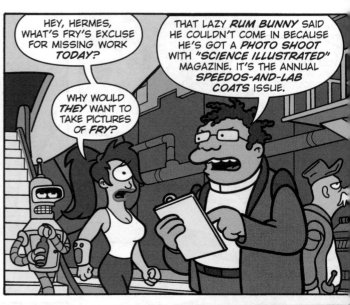

HEY, HERMES, WHAT'S FRY'S EXCUSE FOR MISSING WORK *TODAY?*

WHY WOULD *THEY* WANT TO TAKE PICTURES OF *FRY?*

THAT LAZY *RUM BUNNY* SAID HE COULDN'T COME IN BECAUSE HE'S GOT A *PHOTO SHOOT* WITH *"SCIENCE ILLUSTRATED"* MAGAZINE. IT'S THE ANNUAL *SPEEDOS-AND-LAB COATS* ISSUE.

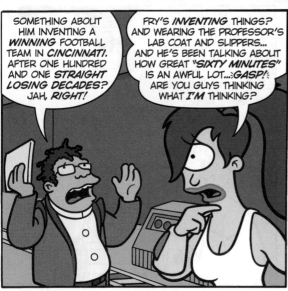

SOMETHING ABOUT HIM INVENTING A *WINNING* FOOTBALL TEAM IN *CINCINNATI.* AFTER ONE HUNDRED AND ONE *STRAIGHT LOSING DECADES?* JAH, *RIGHT!*

FRY'S *INVENTING* THINGS? AND WEARING THE PROFESSOR'S LAB COAT AND SLIPPERS... AND HE'S BEEN TALKING ABOUT HOW GREAT *"SIXTY MINUTES"* IS AN AWFUL LOT...*GASP!*: ARE YOU GUYS THINKING WHAT *I'M* THINKING?

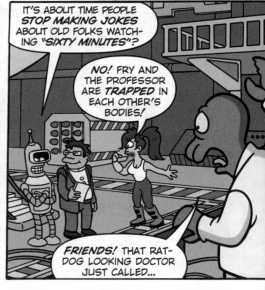

IT'S ABOUT TIME PEOPLE *STOP MAKING JOKES* ABOUT OLD FOLKS WATCHING *"SIXTY MINUTES"?*

NO! FRY AND THE PROFESSOR ARE *TRAPPED* IN EACH OTHER'S BODIES!

FRIENDS! THAT RAT-DOG LOOKING DOCTOR JUST CALLED...

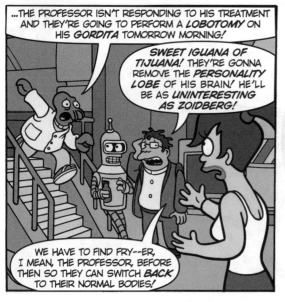

...THE PROFESSOR ISN'T RESPONDING TO HIS TREATMENT AND THEY'RE GOING TO PERFORM A *LOBOTOMY* ON HIS *GORDITA* TOMORROW MORNING!

SWEET IGUANA OF TIJUANA! THEY'RE GONNA REMOVE THE *PERSONALITY LOBE* OF HIS BRAIN! HE'LL BE AS *UNINTERESTING* AS ZOIDBERG!

WE HAVE TO FIND FRY--ER, I MEAN, THE PROFESSOR, BEFORE THEN SO THEY CAN SWITCH *BACK* TO THEIR NORMAL BODIES!

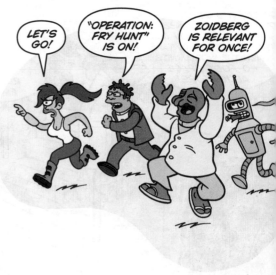

LET'S GO!

"OPERATION: FRY HUNT" IS ON!

ZOIDBERG IS RELEVANT FOR ONCE!

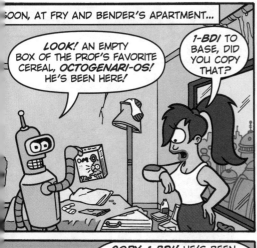

LOOK! AN EMPTY BOX OF THE PROF'S FAVORITE CEREAL, **OCTOGENARI-OS!** HE'S BEEN HERE!

1-BDI TO BASE, DID YOU COPY THAT?

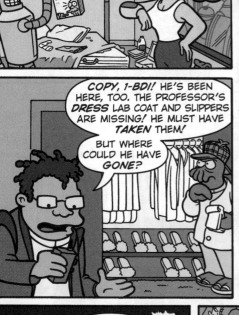

COPY, 1-BDI! HE'S BEEN HERE, TOO. THE PROFESSOR'S **DRESS** LAB COAT AND SLIPPERS ARE MISSING! HE MUST HAVE **TAKEN** THEM!

BUT WHERE COULD HE HAVE **GONE?**

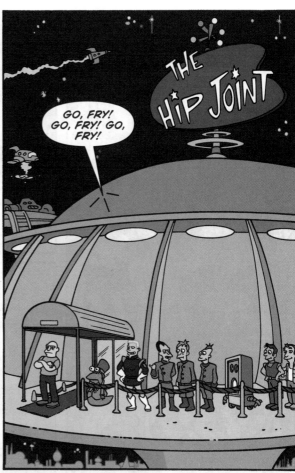

GO, FRY! GO, FRY! GO, FRY!

THE HiP JOiNT

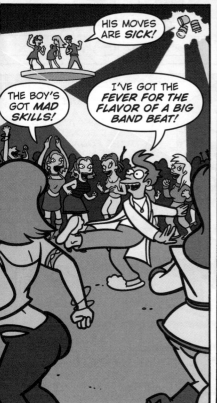

HIS MOVES ARE **SICK!**

THE BOY'S GOT **MAD SKILLS!**

I'VE GOT THE **FEVER** FOR THE **FLAVOR** OF A BIG BAND BEAT!

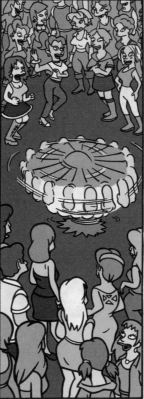

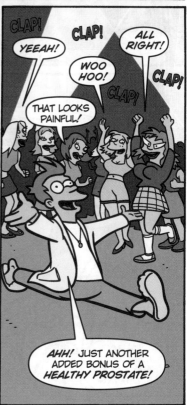

CLAP!

YEEAH!

CLAP!

ALL RIGHT!

WOO HOO!

THAT LOOKS PAINFUL!

CLAP!

CLAP!

AHH! JUST ANOTHER ADDED BONUS OF A **HEALTHY PROSTATE!**

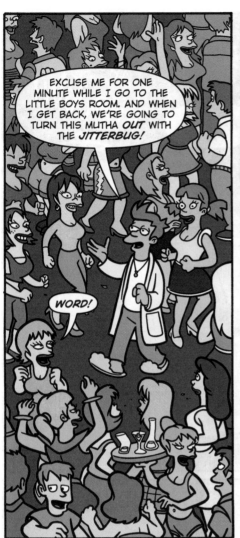

EXCUSE ME FOR ONE MINUTE WHILE I GO TO THE LITTLE BOYS ROOM. AND WHEN I GET BACK, WE'RE GOING TO TURN THIS MUTHA *OUT* WITH THE *JITTERBUG!*

WORD!

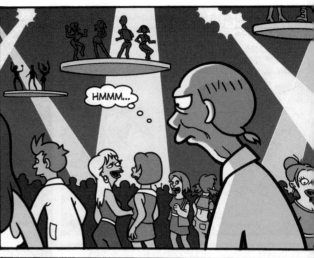

HMMM...

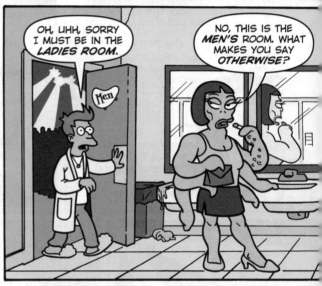

OH, UHH, SORRY I MUST BE IN THE *LADIES ROOM.*

Men

NO, THIS IS THE *MEN'S* ROOM. WHAT MAKES YOU SAY *OTHERWISE?*

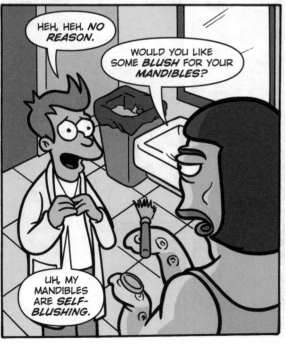

HEH, HEH. *NO REASON.*

WOULD YOU LIKE SOME *BLUSH* FOR YOUR *MANDIBLES?*

UH, MY MANDIBLES ARE *SELF-BLUSHING.*

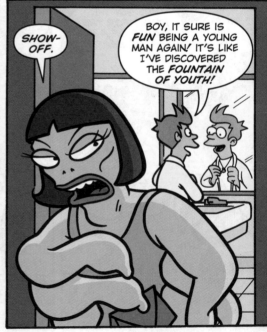

SHOW-OFF.

BOY, IT SURE IS *FUN* BEING A YOUNG MAN AGAIN! IT'S LIKE I'VE DISCOVERED THE *FOUNTAIN OF YOUTH!*

:SIGH.: BUT I GUESS I CAN'T STAY THIS WAY FOREVER. POOR FRY HAS THE REST OF HIS LIFE TO LIVE. *PATHETIC* AS IT MAY BE WITHOUT MY BRILLIANT MIND. OH, WELL. ONE LAST NIGHT OF *JUVENILE DEBAUCHERY*, AND THEN I'LL LET THE OTHERS IN ON OUR SWITCHEROO SECRET...

WHO TURNED OUT THE LIGHTS?! HELLO? IS ANYONE *THERE*?

CLICK!

SLAP!

OOMF!

OOOH!

BAM!

OWW!

POW!

JUDO CHOP!

LATER...

WAKEY-WAKEY, *MR. ATTACKER.* TIME FOR YOUR *MEDICINE*...

HUH? WHO? :GASP!: IT'S *YOU*!

WERNSTROM?!?!? BUT HOW--?
SIMPLE. I GOT THE DROP ON YOU AT THAT CLUB WITH THE HELP OF MY CHINESE GRAD-STUDENT ASSISTANTS. UNFORTUNATELY FOR YOU, THEY'RE GOING TO ASSIST ME IN TEACHING YOU A LESSON IN RESPECTING YOUR ELDERS, WHIPPER-SNAPPER!

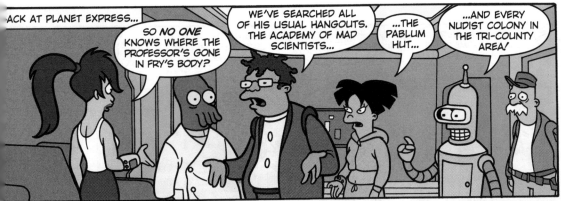

BACK AT PLANET EXPRESS...

SO NO ONE KNOWS WHERE THE PROFESSOR'S GONE IN FRY'S BODY?

WE'VE SEARCHED ALL OF HIS USUAL HANGOUTS. THE ACADEMY OF MAD SCIENTISTS...

...THE PABLUM HUT...

...AND EVERY NUDIST COLONY IN THE TRI-COUNTY AREA!

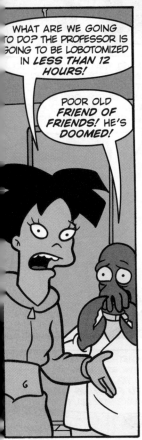

WHAT ARE WE GOING TO DO? THE PROFESSOR IS GOING TO BE LOBOTOMIZED IN LESS THAN 12 HOURS!

POOR OLD FRIEND OF FRIENDS! HE'S DOOMED!

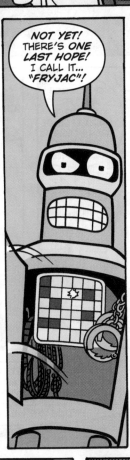

NOT YET! THERE'S ONE LAST HOPE! I CALL IT... "FRYJAC"!

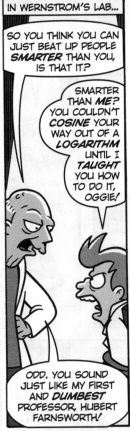

IN WERNSTROM'S LAB...

SO YOU THINK YOU CAN JUST BEAT UP PEOPLE SMARTER THAN YOU, IS THAT IT?

SMARTER THAN ME? YOU COULDN'T COSINE YOUR WAY OUT OF A LOGARITHM UNTIL I TAUGHT YOU HOW TO DO IT, OGGIE!

ODD. YOU SOUND JUST LIKE MY FIRST AND DUMBEST PROFESSOR, HUBERT FARNSWORTH!

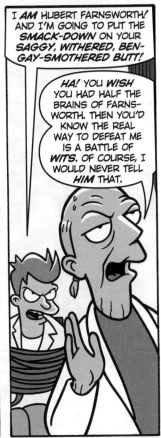

I AM HUBERT FARNSWORTH! AND I'M GOING TO PUT THE SMACK-DOWN ON YOUR SAGGY, WITHERED, BEN-GAY-SMOTHERED BUTT!

HA! YOU WISH YOU HAD HALF THE BRAINS OF FARNSWORTH. THEN YOU'D KNOW THE REAL WAY TO DEFEAT ME IS A BATTLE OF WITS. OF COURSE, I WOULD NEVER TELL HIM THAT.

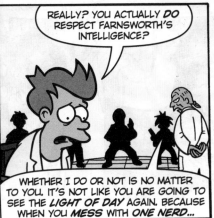

REALLY? YOU ACTUALLY DO RESPECT FARNSWORTH'S INTELLIGENCE?

WHETHER I DO OR NOT IS NO MATTER TO YOU. IT'S NOT LIKE YOU ARE GOING TO SEE THE LIGHT OF DAY AGAIN. BECAUSE WHEN YOU MESS WITH ONE NERD...

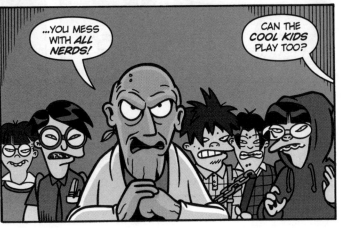

...YOU MESS WITH ALL NERDS!

CAN THE COOL KIDS PLAY TOO?

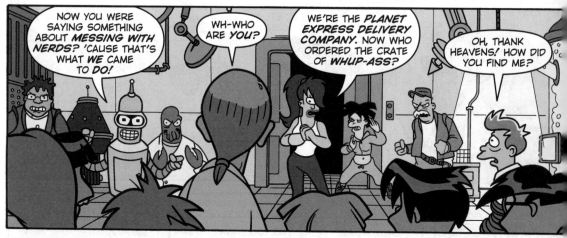

NOW YOU WERE SAYING SOMETHING ABOUT *MESSING WITH NERDS?* 'CAUSE THAT'S WHAT *WE* CAME TO *DO!*

WH-WHO ARE *YOU?*

WE'RE THE *PLANET EXPRESS DELIVERY COMPANY.* NOW WHO ORDERED THE CRATE OF *WHUP-ASS?*

OH, THANK HEAVENS! HOW DID YOU FIND ME?

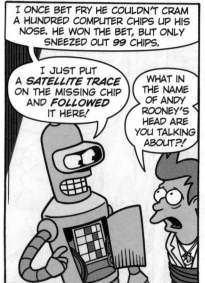

I ONCE BET FRY HE COULDN'T CRAM A HUNDRED COMPUTER CHIPS UP HIS NOSE. HE WON THE BET, BUT ONLY SNEEZED OUT 99 CHIPS.

I JUST PUT A *SATELLITE TRACE* ON THE MISSING CHIP AND *FOLLOWED* IT HERE!

WHAT IN THE NAME OF ANDY ROONEY'S HEAD ARE YOU TALKING ABOUT?!

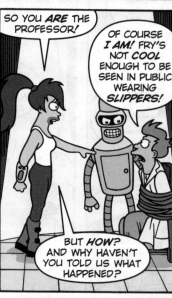

SO YOU *ARE* THE PROFESSOR!

OF COURSE I *AM!* FRY'S NOT *COOL* ENOUGH TO BE SEEN IN PUBLIC WEARING *SLIPPERS!*

BUT *HOW?* AND WHY HAVEN'T YOU TOLD US WHAT HAPPENED?

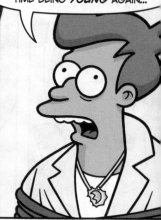

IT MUST HAVE SOMETHING TO DO WITH THESE *GREEN ROCKS* THAT FRY AND I HAVE HANGING AROUND OUR NECKS, BUT I WAS HAVING SUCH A WONDERFUL TIME BEING *YOUNG* AGAIN...

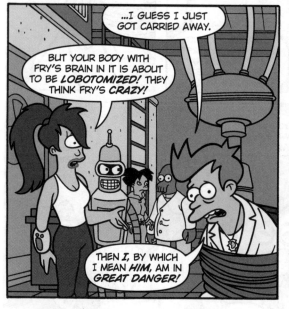

...I GUESS I JUST GOT CARRIED AWAY.

BUT YOUR BODY WITH FRY'S BRAIN IN IT IS ABOUT TO BE *LOBOTOMIZED!* THEY THINK FRY'S *CRAZY!*

THEN *I*, BY WHICH I MEAN *HIM*, AM IN *GREAT DANGER!*

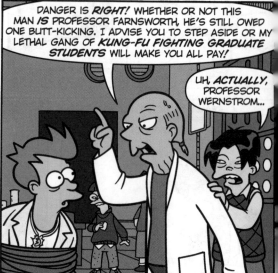

DANGER IS *RIGHT!* WHETHER OR NOT THIS MAN *IS* PROFESSOR FARNSWORTH, HE'S STILL OWED ONE BUTT-KICKING. I ADVISE YOU TO STEP ASIDE OR MY LETHAL GANG OF *KUNG-FU FIGHTING GRADUATE STUDENTS* WILL MAKE YOU ALL PAY!

UH, *ACTUALLY*, PROFESSOR WERNSTROM...

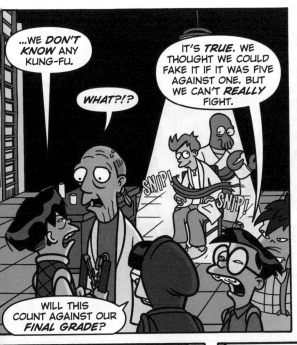

...WE **DON'T KNOW** ANY KUNG-FU.

WHAT?!?

IT'S **TRUE**. WE THOUGHT WE COULD FAKE IT IF IT WAS FIVE AGAINST ONE. BUT WE CAN'T **REALLY** FIGHT.

SNIP!

SNIP!

WILL THIS **COUNT** AGAINST OUR **FINAL GRADE?**

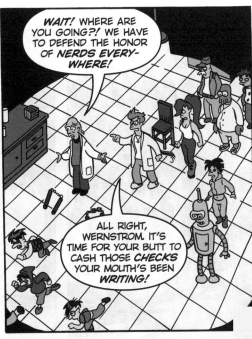

WAIT! WHERE ARE YOU GOING?! WE HAVE TO DEFEND THE HONOR OF **NERDS EVERY-WHERE!**

ALL RIGHT, WERNSTROM. IT'S TIME FOR YOUR BUTT TO CASH THOSE **CHECKS** YOUR MOUTH'S BEEN **WRITING!**

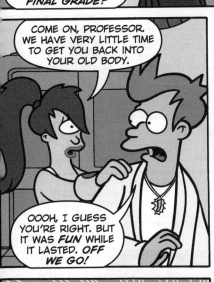

COME ON, PROFESSOR. WE HAVE VERY LITTLE TIME TO GET YOU BACK INTO YOUR OLD BODY.

OOOH, I GUESS YOU'RE RIGHT. BUT IT WAS **FUN** WHILE IT LASTED. **OFF WE GO!**

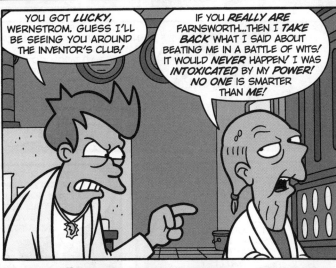

YOU GOT **LUCKY**, WERNSTROM. GUESS I'LL BE SEEING YOU AROUND THE INVENTOR'S CLUB!

IF YOU **REALLY ARE** FARNSWORTH...THEN I **TAKE BACK** WHAT I SAID ABOUT BEATING ME IN A BATTLE OF WITS! IT WOULD **NEVER** HAPPEN! I WAS **INTOXICATED** BY MY **POWER!** **NO ONE** IS SMARTER THAN **ME!**

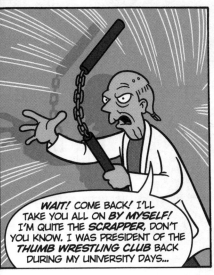

WAIT! COME BACK! I'LL TAKE YOU ALL ON **BY MYSELF!** I'M QUITE THE **SCRAPPER**, DON'T YOU KNOW. I WAS PRESIDENT OF THE **THUMB WRESTLING CLUB** BACK DURING MY UNIVERSITY DAYS...

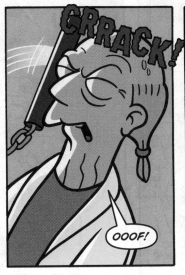

CRRACK!

OOOF!

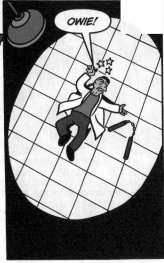

OWIE!

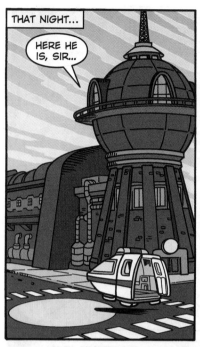

THAT NIGHT...

HERE HE IS, SIR...

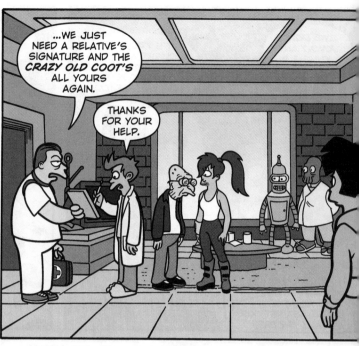

...WE JUST NEED A RELATIVE'S SIGNATURE AND THE *CRAZY OLD COOT'S* ALL YOURS AGAIN.

THANKS FOR YOUR HELP.

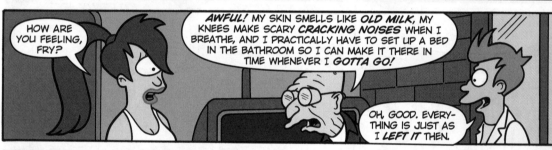

HOW ARE YOU FEELING, FRY?

AWFUL! MY SKIN SMELLS LIKE *OLD MILK*, MY KNEES MAKE SCARY *CRACKING NOISES* WHEN I BREATHE, AND I PRACTICALLY HAVE TO SET UP A BED IN THE BATHROOM SO I CAN MAKE IT THERE IN TIME WHENEVER I *GOTTA GO!*

OH, GOOD. EVERY-THING IS JUST AS I *LEFT IT* THEN.

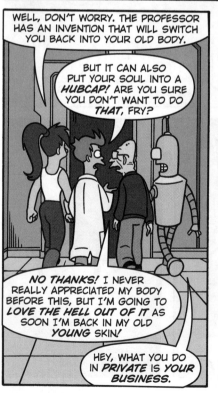

WELL, DON'T WORRY. THE PROFESSOR HAS AN INVENTION THAT WILL SWITCH YOU BACK INTO YOUR OLD BODY.

BUT IT CAN ALSO PUT YOUR SOUL INTO A *HUBCAP!* ARE YOU SURE YOU DON'T WANT TO DO *THAT*, FRY?

NO THANKS! I NEVER REALLY APPRECIATED MY BODY BEFORE THIS, BUT I'M GOING TO *LOVE THE HELL OUT OF IT* AS SOON I'M BACK IN MY OLD *YOUNG* SKIN!

HEY, WHAT YOU DO IN *PRIVATE* IS *YOUR BUSINESS.*

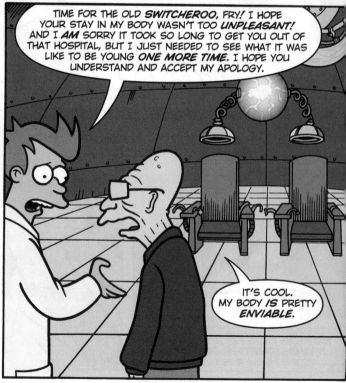

TIME FOR THE OLD *SWITCHEROO*, FRY! I HOPE YOUR STAY IN MY BODY WASN'T TOO *UNPLEASANT!* AND I *AM* SORRY IT TOOK SO LONG TO GET YOU OUT OF THAT HOSPITAL, BUT I JUST NEEDED TO SEE WHAT IT WAS LIKE TO BE YOUNG *ONE MORE TIME.* I HOPE YOU UNDERSTAND AND ACCEPT MY APOLOGY.

IT'S COOL. MY BODY *IS* PRETTY *ENVIABLE.*

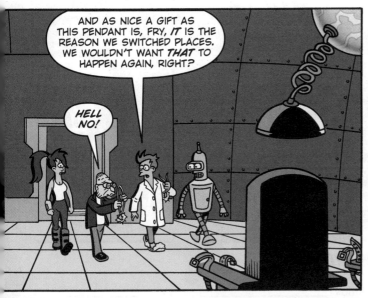

AND AS NICE A GIFT AS THIS PENDANT IS, FRY, *IT* IS THE REASON WE SWITCHED PLACES. WE WOULDN'T WANT *THAT* TO HAPPEN AGAIN, RIGHT?

HELL NO!

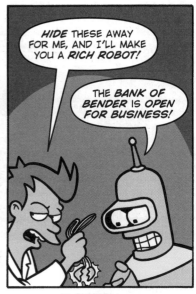

HIDE THESE AWAY FOR ME, AND I'LL MAKE YOU A *RICH ROBOT!*

THE *BANK OF BENDER* IS OPEN FOR BUSINESS!

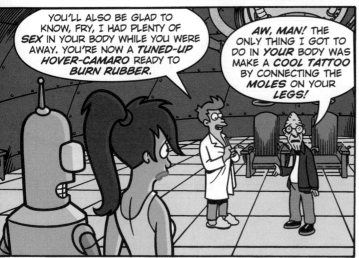

YOU'LL ALSO BE GLAD TO KNOW, FRY, I HAD PLENTY OF *SEX* IN YOUR BODY WHILE YOU WERE AWAY. YOU'RE NOW A *TUNED-UP HOVER-CAMARO* READY TO *BURN RUBBER.*

AW, MAN! THE ONLY THING I GOT TO DO IN *YOUR* BODY WAS MAKE A *COOL TATTOO* BY CONNECTING THE *MOLES* ON YOUR *LEGS!*

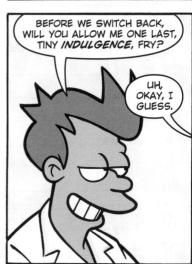

BEFORE WE SWITCH BACK, WILL YOU ALLOW ME ONE LAST, TINY *INDULGENCE,* FRY?

UH, OKAY, I GUESS.

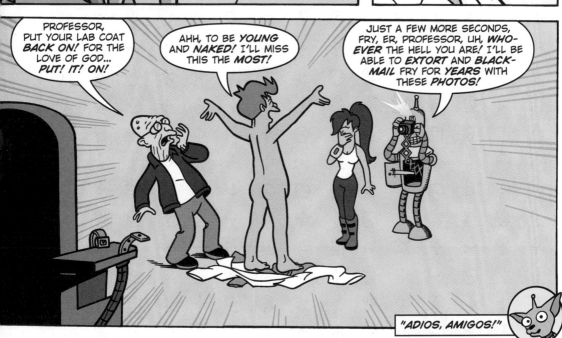

PROFESSOR, PUT YOUR LAB COAT *BACK ON!* FOR THE LOVE OF GOD... *PUT! IT! ON!*

AHH, TO BE *YOUNG* AND *NAKED!* I'LL MISS THIS THE *MOST!*

JUST A FEW MORE SECONDS, FRY, ER, PROFESSOR, UH, *WHOEVER* THE HELL YOU ARE! I'LL BE ABLE TO *EXTORT* AND *BLACKMAIL* FRY FOR *YEARS* WITH THESE *PHOTOS!*

"ADIOS, AMIGOS!"

THE WORD SEARCH THAT ATE MY BRAIN!

HEY, FUTURAMAPHILES! DO YOU LIKE TO SPEND HOURS STARING AT BIG BLOCKS OF LETTERS, TRYING TO FIND HIDDEN WORDS OR PHRASES UNTIL YOUR BRAIN THROBS WITH PAIN AND YOUR BLOODSHOT EYES FEEL LIKE THEY'RE GOING TO EXPLODE OUT OF YOUR HEAD? YOU DO? FANTASTIC! THIS IS THE PUZZLE FOR YOU!

HIDDEN IN THE SLIME-GREEN BOX BELOW ARE 27 WORDS OR PHRASES FAMILIAR TO ALL FUTURAMA FANS. THE WORDS MAY APPEAR HORIZONTALLY, VERTICALLY, OR DIAGONALLY   HINT: THE DIAGONAL WORDS MAY READ FROM TOP TO BOTTOM, OR FROM BOTTOM TO TOP . CIRCLE EACH WORD OR PHRASE YOU FIND, UNTIL YOU HAVE LOCATED ALL 27. WHAT'S THAT? YOU CAN'T READ THIS STRANGE ALIEN LANGUAGE? NOT A PROBLEM. WE'VE LISTED THE WORDS BELOW. USING THE KEY ON THE RIGHT SIDE OF THE PAGE, SIMPLY TRANSLATE FROM ENGLISH INTO ALIENESE IN THE SPACES PROVIDED BEFORE WORKING THE PUZZLE! YOU CAN MAKE A PHOTO COPY OF THIS PAGE IF YOU WANT TO AVOID DEFACING THIS INCREDIBLE ISSUE!

> PENCILS ARE FOR SPINELESS HUMANS! USE A PEN. **IF YOU DARE!!!**

WORD LIST

Oh my no _____	Xmas _____	Fry _____
What up _____	DOOP _____	Donbot _____
Zapp _____	Guh _____	Planet Express _____
Omicronian _____	Ship _____	Panucci's _____
Mars U _____	Leela _____	H.G. Blob _____
Kif _____	Elzar _____	Robot _____	Mom _____
New New York _____		Flexo _____
Laser _____	Amy _____	Dr. Zoidberg _____
Amazonia _____	Bender _____	Url _____

KEY

A=ψ
B=≤
C=⊗
D=⋈
E=⋎
F=▣
G=⌿
H=↓
I=⌢
J=✕
K=⅄
L=ℋ
M=⋈
N=⊙
O=℘
P=ᐁ
Q=✳
R=⊛
S=⊘
T=⋏
U=⅜
V=▢
W=↴
X=⌾
Y=⌇
Z=↯

MATT
GROENING

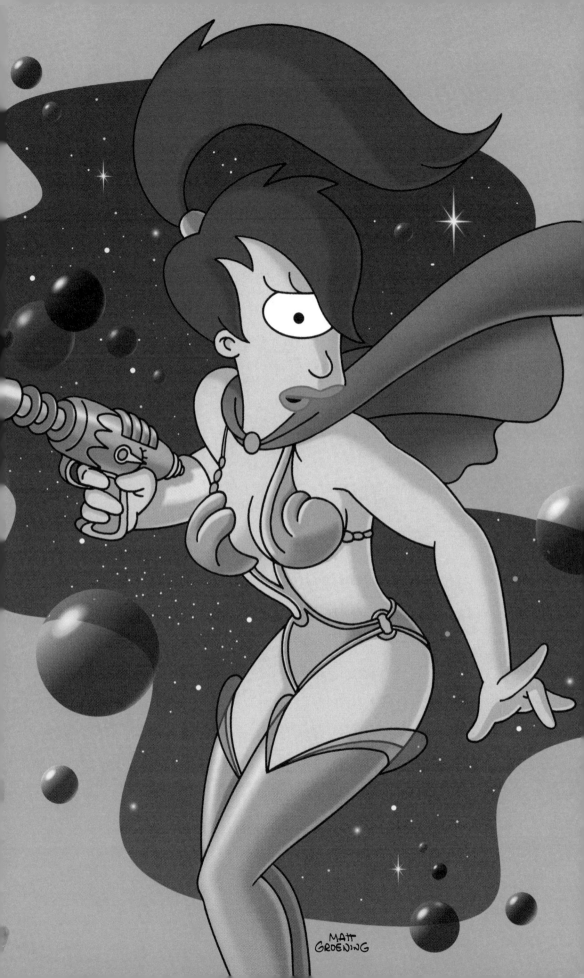